THE IMPACT OF PARENTAL EMPLOYMENT

The Impact of Parental Employment

Young People, Well-Being and Educational Achievement

LINDA CUSWORTH
University of York, UK

ASHGATE

Published by
Ashgate Publishing Limited
Wey Court East
Union Road
Farnham
Surrey, GU9 7PT
England

Ashgate Publishing Company
Suite 420
101 Cherry Street
Burlington
VT 05401-4405
USA

www.ashgate.com

British Library Cataloguing in Publication Data
Cusworth, Linda.
    The impact of parental employment : young people,
    well-being and educational achievement. -- (Studies in cash
    & care)
    1. Parental influences--Great Britain. 2. Children of
    working parents--Great Britain--Psychology. 3. Children of
    unemployed parents--Great Britain--Psychology. 4. Child
    development--Social aspects--Great Britain. 5. Academic
    achievement--Social aspects--Great Britain
    I. Title II. Series
    305.2'31-dc22

Library of Congress Cataloging-in-Publication Data
Cusworth, Linda.
    The impact of parental employment : young people, well-being and educational achievement / by Linda Cusworth.
       p. cm.
    Includes bibliographical references and index.
    ISBN 978-0-7546-7559-4 (hbk.) -- ISBN 978-0-7546-9813-5
     1. Children of working parents--Psychological aspects. 2. Work and family--Psychological aspects. 3. Unemployment--Psychological aspects. 4. Children--Psychological aspects. 5. Academic achievement. I. Title.

    HQ777.6.C87 2009
    155.9'240941--dc22

2009019242

ISBN 9780754675594 (hbk)
ISBN 9780754698135 (ebk)

Mixed Sources
Product group from well-managed
forests and other controlled sources
www.fsc.org Cert no. SA-COC-1565
© 1996 Forest Stewardship Council
FSC

Printed and bound in Great Britain by
MPG Books Group, UK

Contents

List of Figures

List of Tables

Acknowledgments

This book is based on research undertaken at the University of Nottingham for my PhD thesis. I am truly indebted to my PhD supervisors, Professor Robert Walker and Dr Tracey Warren, who continually advised, supported, inspired, guided, challenged and encouraged me throughout the life of the research. I am also grateful to Professor Jonathan Bradshaw and other colleagues in the Social Policy Research Unit at the University of York.

The thesis was funded by the Economic and Social Research Council (award number S42200134013), the Department for Work and Pensions (through a Collaborative Research Studentship Award), and the University of Nottingham. The British Household Panel Survey data used in this thesis were made available through the ESRC Data Archive at the University of Essex.

On a personal note, I would like to thank my family and friends for the endless love and encouragement they have given me through my PhD research and in preparation for this book. A particular thank you goes to Martin – who went from boyfriend to fiancé to husband to father of our baby Cara Grace during the course of this research – for sharing my enthusiasm and achievements, tears and frustrations, for always having faith in me, and for providing a constant supply of coffee and chocolate – I couldn't have done this without you and for that I am forever grateful.

List of Abbreviations

ALSPAC Avon Longitudinal Survey of Parents and Children

BCS   British Cohort Study (1970)
BHPS   British Household Panel Survey
BYP   British Youth Panel

DAWBA   Development and Well-being Assessment
DfEE   Department for Education and Employment
DfES   Department for Education and Skills
DoH   Department of Health
DSS   Department of Social Security
DWP   Department for Work and Pensions

GHQ   General Health Questionnaire

HRBQ   Health-Related Behaviour Questionnaire
HSBC   Health Behaviour Survey of School-Aged Children
HSE   Health Survey for England

ICD-10 International Classification of Diseases

MCS   Millennium Cohort Study (2000)

NCDS   National Child Development Study (1958)
NDLP   New Deal for Lone Parents
NEET   Not in Education, Employment or Training
NSHD   National Survey of Health and Development (1946)

ONS   Office for National Statistics

SDQ   Strengths and Difficulties Questionnaire
SEU   Social Exclusion Unit
SHEU   Schools Health Education Unit
SMP   Statutory Maternity Pay

WFTC   Working Families Tax Credit
WHO   World Health Organisation

YCS   Youth Cohort Study
YJB   Youth Justice Board

Chapter 1

Introduction

What parents do clearly has an impact on children's lives, both in the short-term and later in life, and parental employment patterns have an influence on children in various ways, through the effect on family income, the time parents spend with their children, and the provision of a role-model image. This book is concerned with these effects, and applies a forms of capital approach (Bourdieu 1983) to understanding the impact of parental employment and unemployment on the educational and emotional well-being of children and young people.

The debate surrounding the impact of parental employment, in reality usually just that of mothers, on children has a long and emotive history, with the battle lines drawn between feminists, child psychologists, economists, educational theorists and others. In 1997, Panorama's screening of 'Missing Mum' (BBC 1997) provoked a media furore with its implication that children of working mothers do less well at school, and this controversial issue has also been the subject of radio phone-ins (for example on Woman's Hour, BBC Radio 4, November 2001) and newspaper articles (for example 'Working mothers "bad for children"', *The Guardian*, November, 2003; 'What if mums don't actually want to go out to work?', *The Telegraph*, June, 2005; 'Official: babies do best with mother', *The Observer*, October, 2005).

This introductory chapter defines some of the terms and boundaries of the book. The key issues are introduced, a brief overview of the policy, theoretical and historical background given, and the aims of the book presented. The chapter concludes with an overview of the book, and a brief summary of each chapter.

Some definitions

When investigating the impact of parental employment and unemployment on children and young people, in terms of outcomes and well-being, it is important first to define some key terms. For the purposes of this book a *child* is defined as aged under 11, with a *young person* defined as aged over 11 but under 16, although the term *dependent child* encompasses both child and young person. The term *parental* is used to refer to resident parents, whether natural (birth) parent or stepparent. Thus we consider the employment patterns of the parent(s) who reside with a young person, both currently and during childhood. A *family* is defined as a married/cohabiting couple with or without dependent child(ren) (aged under 16, or aged 16–18 in full-time education) or a lone parent with dependent child(ren), in line with the definition used by the Office for National Statistics (ONS 2005a).

There is no one accepted definition of *well-being*, and the concept of well-being has been debated by a wide range of disciplines, including health economics, advertising, medicine, sociology and psychology. However, the current research focuses on the impact of parental employment and unemployment on children's educational and emotional well-being. This research focuses primarily on the UK, although international research sources are drawn upon where appropriate.

Background

Over recent decades, there have been huge increases in the diversity of household composition, and changes in patterns of cohabitation, marriage and divorce have led to considerable changes in the family environment. There has been a decrease in the proportion of households containing the 'traditional' family unit – couple families with dependent children – and an increase in the proportion of both lone parent families and stepfamilies. The proportion of households in Great Britain comprising a couple with dependent children fell from over a third in 1971 to less than a quarter in 2005. Over the same period the proportion of lone parent households with dependent children doubled, to seven per cent of all households in 2005 (ONS 2006a). The 2001 census (the first census which allowed the identification of stepfamilies) found that ten per cent of all families in the UK with dependent children were stepfamilies, and one quarter were lone parent families (ONS 2005).

There have been dramatic changes too in parental employment patterns. Since the mid-1980s there has been a rapid increase in married mothers' employment rates, especially in full-time jobs and especially among those with pre-school children. Lone mothers have not shared in these trends however, and participation rates amongst lone mothers are lower than those amongst married/cohabiting mothers (ONS 2005b). These trends have contributed to a polarised pattern of 'work-rich' and 'work-poor' households, with a decline in the proportion of one-earner couple families, and these changes may have an impact on family life and experiences.

For many families, being without paid work means a life of low income (Department for Work and Pensions (DWP) 2001). When the current government came to power in 1997 they inherited a country where 11 million people, including 4.5 million children under 16 (one in three) were living in households with below half average income, and nearly one in five working-age households had no one in employment (Department of Social Security (DSS) 2000a). In the first of a series of annual reports, New Labour outlined its commitment to tackling poverty and its causes (DSS 1999). Their approach is encompassed by an awareness of the need to break the cycle of deprivation, to prevent disadvantage being passed on through generations, and their dedication to this aim was affirmed by the Prime Minister in the Beveridge Lecture in March 1999, who said 'our historic aim will be for ours to be the first generation to end child poverty ... it is a 20-year mission but I believe it can be done' (Blair 1999, 17).

The government's strategy is based on the principle that, for most families, paid work is the best route out of poverty (DSS 1999). A variety of policies have therefore been introduced to promote paid work and to make work pay (including the New Deal schemes, Working Tax Credits and Children's Tax Credits, and childcare policies).

The impact of parental employment on children

The social changes outlined above and the government's emphasis on promoting paid work for all, including mothers, brings with it the question of whether parental employment patterns influence children's well-being. Children's well-being can be considered in terms of their outcomes in life, encompassing their experiences, attitudes, aspirations and behaviours, in childhood, adolescence and later in life.

Using the theoretical framework of Bourdieu (1983), parental employment patterns can be understood to impact upon children's outcomes in several ways: through the effect on household income and socio-economic circumstances (economic or financial capital); through the provision of cultural norms and expectations (cultural capital); and through family relationships and interaction (social capital). Parents' qualifications (human capital) also play an important part, and are related to levels of both economic and cultural capital.

Previous research

Previous research into the impact of parental employment and unemployment on children has tended to focus on a fairly narrow range of outcomes, mainly educational achievement and children's own patterns of employment later in life (for example Kiernan 1996; O'Brien and Jones 1999; Ermisch and Francesconi 2001a). Although these are important, children's lives are complex, and there is a need to explore the potential relationships between parental employment patterns and the more social and emotional aspects of these lives, such as attitudes and aspirations, relationships and emotional well-being.

There has also been a focus on the outcomes for very young children (for example, Gregg and Washbrook 2003), or the impact of parental employment patterns when children were very young on their later outcomes (for example, Joshi and Verropoulou 2000). Much less attention has been paid to the impact of parental employment patterns on outcomes for adolescents, and this book aims to address this gap in knowledge. Adolescence is a crucial period in the life course when a young person becomes ready to assume adult responsibility, marking the transition from dependent childhood to independent adulthood (Schoon 2003). Today's adolescents are the parents, teachers, and leaders of the future, and there is clear evidence from life course research that adolescence experiences, and the formation of attitudes and opinions at this stage, have a pronounced influence on adult life. In addition, the opportunities and experiences mark the present quality of young people's lives.

There has been a strong reliance in previous research in this area on data from the birth cohort studies – The National Survey of Health and Development (NSHD, conducted in 1946), The National Child Development Study (NCDS, conducted in 1958), and The British Cohort Study (BCS, conducted in 1970). There are several key limitations to such data, not least that the children being studied were born up to 50 years ago when maternal employment, lone parenthood and other aspects of family life were very different to modern times. More recently, the Millennium Cohort Study (MCS, conducted in 2000) has provided a useful source of data, although the children being studied are still very young.

The current research uses data from the British Household Panel Survey (BHPS) and its associated Youth Panel (BYP) (more details are given in Chapter 3) whereby the young people (aged 11–15) in the BHPS households are interviewed each year. The Youth Panel is a unique and under-utilised resource, which enables the examination of any relationship between parental employment and outcomes in adolescence. The young people in the samples used in the current study were born between 1978 and 1990, and thus the research is more relevant and up-to-date than previous work in this area.

Previous studies have tended to focus on the impact of maternal or paternal employment in isolation (for example, Ermisch and Francesconi 2001a). Although the term *maternal employment* suggests a focus on the mother and her labour force affiliation, the experience of maternal employment (and likewise, paternal employment or unemployment) is embedded in a family system. Therefore, when considering child outcomes, there is a need to study the impact of parental employment patterns within the whole family context.

Aims of the book

The main aim of this book is to investigate any relationships between patterns of parental employment and young people's educational and emotional well-being. As outlined above, a forms of capital approach is used to contextualise and explain these relationships. The research also examines any impact of the timing of parental employment, by exploring whether current parental employment patterns differ in their impact on well-being to patterns of parental employment experienced in childhood. The current work also considers the role of other individual, parental and family factors, both in directly influencing well-being, and in mediating any relationships between parental employment patterns and young people's well-being.

Overview of the book

Six chapters and two appendices follow this introductory chapter.

Chapter 2, *Parental employment and children's outcomes*, presents the social, policy and theoretical background to the impact of parental employment patterns on children and young people.

Chapter 3, *Methodology*, explains how the research was carried out, providing details of the data sources and samples of young people used in the project.

Chapter 4, *Emotional well-being*, considers the meanings, prevalence and nature of the emotional well-being of children and young people. The chapter then examines the support for links between mental or emotional well-being, and parental employment patterns, together with personal, familial and other factors, to include family structure, parents' educational qualifications and own emotional well-being, the quality of family relationships, and young people's age and gender. Data from the youth survey of the BHPS is then used to empirically examine the relationships between parental employment patterns, and other factors, and young people's emotional well-being, using a forms of capital approach to explain and understand these influences.

Chapter 5, *Educational well-being – behaviour and attitudes*, reviews the existing evidence surrounding bullying, truancy, and school exclusion, reflecting on the scale and nature of these issues, and considering the individual, family, school and societal characteristics which may have an influence. Data from the youth survey of the BHPS is then used to investigate links between young people's educational outcomes and parental employment patterns, together with other factors, using a forms of capital approach (Bourdieu, 1983) to explain any associations.

Chapter 6, *Educational well-being – attainment and progression*, sets the importance of educational attainment and post-16 participation in context, before considering the individual, parental, family, and other factors which have an influence on these outcomes. Data from a special follow-on sample from the BHPS is used to consider the impact of parental employment patterns during childhood and adolescence on GCSE attainment, and both the intention and actuality of staying on in full-time education post-16.

Chapter 7, *Conclusions*, discusses the key findings of this book. The main conclusion is that parental employment patterns do have an impact on young people's outcomes, through the impact on family socio-economic circumstances (financial capital), the provision of a role model and cultural norms and expectations (cultural capital), and through a protective or nurturing influence (social capital). Following a reflection on the limitations of this research, there is a discussion of potential areas for future work.

Appendix A contains details of how the samples used in the empirical analysis were constructed, whilst *Appendix B* details parental employment patterns in the BHPS, together with how these compare with employment patterns in other surveys.

Summary and conclusion

This chapter has introduced the topic of the impact of parental employment on children, with a brief review of the social and policy background. The aims of the book have been stated, and an overview of the rest of the book given.

Chapter 2

Parental Employment
and Children's Outcomes

This chapter sets out the social, policy, and theoretical context to this research project. The last few decades have seen dramatic increases in employment amongst women, with the most significant increases amongst mothers, especially those with young children. In addition, particularly since the election of New Labour into government in 1997, policy has been directed towards facilitating labour market participation for a range of socially excluded groups, including women with children, and especially lone mothers. As mothers with an employed partner are themselves more likely to be in paid employment than lone mothers and those whose partners are unemployed, a polarisation has occurred, with increases in the proportions of work-rich and work-poor households. The New Deal for Lone Parents (NDLP), alongside other policies such as the National Childcare Strategy, the Working Families' Tax Credit, and employment regulations all support mothers, both lone and partnered, in taking up paid employment (Dex 1999; Millar 2000). Such welfare to work strategies are complemented by policies which should help all parents at work, for example, parental leave, the minimum wage, and family-friendly workplace initiatives (Dex 1999). The focus on paid work as the best route out of poverty is also a key element of the governments' agenda to eradicate child poverty in the UK by 2020.

These trends and policy changes affect the everyday lives of both parents and children. The increased employment of mothers – supported by recent policies, both as a response to employment trends and because employment is seen as a defence against poverty – brings with it the question of whether that increased parental employment may affect outcomes for children. It is with the potential impacts of parental employment on children and young people that the current research is concerned.

Trends in parental employment patterns

There are clear differences in employment rates between parents and non-parents, between mothers and fathers, and between couple parents and lone parents, and there have been distinct changes in employment trends over the past few decades. This section considers some of these trends, and how patterns have changed, together with some of the possible reasons why. When considering the impact of parental employment and unemployment on children it is important to understand

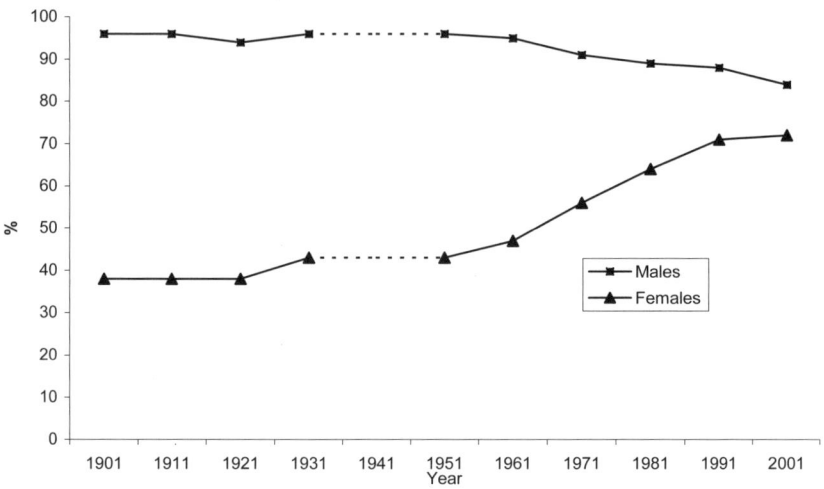

Figure 2.1   Economic activity rates of men and women, 1901–2001

Note: 1941 – no data available.
Source: Labour Force Survey, 1901–1961 from Hakim (1996a); 1971–2001 from ONS (2002).

what patterns and trends exist, and to place current patterns of employment into context.

Men's and women's economic activity

Figure 2.1 indicates the trend in economic activity rates – that is employment and unemployment, or the proportion of the population that is in the labour force – for men (aged 16–64) and women (aged 16–59) since 1901.

It can be seen that throughout the first half of the twentieth century, economic activity rates for men and women remained fairly consistent, at 96 per cent for men, and between 38 per cent and 43 per cent for women. In the later half of the century female economic activity rates virtually doubled, to 72 per cent by 2001. In contradistinction, a general downward trend can be seen in the proportion of men who were economically active, which decreased by over a fifth, to 84 per cent in 2001. The gap between the proportions of men and women who were economically active reduced from 58 percentage points in 1901 to just 12 percentage points in 2001.

At the start of the twentieth century a marriage bar operated to exclude women from employment on marriage, and according to Hakim (1996a, 125) this 'institutionalised the marriage career for women', reinforcing the male breadwinner/ female carer model of the gender division of labour which had emerged with industrialisation and was supported by the policies of the Trade Union movement.

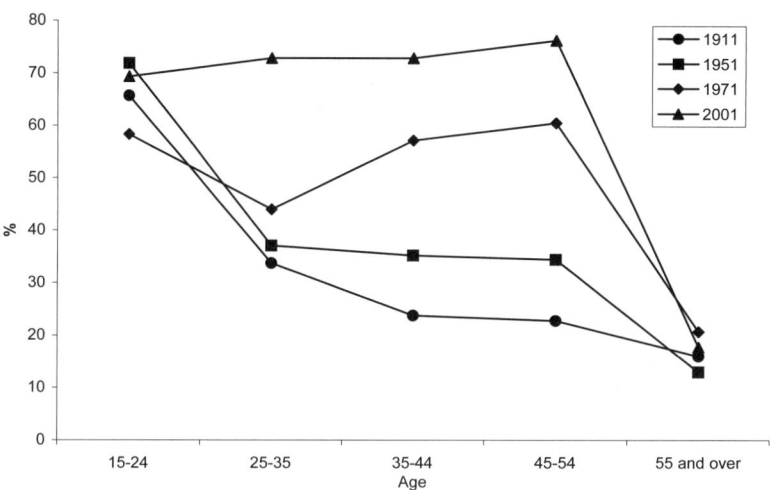

Figure 2.2   Female economic activity rates by age-group, 1911–2001

Source: 1911–1971, Census data, from Halsey, 1988; 2001, Census and Labour Force Survey, from ONS (2001a).

So although 38 per cent of all women were economically active in 1901, this proportion varied from around 70 per cent for single women to just 10 per cent for married women (Crompton 1997, 26). The overall increase in female economic activity from the 1950s onwards stems mainly from an increase in married women's participation, although there were distinct differences across the life course.

Figure 2.2 shows that in 1911, economic activity rates for women were highest for those aged 16–24 as women then withdrew from the formal labour market to bear and rear children, and economic activity rates declined with age. This pattern was still evident in 1951. By 1971, a characteristic double-peaked profile of economic activity amongst women had emerged – the economic activity rates for young women were relatively high, sharply falling as women entered their childrearing years and stayed at home to look after their children, starting to rise again for women in their thirties who returned to paid employment in increasing numbers, usually after the youngest child had started school. By 2001 the dip in women's economic activity for those aged 25–35 had disappeared, as the break taken in employment by women for childrearing reduced in length.

Women's part-time employment

A particular aspect of women's employment in Britain is the close association with part-time work. Almost all of the increase in women's employment between the 1950s and the 1980s was in part-time work. In 1951 part-time women workers constituted 12 per cent of the female labour force; this had risen to 22 per cent in 1961, to 34 per cent in 1971 and to 39 per cent in 1981 (Beechey and Perkins 1987). In 2001, 40 per cent of women in employment were working part-time, which compared with just 7 per cent of employed men; in other words, over 80 per cent of all part-time jobs were held by women (Office for National Statistics (ONS) 2002).

It is well known that part-time jobs on average have lower wage rates than full-time jobs. In some accounts (e.g. Harkness 1996; Burchell et al 1997; Warren 2000) it is suggested that it is the status of a job as either part-time or full-time that explains the lower wages, through discrimination. Others (e.g. Miller 1987; Kidd and Shannon 2001) have argued that the lower wages associated with part-time employment can be wholly or partly attributed to the lower human capital (e.g. education) of the women who work in part-time jobs. In 2002, female employees who worked part-time earned just 73 per cent of the average gross hourly earnings of women who worked full-time (Perfect and Hurrell 2003).

The influence of children

Women's employment patterns have always been strongly influenced by having children, and although in the past mothers used to withdraw from the labour market, in recent decades the rise in women's employment has been most notable amongst those with children (McRae 1991a; Harrop and Moss 1995; Dex et al 1998).

The timing of return to work after childbirth has been cited as of critical importance to labour market outcomes for women (Smeaton 2006). In 1979, 24 per cent of women who were in employment when they became pregnant returned to work within about 9–11 months of the birth. This figure had increased to 45 per cent in 1988, 67 per cent in 1996 (within 10–11 months of the birth) and 80 per cent in 2002 (within 13–17 months) (Callender et al 1997; Hudson et al 2004). There have always been marked differences between women, especially on the basis of class, although recent analysis of birth cohort data has suggested that the predictors of return rates have changed over time (Smeaton 2006). During the 1980s, as a significant growth in the proportion of women returning to work quickly post-childbirth became apparent, it was observed that a polarisation of opportunities was emerging, with professional women becoming the main beneficiaries of change. However, by the mid-1990s, occupational class was no longer the main determinant of return timing, and there had been a decline in the polarisation of class-based employment outcomes. Instead the financial burden of mortgage debt was pushing women into early work returns (Smeaton 2006).

The most recent figures show that in 2004, working-age mothers with dependent children were less likely to be in employment than working-age women without dependent children (67 per cent compared with 73 per cent). For men, the opposite was true – fathers were more likely to be in employment than working-age men without dependent children (90 per cent and 74 per cent) (ONS 2006a). There are important differences however for women by the age of their youngest child and their marital/cohabiting status (see Table 2.1). Employment rates are the lowest for women whose youngest child is aged under five, and increase with the age of the

Table 2.1   **Full-time and part-time employment rates of women, by marital status and age of youngest dependent child, 2004**

| | | | | Percentages | | | | |
| | | | Age of youngest child | | | | No | All |
		Under 5	5–10	11–15	16–18	All	dependent children	women
Not married/	**In employment**	33	56	66	72	52	67	63
cohabiting	**Full-time**	12	22	37	53	24	46	40
	Part-time	21	34	29	19	28	21	23
Married/	**In employment**	58	77	81	80	70	78	74
cohabiting	**Full-time**	20	27	38	43	28	52	40
	Part-time	38	50	43	37	43	26	34
All	**In employment**	53	71	77	78	66	73	70
	Full-time	18	26	38	45	27	49	40
	Part-time	34	45	39	33	39	24	30

Notes: United Kingdom figures for all women aged 16-59; 16-18 year-old children refers to those in full-time education; not married/cohabiting includes single, widowed, separated and divorced women.

Source: Labour Force Survey, ONS, 2006a.

youngest child. More women with a youngest child aged under 11 are in part-time employment than full-time employment, whereas roughly equal proportions of mothers whose youngest child is aged 11–15 work full- and part-time, and those with older children are more likely to work full-time.

For mothers with children of all ages, overall employment rates are higher for married/cohabiting women than those who are not married or cohabiting. The largest gap in economic activity between women who are and are not married/cohabiting is observable when the youngest child is under five (25 percentage points), although this gap reduces as the age of the youngest child increases.

Heterogeneity

Looking at these overall trends masks the heterogeneity of women's employment, particularly in terms of class and educational level differences. Not surprisingly, employment rates were highest among graduates and lowest among those with no qualifications (ONS 2006a), and women with higher-level academic qualifications are more likely to be employed full-time, and more likely to be in professional jobs (Warren 2000).

Household worklessness

So far we have considered trends in employment patterns amongst individuals, observing a convergence of economic activity rates of men and women, and

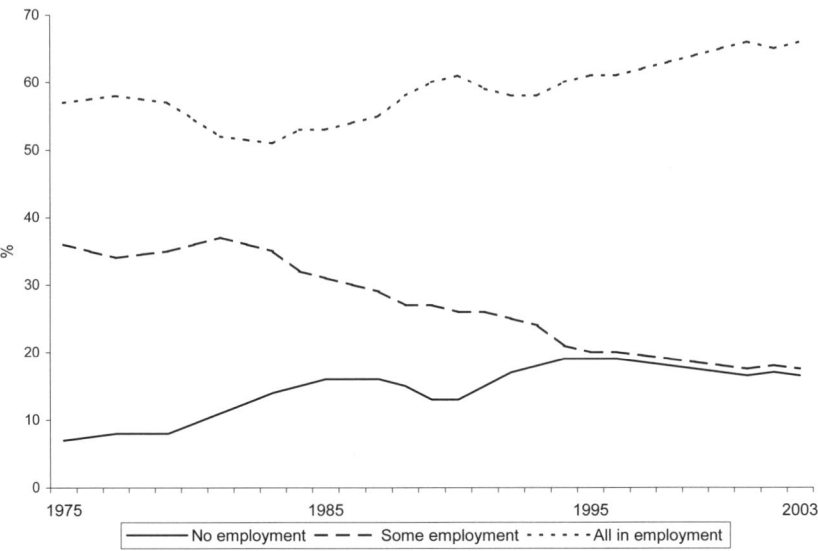

Figure 2.3   Distribution of employment across households, 1975–2003

Source: Labour Force Survey data (taken from Gregg and Wadsworth, 2004).

particularly significant increases in paid employment amongst women with young children. Increases in female employment have disproportionately occurred in households which already contained working members (Gregg et al 1999). These changes have had consequences for the distribution of work across households, with a polarisation of work-rich and work-poor households. Figure 2.3 shows that the proportion of households with no working-age adult in employment has gradually increased since the mid-1970s. At the same time, the proportion of households where all adults of working-age are in employment has also increased, and these increases are offset by a reduction in households where some adult members are in employment, but some are not.

Table 2.2 indicates the proportions of all households without an adult in employment, together with the rates of worklessness amongst lone parent families and couples with children. It can be seen that rates of worklessness for lone parent households are consistently much higher than those for couples with children, but that for both groups reached a peak in the mid-1990s with a reduction since then.

Explaining the trends

So far, this chapter has briefly reviewed some of the historical trends and current patterns in women's employment, focusing particularly on how the relationship for women between marriage, motherhood and employment has been challenged.

Table 2.2   Household worklessness by family type, 1968–2004

	All households	Percentages Lone parents	Couples with children
1968	4	23	2
1975	6	37	3
1981	11	41	7
1985	16	30	11
1990	13	49	6
1992	17	54	9
1993	19	55	9
1994	19	54	9
1995	19	53	8
1996	19	52	8
1997	18	50	7
1998	18	49	7
1999	17	48	6
2000	17	45	6
2001	17	44	6
2002	17	44	6
2003	16	43	5
2004	16	42	5
2005	16	41	5
2006	16	39	5

Source: 1968–1990, Family Expenditure Survey (from Gregg et al, 1999); 1992–2006, Labour Force Survey (ONS, 2006b).

Parental employment rates have also been considered, together with rates of worklessness amongst all households and those with children.

Many different, often conflicting, explanations have been suggested to explain the trends and patterns in female employment in Britain. Some focus on supply-side factors, such as human capital resources, work orientations and preferences. Others focus more on demand-side factors, emphasising the structure of the labour market and the role of institutions, such as the welfare state or the family.

Human-capital theorists explain women's labour market outcomes in terms of their sex-role preferences, their human capital investments and an efficient beneficial family division of labour (Becker 1964, 1981; Polachek 1981; Hakim 1991, 1995, 1996a). Men and women behave rationally in order to maximise their individual utility, with the sexual division of labour in the home, particularly women's role in childbearing and childrearing, making it efficient for women to specialise in domestic work and men to specialise in employment. Women have thus traditionally invested less in their human capital, in terms of education, training and work experience, because of their family commitments and a need to balance home and work. Part-time employment has often been highlighted as a mechanism of enabling women with children to combine a work career with domestic responsibilities (for a review see Warren and Walters 1998). Becker (1993) has argued that changes in the labour market, the growth in divorce rates, and the decline in family size have all served to encourage women's participation in the labour market, increasing the incentive for them to invest more in their own human capital. Women have responded as rational economic actors to the changing costs and benefits of the situation, and have sought to maximise their self-interest, with a resulting rise in earnings and employment opportunities.

Whilst building on this rational action approach, the prolific work of Hakim (1991, 1995, 1996a, 1996b, 1998, 2000, 2002, 2003), Preference Theory, asserts that women are not homogeneous in their priorities and preferences in relation to the conflict between work and family life, and that it is these differences which account for both within- and between-gender difference in labour market activities and outcomes. On the basis of their work-life preferences, Hakim classifies women into three qualitatively-different groups: home-centred women, for whom children and family life are the main priorities throughout life; adaptive women, non-career oriented women who wish to combine work and family, or who have unplanned careers; and work-centred women, for whom employment is the main priority in life. Adaptive women form by far the largest group, potentially 80 per cent (Hakim 2000, 165) and the most diverse group, including those who want to combine employment and family, without either taking priority, those with unplanned careers, and a large number of 'drifters'. Hakim proposes that adaptive women adopt strategies that enable them to combine paid work with family life, either through entering part-time or intermittent work, careers which suit family life, such as teaching, or through only having one child.

Critics (Bruegel 1996; Ginn et al 1996; Crompton and Harris 1998a; Crompton and Harris 1998b; Procter and Padfield 1999; Barlow and Duncan 2000; Crompton 2002; McRae 2003) have argued that human capital and preference theories make strong assumptions on rationality and stability of preferences that do not seem to hold in reality, and disregard the role of structural, institutional and cultural factors. According to these critics, women do make choices, but these choices are made within available opportunities and constraints.

The changing structure of the economy can be argued to have contributed to the position of women in the labour market. In pre-industrial Britain the household was the basic unit of production, and all family members were involved in different aspects of this production. But during the early stages of industrialisation the factory steadily replaced the family as the unit of production, and although women and children were employed within the factories initially, a series of factory acts, beginning in 1819 gradually restricted child labour. Children became more dependent on their parents and the caring role was taken on by women, isolating housework and childcare from other work. It has been argued that 'the increased differentiation of child and adult roles, with the child's growing dependence, heralded the dependence of women in marriage and their restriction to the home' (Oakley 1974, 43). Victorian ideology of femininity and domesticity, particularly amongst the middle classes stated that a woman's place was in the home. This was reinforced through educational provision, exclusion of women from the trade unions, and increasing restrictions on women's employment in certain industries, such as mining, through legislation. It was this combination of factors which locked the majority of women into the mother-housewife role. In this way, changes in the labour market, as a result of industrialisation could be argued to be the origin of women's position in the labour market in the late nineteenth century. These structural changes were however heavily dependent on ideological assumptions about women's roles within the family for their effect.

The UK experienced structural change in the post-war period, with a decline in the manufacturing sector and an increase in the service industries, leading to the continued growth of female part-time employment, as employers continually sought increased flexibility. Fagan and O'Reilly (1998) discuss the demand-side factors relating to women's employment, especially part-time work. They argue that, as opposed to an increase in the supply of workers wanting part-time jobs, changes occurred in employers' demand for part-time workers. Specifically 'if the employment share of industries with a high rate of part-time employment increases, the demand for part-time workers will increase, all else being equal' (Fagan and O'Reilly 1998, 243). The service sector lends itself to flexible working patterns, thus drawing in women's labour. This links into Marxist-feminist 'reserve army of labour' theories (Bruegel 1979; Beechey and Perkins 1987) which assert that women, particularly married women, make up a labour reserve, because their role within the family makes them a cheap, flexible and disposable source of labour. Alternative but similar 'segmentation of the labour market' theories (Barron and Norris 1976; Rubery et al 1994) suggested that the labour market was structured into two distinct sectors, with women constituting the secondary sector, characterised by lower wages, security and conditions. Second-wave feminists, such as Walby (1986, 1988, 1990, 1997) and Hartmann (1976), point to patriarchal practices as maintaining women's position in the labour market. In traditional terms, patriarchy means 'the rule of the father', and has come to be used as a term to describe the domination of women by men. Walby (1990) argues that patriarchy shifted from private patriarchy in the nineteenth century, with women serving individual patriarchs (their husband) through domestic work, to public patriarchy in the twentieth century where women in paid employment were collectively exploited by employers, to maintain occupational segregation. Exclusionary strategies, the trade union campaign for the principle of the family wage, and segregation strategies operated as structural aspects of the labour market to maintain the domestic division of labour, and constrain women's position in the labour market (Hartmann 1976). Although formal restrictions on women's participation have been removed, through the introduction of equal opportunities legislation, occupational segregation has deep roots in a historical period when discriminatory practices were legal (Walby and Olsen 2002).

Other structural constraints, such as the cost and availability of childcare, face women in choosing how to balance market work and family work. Institutions, such as the Welfare State and the family, together with social attitudes and stereotypical gender roles, and breadwinner ideologies (Oakley 1974; Esping-Anderson 1990; Fraser 1997; Pfau-Effinger 1999; Marks and Houston 2002) have also had an important part to play in structuring the labour market, and women's role within it.

This section has considered a number of potential theoretical explanations for trends and patterns in female employment, encompassing both supply- and demand-side factors. Human capital and preference theories, which emphasise the role of individuals rational choices and preferences have been criticised as neglecting the role that the structure of the labour market itself plays. Individuals do make choices, but these choices are made within available opportunities and constraints, and are strongly affected by the welfare state, the family, and the regulation of the labour market.

Policy context

In the previous section we saw that over the last few decades there have been significant changes in the employment patterns of men and women, with particularly noteworthy increases in employment rates among mothers. But what policy changes have accompanied this increase, and how have families been supported in balancing work and family life? This section reviews relevant government policy in this area, including maternity rights, pay and leave, the National Childcare Strategy, and welfare to work strategies.

It has been argued that the fast growth in maternal employment in Britain was not facilitated by appropriate economic and social policies until the mid-1990s (Hewitt 1993; Ferri and Smith 1996; Lewis and Lewis 1996; Brannen et al 1997). Until this time the primary emphasis was on social policy measures which incurred little cost to the state, and on employment policies that relied mainly on voluntary action rather than regulation (Bradshaw et al 1996; Moss 1996). Social polices were slow to react to work and family change, and had a tendency to 'ignore the tide of women entering the labour market' (Pascall 1997, 301).

Under the current Labour government the reconciliation of paid employment and home life has been given higher priority than in the past (for example Department for Education and Employment (DfEE) 2000a; Department of Trade and Industry 2000) and this section briefly considers government policy with regards parental employment, maternity and parental leave, family friendly policies and work-life balance. In addition, since the advent of New Labour policies to promote paid work and make work pay have been at the heart of the anti-poverty agenda, to support the aim of eradicating child poverty in the UK by 2020, and these policies have implications for parents and their children.

Maternity rights

In Britain, national maternity leave legislation was first passed in 1978, but less than half of working women were eligible for cover, because a woman had to have worked two years full-time or five years part-time to qualify. Maternity pay, or at a slightly lower rate, maternity allowance, was payable to those who qualified for a period of 14 weeks leave, and eligible women retained the right to return to their job at any time for a total of 40 weeks (11 weeks before and 29 weeks after childbirth) (McRae 1991b; Waldfogel 1998). In 1993, in line with the European Economic Community (EEC) Pregnant Workers Directive (EEC 1992) maternity leave coverage was extended in the UK as qualifying rules were relaxed, and all female employees, regardless of length of service and whether they worked full or part-time, were entitled to a minimum of 14 weeks' maternity leave (sometimes unpaid, although maternity pay or maternity allowance was usually payable). The period of entitlement was later extended to 18 weeks. Although framed as a right to return to the same job up to 29 weeks after childbirth, an additional period of unpaid additional maternity leave was available to women who had been in employment for a year.

Significant changes were introduced in 2003, with new mothers being entitled to a period of 26 weeks Ordinary Maternity Leave (OML), regardless of how long they had been with their employer. Women who had been employed for minimum of 26 weeks by 14 weeks before their estimated due date were also entitled to a further 26 weeks of Additional Maternity Leave (AML) after this. The level of Statutory Maternity Pay (SMP) and Maternity Allowance (MA) increased significantly (£117.18 at 6 April 2008), with SMP paid at 90 per cent of earnings for the first six weeks to eligible women (based on the same qualifying rules as for AML). A report published alongside the 2004 Pre-budget report (HM Treasury 2004a) indicated the government's intention to extend paid maternity leave from six months to nine months from April 2007 (and thus now in effect), and to a year before the end of the next parliament. From April 2007, all female employees have qualified for 12 months maternity leave (6 months OML and 6 months AML).

Maternity leave enables a mother to spend time caring for her young baby. Evidence suggests that paid maternity leave is associated with a range of significant benefits, such as lower maternal depression, lower infant mortality (4 per cent reduction when leave is extended 10 weeks), fewer low birthweight babies, more breastfeeding and more use of preventative health care (Chatterji and Markowitz 2004). Although unpaid leave does not have the same protective effects, it helps keep mothers engaged with the labour market, which may be important both for child development and wider economic reasons. Whilst the government has extended a mother's right to maternity leave to a full year and extended the statutory paid period to 9 months, the final 3 months of maternity leave is unpaid. As a result, many families find it hard to afford to make use of the full 12 months. Seventy five per cent of mothers surveyed in 2002 who were entitled to AML but returned to work early said they did so for financial reasons. Only 11 per cent of mothers said they were ready or wanted to go back to work (Hudson et al 2004). Thus the proposals to increase the period of paid maternity leave have potential benefits for both mothers and children.

Paternity rights

Paid paternity leave was introduced for the first time in 2003, with fathers being eligible for two weeks paid leave (at the same rate as SMP) after the birth of their child. The Work and Families Bill 2005 proposed that when maternity leave was increased to 9 months in 2007 fathers may be eligible to take up to three months of this (paid) leave, providing the mother has returned to work. This policy is yet to implemented.

Parental leave and the right to time off to care for dependents

An entitlement to 13 weeks of unpaid parental leave was introduced in 1999 for all parents (of children up to age six, or age 18 if the child is disabled) who have worked for the same employer for a year. In addition to these pay and leave entitlements, parents also have the right to request flexible working arrangements. Employers have a responsibility to consider these requests seriously, and to provide good business reasons if they are turned down.

National Childcare Strategy

Until 1997, childcare in Britain was seen mainly as a private concern and very limited publicly funded childcare was available. This reflected the belief in the privacy of the family, whereby the state should only intervene if there was a clear failure on the part of the child's natural carer (Daycare Trust 2004). But the lack of good quality, affordable childcare is a significant barrier to parents, particularly mothers, of young children wishing to take up paid employment. Evidence from a survey on parents' demand for childcare (Woodland et al 2002) illustrates some of the frustration and dissatisfaction that parents feel about the choices open to them. The survey found that nearly two thirds (63 per cent) of non-working mothers would prefer to work or study if they had access to good quality, convenient, reliable and affordable childcare. Most mothers in work (85 per cent) said they would like to use some formal childcare if it was readily available and was affordable, but less than half of working mothers had used formal childcare in the previous year. On the other hand, the study also found that nearly two thirds (63 per cent) of mothers who were currently in employment wanted to work fewer hours and just under half (44 per cent) of working mothers would prefer to give up work and stay at home with their children if they could afford it. Bradshaw and Finch (2002) compared child benefit packages across 22 countries, and although the UK came 7th overall (an improvement from a similar study in 1992 (Bradshaw et al 1993)) it had amongst the highest childcare costs for better-off couples.

The first National Childcare Strategy (Department for Education and Employment (DfEE) 1998a) was launched in 1998, with the aim of increasing the level and quality of childcare, both to promote children's well-being and development, and to offer more parents the opportunity to work and enhance their employability. From September 1998 the government made a commitment to provide a free part-time nursery place for all 4-year-olds whose parents wanted it; this was extended to all 3-year-olds in September 1999. Since 2002, the government has recognised the importance of a more integrated approach to children's services, and in December 2002, the Sure Start Unit was created, which brought together responsibility for early education, childcare, health and family support. Help with paying for childcare came with the introduction of tax credits (see below), and from 2005 changes in the existing tax and national insurance rules introduced incentives for employers to support the provision of childcare for their employees.

Welfare to work

The central theme of the incoming Labour government's first social security green paper (Department of Social Security (DSS) 1998a) was the focus on getting people into work, with the introduction of the mantra 'work is the surest route out of poverty'. The implementation of a number of New Deal programmes began in 1997 with the New Deal for Lone Parents (NDLP), which is the only programme specifically targeted upon families with children. The original target group was lone parents receiving Income Support for at least three months and who had a youngest child aged five or above, although others could put themselves forward for the programme. Lone parents are now required to attend work-focussed interviews as a condition of benefit receipt, but participation in the NDLP remains voluntary. Personal advisers provide an integrated service of advice and support, covering job search, advice on training, help in finding childcare services, advice on benefits and help with claiming benefits. Lone parents who start work are able to receive continuing in-work support from the personal adviser. For those who are not ready to start work, the aim is to assist lone parents become work-ready, for example by finding appropriate education or training as a step towards employment. The other New Deal programmes (Over-50s, Young People, Partners, Disabled People, 50 Plus, and Musicians) operate in a similar way, with the focus on enabling individuals into work through a combination of advice, support and training.

A number of evaluations, both qualitative and quantitative, of the various New Deal programmes have been carried out (reviewed in Millar 2000), with generally positive findings, with a positive, although fairly small, impact on exits from income support, although take-up has been low (Millar and Ridge 2001).

Making work pay

Improving work incentives – that is incentives, not necessarily just financial, for individuals to move from welfare into work and incentives for employers to take them on – was another key theme of New Labour's policy. To help 'make work pay' the government brought in the UK's first National Minimum Wage in April

1999. At the same time, various reforms to income tax and National Insurance Contributions reduced the tax burden on the low paid and their employers (Gregg et al 2005). Additionally, in October 1999 the government introduced a new tax credit, the Working Families Tax Credit (WFTC), for couples with children or lone parents who worked 16 or more hours per week (with higher benefits if they worked 30 or more hours) (HM Treasury 1998). This had the aim of ensuring families were better off in work than on benefit by tackling the poverty trap inherent in Family Credit, whereby families were little, if at all, better off when they increased their earnings because up to 90 per cent of every extra pound they earned was taken away in tax or reduced benefits (HM Treasury 2000). Alongside this a Children's Tax Credit was introduced from April 2001, essentially a tax relief reducing the tax paid by working families with children aged under 16, which doubled in value when a baby was born during the tax year. The Labour government also introduced a series of benefit changes aimed at reducing child poverty, including significant real increases in the value of the universal child allowance, Child Benefit, and substantial increases in allowances for children under age 11 in non-working families receiving Income Support.

A substantive change in financial support for childcare costs occurred with the introduction of WFTC. Seventy per cent of childcare costs, up to a maximum of £135 per week for one child and £200 per week for two children, was available to both lone-parent and couple families, provided both parents worked over 16 hours a week (Blundell 2001). This represented a substantial increase in generosity in the treatment of childcare costs and a major improvement in work incentives where claimants had to pay for childcare.

The evidence suggests that the success of WFTC reforms varied with family structure. Based on simulation modelling, Blundell (2000) argued that for lone-parent families WFTC increased incentives to work, as it did for couple families with neither parent in employment. However, for couples where both partners were employed there appeared to be some incentive for a reduction in hours by one partner or a move out of employment altogether.

In April 2003, all of the various benefits and tax credits for children (apart from Child Benefit) were combined into a single integrated Child Tax Credit, to provide a single, seamless system of support of families with children, payable irrespective of the work status of the adult(s) in the household (HM Treasury 2002). This came alongside the introduction of another new tax credit, the Working Tax Credit to support those on low incomes, with and without children. Although complex, these two tax credits aimed to provide a more transparent, responsive and fairer system. It is mainly in the realm of responsiveness that criticisms have been levelled at the tax credit system. In drawing up the new Tax Credits scheme, the government looked at systems in other countries, in particular, Canada – which has a relatively simple and unresponsive system, with awards based on income from the previous year – and Australia – which has a highly responsive system (Whiteford et al 2003). The government concluded that neither model could be replicated precisely in the UK and sought to design a system that steered 'a course between the two'

(HM Treasury 2002, 22). It was decided that the UK system would be responsive to changes in circumstances (such as family size, childcare costs and disability); to all falls in annual income; and to rises in annual income of more than £2,500 a year. Awards are annual and therefore 'the system has an element of financial uncertainty built into it, sometimes causing significant problems for people who have to plan carefully to manage their family budgets' (Parliamentary and Health Service Ombudsman 2005, 5). There have been criticisms of the complexity of the system and the extent of overpayments, which represented about one-third of all tax credits awards paid, at a cost of nearly £2 billion in 2003–04 (House of Commons Treasury Committee 2006).

Theoretical context

We have seen how patterns of parental employment have changed, and explored the increasing policy emphasis on paid work. But what does this mean for children? And what are the possible mechanisms of impact of parental employment and unemployment impact on children's outcomes? This section discusses some of these possible mechanisms of transmission, and outlines the theoretical framework adopted in this research, based on a forms of capital approach.

Meritocracy and social mobility

In a truly meritocratic society 'individuals get out of the system what they put into it based on individual merit' (McNamee and Miller 2004, 1). If life is considered to be a race to get ahead and succeed, then if a true merit system existed everyone would start at the same place and have an equal opportunity to do well through their own individual ability and effort, rather than class background, gender or ethnicity. In this sense, children would all have the opportunity to do well in life based on their ability, regardless of their parents' occupational or class background. But the evidence suggests that merit is only part of the story. The reality is that, as McNamee and Miller write, 'the race to get and stay ahead is more like a relay race in which we inherit our starting positions from our parents. The passing of the baton between generations profoundly influences life outcomes' (197–8). Thus children of successful parents are more likely to experience success in their own lives. This intergenerational transmission of advantage and disadvantage refers to the extent to which inequalities persist across generations, generally in terms of income, employment and class.

Conversely, social mobility describes the movement or opportunities for movement between different social groups, or doing better than expected on the basis of your background. Intragenerational mobility refers to social mobility within a single generation and is measured by comparing the occupational or social status of an individual at two or more points in time. Thus a person who begins her or his working life as an unskilled manual worker and ten years later is employed as an accountant has experienced intragenerational mobility. Intergenerational mobility refers to social mobility between generations and is measured by comparing the occupational or social status of sons with that of fathers (and only rarely the occupational status of fathers or mothers with that of their daughters). Thus, if the son of an unskilled worker becomes an accountant, he is socially mobile in terms of intergenerational mobility (for a good discussion of social mobility see Aldridge 2001).

The first studies of social mobility appeared at the beginning of the twentieth century. They were small scale, focusing on the recruitment to particular occupations (Chapman and Marquis 1912; Chapman and Abbott 1913; Ginsberg 1929). Considerable openness and mobility was observed, but it was not possible to generalise the findings to the society as a whole. The first major nationally-representative study was that of Glass and his associates (the 1949 mobility survey), which provided a picture of mobility trends over the first half of the century, and claimed that 'the general picture so far is of a rather stable social structure, and one in which social status has tended to operate within, so to speak, a closed circuit' (Glass 1954, 21).

Later research by John Goldthorpe and his colleagues at the Social Mobility Group, Oxford, in the early 1970s told a different story (Goldthorpe 1980; Heath 1981; Goldthorpe and Payne 1986). By the time of the 1972 survey of men's mobility in England and Wales there was increasing 'room at the top' and a considerable surplus of upward over downward mobility. The driving force behind this change was the expansion of professional and managerial occupations and decline of manual occupations. Hence mobility rates, especially upward mobility, increased substantially in the post-war period. However, Goldthorpe also noted considerable stability in class relations. Children of middle-class origins were still much more likely to arrive at middle-class destinations than those with working class parents. In this sense, although chances of upward mobility had increased for everyone, relative rates of mobility – the relative chances of people from different social origins ending up in the middle classes – had not changed from the 1940s.

One of the major problems with the Oxford Mobility Study is that it ignores women (see Crompton 1980) as Goldthorpe strongly believed in the male breadwinner family as the unit of stratification in industrial societies. Later studies have tried to establish a picture of women's mobility patterns (comparing the social class of daughters with their fathers), finding that in general women have not enjoyed as much social mobility as men, although this has been complicated by the substantial proportion of women who are not in the labour market (Heath 1981; Marshall et al 1988; Johnson and Reed 1996).

Looking specifically at the impact of parental employment on the outcomes of children and young people, the study of social mobility based on occupational status is necessarily limiting, because we have to wait until children are grown up to compare their occupational status with that of their parents. Studies of social mobility also give no insight into the impact of parental employment on other areas of children's lives, or into the mechanisms of transmission, with which the next section is concerned.

Mechanisms of intergenerational transmission

As Machin (1998) writes 'for an offspring to be in an advantageous or disadvantageous position simply because of their parents' achievement has a distinct feel of unfairness to it, particularly from an equality of opportunity perspective' (55). Thus the ways in which advantage or disadvantage is transmitted between generations has been the subject of many studies, and theories abound as to the processes of transmission. These theories inform the debate about the impact of parental employment and unemployment on children and young people.

Children inherit their genetic make-up from their parents providing the groundplan for development (Smith et al 1998). But although genetics may have a role in understanding intergenerational transmission (see Neiderhiser and Reiss 2002, for a discussion of some of the literature on genetic influences on measures of family process and child adjustment) there is no doubt that other factors play a greater part. Thus as Gittins (1998) writes 'biology is not necessarily fixed and static, but is also changed by social and environmental factors, the two more often than not interacting' (24).

Goldthorpe (1980) argued that those at the higher echelons of the class structure (middle classes) enjoy greater economic resources or income, and the power that comes with them, than those in the lower echelons (working class). These advantages enable them to maintain their position in society, and through the transmission of these resources to their children, establish their position as well. In this sense children benefit from their parents employment via the income it provides to the household. But there are two main competing hypotheses about the role of income in the intergenerational transmission mechanism – the investment theory and the good parent theory (Mayer 1997; Mayer 2002). The former holds that income has a direct effect on outcomes; the second maintains that is has an indirect effect.

Investment theory dominates economic models of intergenerational transmission (Becker 1981; Becker and Tomes 1986; Ermisch and Francesconi 2001b). In this theory the relationship between parents' and children's economic success is the result of the biological and other endowments that parents pass on to their children, combined with what parents invest in their children. Parents invest both time and money in their children, especially by investing in their education, but also by purchasing health care, 'good' neighbours, and other inputs that improve children's chances of future success in education, employment, and more generally. How much parents invest in their children is determined by their ability to finance investments (which is determined by their income and access to capital). The return on investments in children may depend on children's biological endowments, so these may also influence the amount parents are willing to invest. Parents' own values and norms may also help to determine their willingness to invest in their children. These economic models predict that children raised in affluent families succeed more often than those raised in poor families, both because rich parents pass on superior endowments and because they can invest more in their children.

In contrast to the investment theory, good parent theories hold that low income hurts children not because poor families have less money to invest in their children, but because low income reduces parents' ability to be 'good parents' (see Mayer 2002). There are two main variations of the good parent theory: the parental stress version and the role model version. In the parental stress version, poverty and low income are held to be stressful and it is this stress that diminishes parents' ability to be supportive, consistent and involved with their children. Poor parenting and interactions in turn hurt the social and emotional development of children, which limits their educational and social opportunities.

The other version of the good parent theory, role model theory, also emphasises parents' interactions with their children. Low income reduces children's chances for socio-economic success and high levels of individual well-being, not because poor families have less money to invest in their children, but because low income decreases the quality of non-monetary investments, such as parents' interactions with their children (Ermisch et al 2001; Mayer 2002). The economic circumstances of parents may be reflected in the underlying family values and processes. For example, the labour income of the father or mother may convey information to the child about the role model provided by that parent. Similarly, the receipt of Income Support may reflect the extent to which a household has (more or less rationally) adopted the norms and values that are sometimes believed to be associated with a 'culture of poverty' or 'welfare culture' (Wilson 1987). These values may not provide children with enough incentives to invest in their own education.

A further suggestion is that there is some element of spuriousness between parental low income and young people's outcomes, with the sharing of some other unmeasured or measurable factors. For example, behavioural and medical problems such as alcoholism, depression or drug addiction may make a parent less likely to work, reducing income, and affecting his or her child's life. A father's alcohol problem may directly affect his investment in his child, by providing smaller material, time and emotional resources, but in addition the father may lose his job or have a less stable attachment to the labour market, and the child's parents may divorce because of the father's alcohol addiction, which in turn may impact upon the child's life experiences and outcomes (Ermisch et al 2004).

So far the discussion has focussed on the role of income in intergeneration transmission, although direct and indirect influences have been mentioned. But parental employment represents more than just a source of income, and thus a theoretical framework which incorporates the different aspects of employment and how they impact on children's outcomes needs to be developed.

Forms of capital approach

One useful framework which can be used to consider the impact of parental employment and unemployment on children's lives is to distinguish between the resources available to a family in terms of different forms of capital – economic capital, social capital and cultural capital (Bourdieu, 1983) – to examine how employment and unemployment might impact on each form of capital, and thus on children's outcomes.

Economic capital Economic (or financial) capital represents the economic resources, derived from employment, savings, or other sources, which an individual possesses (Bourdieu 1983) and is related to class divisions in terms of economic resources as discussed above. Thus parents' employment status and income clearly influence the economic capital they have available. In addition to income, an individual's social class, housing tenure, and car ownership are indicative of their economic capital, and more broadly of their socio-economic circumstances. Bourdieu (1983) challenged economic theory for narrowly focussing only on economic capital, and identified cultural and social capital as well.

Social capital Social capital has been defined as 'the aggregate of the actual or potential resources which are linked to possession of a durable network of more or less institutionalised relationships of mutual acquaintance and recognition' (Bourdieu 1983, 248). In other words, the social networks and connections that an individual possesses, through participation in social activities, group memberships and other networking opportunities, such as employment, all contribute to their social capital. Comparative research demonstrates that individuals occupying positions associated with educational success and employment in professional occupations tend to belong to different social networks from people occupying positions associated with poor educational attainment and unemployment, or employment in poorly paid, unskilled occupations (Burt 2000; Putnam 2000). All of these networks represent potential sources of social capital for their members, but the social capital associated with the networks of the poorly educated and underemployed will tend not to have currency in the networks of the well-educated and professionally employed, and vice versa.

Social capital also encompasses the quality of relationships within the family, and the ways that parents interact with their children and each other, the educational aspirations parents have for their children, the home environment, and even the time that family members have to devote to each other (Winquist Nord et al 1997). Putnam, in his book, *Bowling Alone*, which posits a decline in social capital in the US, demonstrates that child development is powerfully shaped by social capital, that 'trust, networks, and norms of reciprocity within a child's family, school, peer group, and larger community have far reaching effects on their opportunities and choices, and hence on their behaviour and development' (Putnam 2000, 296).

Cultural capital According to Bourdieu (1983), cultural capital represents the collection of non-economic forces such as family background, social class, varying investments in and commitments to education, and different cultural resources at play in an individual's life. Three forms of cultural capital can be distinguished: embodied state (cultural habitus, a person's character and ways of thinking), objectified state (cultural assets, such as paintings and books), and institutionalised state (educational qualifications). Becker's notion of human capital (Becker 1964; Becker and Tomes 1986) – educational qualifications, training and work experience – is seen by Bourdieu as an integral form of cultural capital. Sullivan (2001) asserts that cultural capital is comprised of familiarity with the dominant culture in society and emphasises that the ability to understand and use 'educated language' is a key feature. Employment status, occupation and income are therefore important markers of an individual's cultural capital in terms of the development of cultural values, norms and expectations. The role model which parents present to their children will reflect these cultural values, norms and expectations. Unemployment may also restrict both parents' and children's access to the 'signals of cultural knowledge' and limit the appreciation of 'highbrow cultural activities' (Robson 2003, 2–4).

These forms of capital do not exist in isolation from one another, but are inextricably linked and convertible from one form to another. Bourdieu (1983) recognises that all forms of capital can be derived from economic capital through varying efforts of transformation, but equally that economic reward can be derived from both social and cultural capital. Having considered the main forms of capital proposed by Bourdieu – economic, social and cultural – and how access to each may be affected by an individual's employment and occupational status, we turn to consider how the impact of parental employment patterns on children may be conceptualised using this forms of capital approach.

Parental employment, capitals, and the impact on children

Parental employment, and conversely unemployment, can have both positive and negative effects on children, through its effect on both individual and family levels of economic, social and cultural capital. This could be both deliberate, such as the purchase of books or private tuition, and inadvertent, such as the unwitting development of expectations and norms, which then reflect on children's lives.

Parents' human capital may be important for children's outcomes, not only through the passing on of hereditary endowments, in the form of innate ability, but also through the provision of a culture of learning for children (Coleman 1988). Parental employment or worklessness (and thus income) has a direct effect on children's life outcomes, because it affects the amount of money parents have available to invest in their children. This relates to the economic theories of intergenerational transmission discussed above (Becker 1981; Becker and Tomes 1986; Ermisch and Francesconi 2001b). These investments could be in educational resources, for example seeking better schools, purchasing additional books, visits to the library or access to computers and the internet. Parents with greater economic capital may also be able to invest more in their children's social and cultural capital, driving children to their friends houses, funding trips to the theatre or museums, and paying for musical instrument lessons. Devine (2004) draws on qualitative research with parents in the UK and US to investigate how middle-class parents mobilise their economic, cultural and social resources to increase their children's chances of educational success and occupational advancement.

Investment of resources in children's cultural capital, through the purchase of cultural goods, such as books, cultural visits, etc, is seen as an important way of developing their ability and talent (Bourdieu 1983). In addition, employment status, occupation and position at work have important implications for an individual's cultural capital, through the development of cultural values, norms and expectations, which can then influence their children. Children's attitudes and aspirations can be shaped partly by the family values and expectations to which they are exposed. Thus, the labour market income and occupation of the mother or father may convey information to a child about the role model provided by that parent, and heighten their expectations for their own future.

Parental employment may have both positive and negative effects on children, through its effect on both individual and family social capital. Employment, through an increase in parents' socialising opportunities, is a way of developing parental social capital, and may therefore impact on children in a number of ways. Buchel and Duncan (1998) studied the impact that parent's socialising had on children's educational achievement (using German Socio-economic Panel data), showing both positive and negative consequences, and this could be extended to encompass the implications of parental employment for other child outcomes. They suggested that parents' socialising could have positive effects through the development of social networks, resulting in an increased flow of information to parents, and thus to children, regarding education and employment (see also Coleman 1988). Social networks can also play a part in finding employment (Granovetter 1973; Granovetter 1974) through exposure to information, work experience and vacancies. Thus parental unemployment may limit children's access to social networks and therefore impede recruitment through those networks.

One indirect effect of parental employment, through increasing the opportunities for parent's socialising, is the potential to help develop children's own social skills, important for their future networking and job search activities. Inasmuch as socialising contributes to the happiness and well-being of the parent, it may also have positive effects on the child, and this may also hold true for parental employment (Buchel and Duncan 1998). Arendall (2000) suggests that employed mothers experience higher levels of general well-being and lower levels of depression and anxiety than full-time mothers, and that this may have positive implications for their children. Similarly, unemployed fathers are more likely to be depressed and anxious than employed fathers, which may impact on a child's anxiety and the father-child relationship (Ray and McLoyd 1986).

Coleman (1988) illustrated the importance of social capital within the family for a child's intellectual development, stressing that although children are strongly affected by the human capital possessed by their parents, access to this depends upon both the physical presence of adults in the family and on the attention given by the adults to the child. Although primarily concerned with the 'structural deficiency' in social capital inherent in lone-parent families, he also stated that 'the nuclear family itself, in which one or both parents work outside the home, can be seen as structurally deficient, lacking the social capital that comes with the presence of parents during the day' (111). Coleman expressed concern that job-holding mothers were diminishing family social capital, by reducing women's emotional investment in building relationships with their children at home. He was thus critical of any parental employment that reduced the time that parents spend with their children, neglecting to consider the potential financial benefit of such employment for children.

The impact of parental employment on the amount of time they spend with their children is an important issue. Some commentators have suggested that the 'mass' entry of women into the labour market has created untenable stresses in couple and parent-child relationships because of the lack of time available to devote to family life (Davies 1993; Halsey 1993; Murray 1994; Phillips 1999). However, one local study analysed children's time-use diaries and found that children in two parent families whose parents were both employed full-time actually reported spending more time with their parents than those living in families where the mother was employed part-time, or where she was not in the labour market (O'Brien and Jones 1999). In this study, children in father sole-earner families actually reported the least combined parental time (that is, the total time spent with both parents) of all three groups. This would suggest that parental employment per se might not actually reduce the amount of time that parents spend with their children, although it has to be stressed that this was a relatively small study in one working class locality, and might thus reflect local traditions. There is also an important distinction to be made here between the quantity and quality of parent-child time, as it could be suggested that social capital in terms of the quality of relationships between family members is less dependent upon the amount of time children spend with their parents, and is more to do with the quality of that time. O'Brien and Jones (1999), also found that in terms of parent-child relationships, children were more satisfied with the quality of their mother's time when she was working part-time, although the differences were not significant and satisfaction levels were generally high (617). Thus the effect of parental employment on the time that they spend with their children is complex.

This section has considered the ways in which parental employment and unemployment might be expected to impact on children, employing the use of a forms of capital approach. Employment and unemployment impact on individuals' financial resources (economic capital), qualifications and experience (human capital), social networks and relationships (social capital) and cultural norms and expectations (cultural capital), and in different ways these may be thought to have implications for children. The next section considers some of the evidence from previous research on the impact of parental employment and unemployment on a wide range of outcomes for children.

The impact of parental employment on children's well-being

There is no one accepted definition of well-being, and the concept of well-being has been debated by a wide range of disciplines, including health economics, advertising, medicine, sociology and psychology. Indeed Liu (1976, cited in Felce and Perry 1995) said that there are as many definitions of well-being as there are people, since it is a matter of personal opinion. There is general agreement however that well-being encompasses all aspects of life, and can be broken down into constituent parts (see Hird 2003). A large body of work has sought to devise scales, measures and indicators of well-being (including Bradshaw 2002a; Hird 2003; Bradshaw and Mayhew 2005) and various measures and indicators are used by the government to assess the impact of policies on the incidence of poverty and disadvantage (see the annual 'Opportunity for All' reports: DSS 1999; DSS 2000b; Department for Work and Pensions (DWP) 2001; DWP 2002; DWP 2003; DWP 2004; DWP 2005; DWP 2006a).

Children's lives are complex and thus children's well-being encompasses many aspects of their lives. A wealth of research has been undertaken in the UK, US and other countries, to consider the potential effects of parental employment on children's well-being, in terms of their early development, cognitive ability, educational achievement, and behaviour, together with outcomes in early adulthood, such as early parenthood and economic activity. Although most of this research considers the effect of maternal employment, a small, but growing literature is emerging on the effect of father's employment and unemployment on children.

The current research focuses on the impact of parental employment and unemployment on children's educational and emotional well-being. Although discussed in more detail in the relevant chapters, this section provides a brief review of some of the evidence, focussing particularly on the mechanisms by which parental employment and unemployment effects children's outcomes.

Cognitive development and education

The development of children's cognitive ability is undoubtedly multi-faceted, and could potentially be affected by parental working patterns in a number of ways. As discussed above, increased income derived from employment enables parents to invest more in their children's human capital, thus spending more on their children's education and learning, through the purchase of books, personal tuition or private education (Becker, 1981; Ermisch et al, 2001). But Weinberg (2001) criticises this investment model as ignoring children's own agency and decision-making, and suggests that increased income enables parents to offer children pecuniary incentives to improve their own performance and achievement, whereas those with low incomes are unable to do so.

Living in a low income family may increase levels of parental distress, which could hinder children's social adjustment and limit cognitive development

(Parcel and Menaghan, 1994). Growing up with an unemployed parent might lower a child's own expectations and aspirations, by conveying a negative image to children, and not providing them with the incentives to invest in their own education (Ermisch et al, 2001). Parents' own human capital, in the form of education, qualifications and knowledge also clearly plays a part here, not only through the passing on of hereditary endowments, in the form of innate ability, but also through the provision of a culture of learning. White and Kaufman (1997) found that family social capital, such as parents or siblings helping children with homework regularly, can be an effective buffer against the negative impact of low socio-economic status and low parental education attainment on children's academic outcomes.

But parental employment impacts on more than just the financial resources available to the family. Employed parents may have less free time to spend interacting with children, reading to them and assisting with homework, which may have negative implications for cognitive development. Parental involvement in children's education, in terms of attending school or class events, or volunteering at the school may be affected by patterns of parental employment, at least in part because employment competes for time that could be used participating in school activities (Winquist Nord et al, 1997).

The empirical evidence relating to the effects of early and current parental employment on children's cognitive ability is mixed and inconclusive. Indeed, Haveman and Wolfe (1995), in a review of the evidence (mainly from the US) concluded that some studies identify significant adverse effects on children's educational achievement, whilst others find no significant effect, or even suggest a favourable impact. UK evidence mainly comes from studies which make use of data from the Birth Cohort Studies, and similarly elicits varying results. Joshi and Verropoulou (2000) studied two samples – 1,700 school children whose mothers had been part of the 1958 birth cohort study (National Child Development Study (NCDS)), and children from the Birth Cohort Study (BCS), who were born in 1970, and tracked into adulthood – with mixed findings. Maternal employment in the first year of a child's life had a significant negative effect on their later reading ability, although some employment by the mother when the child was aged one to four had a positive significant effect on children's later mathematics scores, but no significant effect on their reading (NCDS). Looking at later educational achievement (BCS), both males and females were slightly less likely to obtain higher levels of qualifications if their mothers had been employed before they were age five. This finding was echoed in research by Ermisch and Francesconi (2000, 2001a), who used various samples of young people drawn from the British Household Panel Survey (BHPS) born between 1970 and 1981. They found that longer periods of full-time work for mothers of pre-school children tended to reduce the chance of gaining an A level or equivalent, and there was a similar although less pronounced effect of periods of part-time employment. However, longer periods of full-time work when the children were aged 6–10 increased their chance of achieving A level or higher qualifications. That later maternal employment may have benefits of young people's academic achievement is also supported by Kiernan (1996). Her analysis of longitudinal data for British children born in 1958 (the 1958 National Child Development Study) found that having a mother in work when the child was 16 was associated with a higher probability of young women gaining qualifications, that this was particularly true in lone parent families, but that there was no similar statistically significant association for young men.

These results suggest that maternal employment when children are very young impacts in different ways to that when children are older. For pre-school children, it could be suggested that the time employed mothers spend away from their children has some negative implications for their cognitive development, both in the short-term (although this evidence is weak), and in terms of later academic achievement. However, when children are older and attending school, maternal employment appears to have positive implications for children's educational achievement, perhaps through the increase in financial resources which maternal employment may bring to a family, and the provision of a role model image to children.

Emotional well-being

The impact of parental, particularly maternal, employment on children's early development has been the topic of much research and debate, both in the UK and the US, with the focus being mainly on the development of attachment relationships. Bowlby (1969) suggested that infants who were separated from their mothers for prolonged periods of time would be less securely attached, which was thought to have a negative impact on their later psychological well-being. Although the formation of attachment relationships is important, Bowlby's hypothesis of maternal deprivation has on the whole been discredited (see Belsky 1988; Phoenix et al 1991; and Buxton 1998, for a discussion of this debate). This section will therefore consider the potential impact that parental employment and unemployment might have for children's emotional well-being both in childhood and early adulthood.

Joshi and Verropoulou (2000) used data from the second generation NCDS to investigate the effects of both early and current maternal employment on emotional adjustment. Using standard scales, mothers were asked to report if their children displayed aggressive (including bullying, disobedience or restlessness) or anxious (including being worried or unhappy) behaviours. That children's anxiety was reported by mothers may result in a possible bias, as mothers may be reluctant to acknowledge any signs of anxiety in their children, particularly if concerned that this may stem from their employment. Children whose mothers had been employed at any time between infancy and compulsory school age displayed lower levels of anxiety at the time of interview in 1991 (when they were aged 5–17) than those whose mothers had not been in employment. There was also a positive association between mothers' current employment and non-anxiety, and this was greater where the mothers were in part-time employment. In addition, when the employment of both parents was considered, living in a family with no earners was associated with higher levels of anxiety.

Another study (Ermisch and Francesconi 2001a) used various samples of young people drawn from the BHPS born between 1970 and 1981. They derived a measure of psychological distress experienced by the young people from questions about a set of subjective indicators of personal well-being (the GHQ 12-point measure). They found an adverse effect on young adult's psychological well-being associated with mothers' full-time working when children were preschoolers, but that more full-time working when a child was aged six to ten was associated with lower risk of later psychological distress, as were periods of part-time employment when the child was aged one to five. Longer periods of employment by fathers when their children were aged one to five reduced the chances that children suffered high levels of psychological distress as young adults.

The effect of parental employment on children's levels of anxiety then is complex, and suggests something of a 'trade-off' between time and income. The impact that maternal employment may have on the time she spends with her child has been discussed elsewhere, but full-time employment may reduce or constrain in some way this time, potentially contributing to the negative effect on anxiety. However, observation of higher levels of anxiety amongst children in workless households would suggest that the increased income derived from maternal employment in some way reduces children's levels of anxiety. Living in a household with low income can increase parent's levels of stress, and in turn this can affect their relationships with their children (which will be discussed in more detail in a later section). Although not considered separately by Joshi and Verropoulou 2000, father's employment appears to have a positive influence on children's emotional well-being, both in childhood and early adulthood. There is also some question of which direction the positive effect of maternal employment on children's anxiety levels operates. Does maternal employment really have a positive effect, or are mothers of less anxious children more likely to go out to work?

The impact that parental employment and unemployment could have on children's emotional well-being is important, as emotional security in childhood and early adulthood has implications for other areas of life, such as the formation of secure relationships, and job prospects. Although there are some inconsistencies, previous research has generally shown that maternal employment tends to reduce children's later levels of anxiety. Father's employment had the same effect, potentially by keeping a family out of a workless household. Both these studies made use of scales, combining measures on various aspects of emotional well-being, and it would be interesting to consider whether the impact of parental employment and unemployment is the same when these items are considered separately. As with other areas of children's lives, there is also a need to study the impact of maternal and paternal employment patterns not individually, but as a whole.

Limitations and gaps in the literature

The current research aims to address a number of gaps in the existing literature and overcome some of the data limitations of previous work.

Much of the empirical research discussed above uses data from the 1958 National Child Development Study (NCDS) and the 1970 British Cohort Study (BCS). There are several key limitations to such data, not least that the children being studied were born up to 50 years ago, when maternal employment, lone parenthood and other aspects of family life were very different to modern times. Joshi and Verroupoulou 2000 use a NCDS second-generation sample, but there are some problems with representativeness, as it consisted only of children born to female members of the NCDS by the time they were 28. This excludes older mothers, who are likely to be more highly educated (Dex et al 1996), and this in itself may have a positive effect their children's maths and reading scores. Thus any effects that are derived for this sample suffer from possible sample selection bias. A further problem with the British cohort data is that parental employment patterns are only recorded at a number of fixed points in time, with limited information available about employment between the surveys.

The BHPS has some general advantages over the birth cohort data. Firstly, the data are more recent and a better reflection of contemporary family life. Ermisch and Francesconi 2000; 2001a, used various samples of young adults drawn from the BHPS, who were born between 1970 and 1981, when maternal employment and lone parenthood were becoming much more common. The BHPS also yields more detailed information on parent's employment patterns, enabling a fuller picture to be built up of parent's employment throughout their children's upbringing, rather than just at particular points in time.

The current research uses data from the BHPS and its associated Youth Panel (BYP; more details are given in the next chapter) whereby young people (aged 11–15) in the BHPS households are interviewed each year. The Youth Panel is a unique and under-utilised resource, which enables the examination of any relationship between parental employment and outcomes in adolescence. The young people in the samples used in the current study were born between 1978 and 1990, and thus the research is more relevant and up-to-date than previous work in this area.

Previous research into the impact of parental employment and unemployment on children has tended to focus on a fairly narrow range of outcomes, mainly educational achievement and children's own patterns of employment later in life (for example Kiernan 1996; O'Brien and Jones 1999 Ermisch and Francesconi 2001a). Although these are important, children's lives are complex, and there is a need to explore the potential relationships between parental employment patterns and the more social and emotional aspects of these lives, such as attitudes and aspirations, relationships and emotional well-being.

There has also been a focus on the outcomes for very young children (for example, Gregg and Washbrook 2003), or the impact of parental employment patterns when children were very young on their later outcomes (for example,

Joshi and Verropoulou 2000). Much less attention has been paid to the impact of parental employment patterns on outcomes for adolescents, and this book aims to address this gap in knowledge. Adolescence is a crucial period in the life course when a young person becomes ready to assume adult responsibility, marking the transition from dependent childhood to independent adulthood (Schoon 2003). Today's adolescents are the parents, teachers, and leaders of the future, and there is clear evidence from life course research that adolescence experiences, and the formation of attitudes and opinions at this stage, have a pronounced influence on adult life. In addition, the opportunities and experiences mark the present quality of young peoples' lives.

Previous studies have tended to focus on the impact of maternal or paternal employment in isolation (for example, Ermisch and Francesconi 2001a). Although the term 'maternal employment' suggests a focus on the mother and her labour force affiliation, the experience of maternal employment (and likewise, paternal employment or unemployment) is embedded in a family system. Therefore, when considering child outcomes, there is a need to study the impact of parental employment patterns within the whole family context.

Research questions

In light of the literature review, the main aim of this book was to investigate any relationships between patterns of parental employment and young people's educational and emotional well-being. As outlined above, a forms of capital approach is used to contextualise and explain these relationships. The research also examines any impact of the timing of parental employment, by exploring whether current parental employment patterns differ in their impact on well-being to patterns of parental employment experienced in childhood. The current work also considers the role of other individual, parental and family factors, both in directly influencing well-being, and in mediating any relationships between parental employment patterns and young people's well-being.

Summary and conclusions

This chapter has mapped out the background to this research project, setting out the social, policy and theoretical context. Over recent decades there have been dramatic changes in the employment patterns of men and women, with particularly significant increases in employment rates among mothers. Government policy has also increasingly given attention to encouraging parents, particularly lone mothers, into work, with a focus on paid work as a defence against poverty. These trends and policy changes affect the everyday lives of both parents and children, and give rise to questions about the potential impact that parental employment patterns have on children and young people.

The current research builds on the existing evidence in this area, by considering the impact of parental employment on the well-being on adolescents, an age-group often neglected by previous research, using data from the youth panel of the BHPS. A forms of capital approach is adopted, to explain the relationships between employment patterns and parents' social, cultural and economic capital, and thus the direct and indirect effects of parental employment and unemployment on the well-being of young people.

Chapter 3
Methodology

Introduction

Having set out the research questions at the end of the previous chapter, this chapter outlines the methodological strategy adopted in this research project, and details the research techniques used. The aim of the research was to explore the relationship between parental employment patterns and outcomes for young people. A quantitative approach was adopted, undertaking secondary analysis of data from the British Household Panel Survey (BHPS), a long-running, large-scale panel survey. The following sections outline the research design and strategy; strengths and weaknesses of secondary analysis; details of panel survey data and the BHPS; a brief look at how the samples were established (with further details given in Appendix A) and their key characteristics; details of measures of well-being, parental employment, and other variables included in the analysis; and an appraisal of the analytical techniques employed.

Research design and strategy

'Design is concerned with turning research questions into projects … The general principle is that the research strategy or strategies, and the methods or techniques employed, must be appropriate for the questions you want to answer' (Robson 2002, 79–80). For the current research, the research questions related to examining and explaining any relationships between parental employment patterns and children's well-being. Such questions lend themselves to being answered using quantitative methods, which permit statistical analysis in order to produce explanations about how the social world operates. If we had been interested in the opinions or attitudes of children or young people to their parents' employment patterns then a qualitative approach may have been more appropriate, and indeed such research would complement the current work.

Secondary analysis

Secondary analysis has been defined as the 'further analysis of an existing data set which presents interpretations, conclusions or knowledge additional to, or different from those presented in the first report' (Hakim 1982, 1). Official statistics are routinely collected on a range of issues, including the numbers of births, marriages, deaths, criminal convictions, and immigration. Government departments also carry out regular surveys (for example, Labour Force Survey, General Household Survey, Health Survey for England) to collect information on issues such as health, crime, income, employment, and so on. In addition, a number of other surveys have been carried out on an ad-hoc or regular basis (for example, Poverty and Social Exclusion Survey, Families and Children Study, British Household Panel Survey). Secondary analysis is usually though of in terms of quantitative research, but in recent years there have been attempts to encourage secondary analysis of qualitative data, for example through the development of an archive for qualitative data at the University of Essex (Corti et al 1995).

That the data has been collected for some other purpose than for your use as a researcher presents certain advantages and limitations. It can be an attractive strategy as it permits you to capitalise on the efforts of others in collecting the data, providing a relatively cheap and potentially quick method of research (Rowlingson 2004). In addition, access is available to surveys with massive sample sizes, which provides scope for considerable subgroup analysis. Repeated surveys (such as panel surveys, discussed in more detail below) also enable comparisons to be made over time. Many government surveys collect data on all adults (and sometimes children) in a household, allowing the researcher to analyse the interrelationships between the characteristics of different household members (Dale et al 1988). In the current research, a sample of several thousand young people was established quite easily, and the structure of the survey enabled young people to be matched to their parents to consider the intergenerational nature of the research.

There are however some disadvantages to secondary analysis. One of the challenges of secondary analysis for the research is to use sociological imagination to construct theoretically informed research questions that can be addressed by somebody else's data, or data not collected specifically for the purpose. Deciding how to measure concepts of theoretical interest, in this case parental employment patterns and children's well-being, is one of the creative aspects of secondary analysis (Arber 2001). The available data do not always fit the secondary analyst's research questions, and pre-set questionnaires limit the analysis that is possible. Certain key questions may have either not been asked at all, or not been asked in the way that the secondary analyst would have liked, and fixed question response categories also limit the use of data to fulfil theoretical questions. A high level of skills in data handling and management are required to conduct secondary analysis, as some surveys consist of many different data files, often at both household and individual level. For example, in May 2006, when data were available from 13 waves, the BHPS consisted of 134 separate data files, and thus complex data manipulation is necessary before analysis can take place. Despite these limitations, if careful consideration is paid to issues of reliability, validity and representativeness (discussed in more detail below) secondary analysis represents an effective strategy for investigating the potential relationships between aspects of social life.

Cross-sectional and longitudinal data

There are several types of survey available for secondary analysis, and a useful overview is provided in Gilbert 2001. A cross-sectional survey provides a snapshot of the characteristics of either a population (for example, the decennial population census in the UK, see Office for National Statistics (ONS) 2005c, for details), or a sample of the population (for example the Women and Employment Survey, see Martin and Roberts 1984) at a particular point in time, although many are repeated either every few years or every year, using a similar (but not the same) sample. Although both single and repeated cross-sectional surveys can provide useful information about an area of theoretical and policy interest, there are limitations to the research questions which can be answered using this type of data. When considering the impact of parental employment patterns on outcomes for children, cross-sectional data would enable the study of the impact of current parental employment and current outcomes. However the study of the impact of parental employment patterns when children were growing up on their later outcomes would be more difficult, and would rely on the collection of retrospective data, asking respondents about their past work and family histories. In this instance a longitudinal design would be more appropriate, and indeed has been adopted in the current study.

Longitudinal studies are conducted by collecting data at a number of points in time from the same set of people, that is, prospectively. A more accurate way of recording individual's attitudes and behaviours over time than retrospectively in cross-sectional surveys, this allows analysis of how individuals and households experience change in their socio-economic environment and how they respond to such changes. It also enables us to examine how experiences, behaviours, conditions and values are linked with each other dynamically over time. As events and conditions are temporally ordered it is possible to test causal hypotheses and models, and potentially establish the direction of these causalities (Rose 2000).

Clearly, longitudinal designs enjoy major advantages over both single and repeated cross-sectional surveys. There are, however, also some disadvantages, with one of the key problems being the cost of maintaining contact with and repeatedly interviewing the same group of people. Panel attrition is a further problem, as respondents are lost between waves (due to refusals, untraceable changes of residence, or death). Single cross-sectional surveys often find that certain groups, such as ethnic minorities or people from lower social classes, are less willing to participate than others. This problem of response bias is multiplied up in panel surveys where these groups tend to drop out between waves at a higher rate, thereby progressively skewing the representativeness of the sample over time (Buckingham and Saunders 2004). Weighting variables can be used to largely mitigate under-representation (see for example, Taylor et al 2001, for a discussion of weighting in the BHPS). Panel conditioning can also occur, in that because the same respondents are repeatedly interviewed it is possible that responses given in one wave will be influenced by those given in the previous waves (Trivellato

1999). In addition, the behaviour and attitudes of people who have participated in a panel survey over many years may be affected by virtue of having been exposed to research for such a long period. Being asked about your life and opinions at regular intervals may lead you to reflect on these things more than you otherwise would, and this in turn may lead you to change them.

Whilst there are several different types of longitudinal design, there is a crucial and basic distinction between the two main types: panel design and cohort design. A cohort design takes everyone born in a particular period and follows them over their life course. Britain is fortunate to have four birth cohort studies, based on births in one week in March 1946 (National Survey of Health and Development, NSHD), in March 1958 (National Child Development Study, NCDS), and in March 1970 (the British Cohort Study, BCS). The 1946 and 1958 studies have also surveyed the next generation, collecting data about the children of cohort members. The Millennium Cohort Study (MCS) is a new cohort study of babies born between September 2000 and August 2001, ruling this out as a source of data for the study of adolescence for a number of years. There are several problems associated with cohort studies, partially as a result of all participants having been born at a similar time and thus being of a similar age. Such cohort effects relate to the impact of the particular period during which they experienced stages of life such as childhood or middle age. In addition, related to the study of outcomes for adolescents, the latest available data come from the BCS whose respondents were teenagers during the 1980s, since which time parental employment patterns, lone parenthood, and other aspects of society have changed dramatically.

The other main type of longitudinal design is the panel survey, which takes a representative random sample of respondents and collects data from them at fixed intervals. This overcomes the possibility of cohort effects, since members of the sample will have been born at different times. Data from panel surveys also enable the study of a broader range of issues, as individuals of all ages are represented. Among the best-known panel studies are the US Panel Study of Income Dynamics (PSID, begun in 1968), the German Socio-Economic Panel, (SOEP, begun in 1984) and the British Household Panel Study (BHPS, begun in 1991). The use of panel survey data, specifically the BHPS and it's associated British Youth Panel (BYP), offered the most appropriate option for the current research, as it allowed a diachronic analysis of parental employment patterns and the impact on children. These data are far more recent, thus better reflecting contemporary life, than data from the NCDS (1958) and other birth cohorts, on which previous investigations in this area have been based (Joshi and Verropoulou 2000; Kiernan 1996). More details are provided about the data used in the next sections.

The British Household Panel Survey (BHPS)

The BHPS commenced in 1991 as an annual survey of each adult (aged 16+) member of a nationally representative sample of more than 5,000 households, making a total of approximately 10,000 interviews in Wave One. The initial selection of households for inclusion in the panel survey was made using a two-stage clustered probability design and systematic sampling. In the first stage of selection an implicitly ordered listing of all sectors on the Postcode Address File (PAF) was established, stratified by region and three socio-demographic characteristics. Using a systematic procedure, 250 Primary Sampling Units (PSUs) were selected from this listing, on average containing 2,500 delivery points (equivalent to addresses). Stage two involved the selection of around 30 delivery points from each PSU (resulting in a total of 8,166 delivery points being selected) using a systematic sampling procedure, with each delivery point in England and Wales having an equal probability of selection (with proportional probability applied in Scotland, to allow for possible multiple occupancies). Stratified sampling is designed to produce more representative and thus more accurate samples (de Vaus 1996), and the selection of geographically clustered units (postcode sectors) reduces field costs by locating the sample in defined areas (see Taylor et al 2001 for full details of the sampling procedures).

Interviews were attempted at all private households found at these delivery points (subject to sampling where multiple households were found), and all individuals enumerated became part of the longitudinal sample, becoming known as Original Sample Members (OSMs). The same individuals are re-interviewed each successive year, and if they split off from original households, all adult members of their new households are also interviewed. Children born to OSMs after the start of the study automatically count as OSMs, and are interviewed in the adult survey once they reach age 16. From Wave Four onwards there is also a special survey of all household members aged 11–15, which will be discussed in more detail below.

Calculating response rates is highly complex, as this can be established at both the household and individual level, and can take the form of both wave-on-wave response rates (i.e. how many of the people interviewed last wave are re-interviewed in the current wave), and longitudinal response rates (i.e. how many of the people interviewed at Wave One are interviewed at the latest wave). Individuals' eligibility for interview may change, they may die or move out of scope, or children may reach the age of 16 and become eligible for interview. Some 88 per cent of Wave One respondents were re-interviewed at Wave Two, and subsequent wave-on-wave response rates have consistently reached at least 95 per cent. In general, there is confidence that the BHPS are unlikely to suffer from any serious bias resulting from attrition, meaning that the sample remained broadly representative of the population of Britain as it changed during the 1990s (Taylor et al 2001). Nathan (1999) undertook a systematic analysis of the effects of attrition upon the BHPS. He compared responses to those from Census data, the General Household Survey (GHS) and the Family Expenditure Survey (FES), with respect to age, sex, marital status, socio-economic group, ethnicity, employment status and household characteristics, concluding that cumulative attrition in the BHPS is limited and does not lead to serious bias.

With respect to response rates for the youth panel, these are complicated by the fact that each year some young people are 'lost' to the adult survey. In Wave Four (the first wave for the youth panel) the response rate was 89 per cent, and in subsequent waves the overall response rates (that is completion of either the young person's questionnaire or the adult questionnaire) stand at over 90 per cent (Taylor et al 2001). Although there is no specific evidence relating to the continued representativeness of the youth survey, that other researchers (including Bergman and Scott 2001; Ermisch et al 2001) have used data from the youth panel increases confidence in its use.

The questionnaire package consists of several components. The household coversheet records the final household interview outcomes, and contains the interviewer call record and observations on the type of accommodation. The household composition form records a complete listing of all household members with some brief summary data of their sex, date of birth, marital and employment status and their relationship to the household reference person – defined as the person legally or financially responsible for the accommodation, or the elder of the two people equally responsible. A short household questionnaire is administered with the household reference person and contains questions about the accommodation and tenure and some household level measures of consumption. The individual schedule is administered with every adult member of the household (aged 16 and over), and covers topics including neighbourhood, individual demographics, residential mobility, health and caring, current employment and earnings, employment changes over the last year, lifetime childbirth, marital and relationship history (Wave Two only), employment status history (Wave Two only), values and opinions, household finance and organisation. A self-completion questionnaire is also filled in by respondents, and this includes questions which are particularly sensitive, or vulnerable to the influence of other people's presence during completion. The self-completion questionnaire contains a reduced version of the General Health Questionnaire (GHQ), which was originally developed as a screening instrument for psychiatric illness, but is often used as an indicator of subjective well-being. It also contains attitudinal items and questions on social support. A proxy schedule is used to collect information about household members absent throughout the field period or too old/infirm to complete the interview themselves. It is administered to another member of the household, and is a much shortened version of the individual questionnaire. If all other efforts to achieve a face-to-face interview fail, a telephone questionnaire, developed from the proxy schedule is conducted.

The British Youth Panel (BYP)

The British Youth Panel began in 1994, at Wave Four as a supplement to the main BHPS, and has been repeated annually since. The BYP is a valuable resource, as youth panel data is scarce, and it offers real opportunities for the study of the transitional period of adolescence. Of importance to the current study is the fact

Table 3.1   Cohorts of the BYP across waves, with numbers of achieved interviews

Year	N	Panel	BYP					BHPS			
		Age	11	12	13	14	15	16	17	18	19
1994	773	Wave 4	**E**	**D**	**C**	**B**	**A**				
1995	749	Wave 5	**F**	E	D	C	B	*A*			
1996	748	Wave 6	**G**	F	E	D	C	*B*	*A*		
1997	720	Wave 7	**H**	G	F	E	D	*C*	*B*	*A*	
1998	946	Wave 8	**I**	H	G	F	E	*D*	*C*	*B*	*A*
1999	938	Wave 9	**J**	I	H	G	F	*E*	*D*	*C*	*B*
2000	1414	Wave 10	**K**	J	I	H	G	*F*	*E*	*D*	*C*
2001	1413	Wave 11	**L**	K	J	I	H	*G*	*F*	*E*	*D*

Source: Adapted from Ermisch et al (2001). Letters represent cohorts, bold letters represent the first wave for each cohort, and italicised letters indicate cohorts moving into the main BHPS panel.

that the full range of household information is available, which enables analysis of the impacts of both home context and of specific relationships, whether with parents, siblings, or other household members.

Youths become eligible for interview when they reach age 11 (although those ten-year-olds turning 11 by December 1 are included), and are interviewed each successive year until they turn 16, when they move into the adult survey. Thus the BYP is effectively a variant of the standard rotating panel. That is, while a core group remains within the panel for some time (a maximum of five waves) at each wave a year group transfers to the adult survey and a new group of rising-elevens enters.

Table 3.1 shows how the panel is replenished each year, with each letter representing a specific cohort and their movement across the waves of the BYP and transition to the BHPS. For example, cohort E were born in 1983, were aged 11 in 1994 (Wave Four), were interviewed five times before leaving the BYP and entering the adult survey at age 16 (Wave Nine). Cohort L were born in 1990, were aged 11 in 2001 (Wave Eleven) and have been interviewed just once, in that year. In Wave Four there were 605 households containing eligible, co-operating children, realising a baseline response rate of 89 per cent. Numbers of youth interviews for each wave are detailed in Table 3.1.

The development of the youth questionnaire included a series of focus groups and pre-testing within schools for the relevant age group. The methodology used for collecting the youth questionnaire was extensively tested. The questions for the children are tape-recorded and delivered through the use of a personal stereo system, which respondents can control at their own pace. The child can therefore also complete the questionnaire while adult members of the household are being interviewed. The main purpose of the personal stereo system is to ensure confidentiality even where family members might be present. This is further assisted by printing only the response categories, that is without the questions themselves, on the questionnaire form. Any household members scanning the child's responses would therefore not be able to link these with the original questions. The methodology also overcame potential literacy problems for some children. For a full description of the development of the youth questionnaire see Scott et al (1995) and Scott (2000). The questions are different from the adult survey. While about two-thirds of these have been retained throughout the life of the BYP as a continuous core, some non-core questions are therefore replaced or rotated every two years. In Wave Four the main focus was the health, health behaviour, psychological well-being and aspirations of young people. In Waves Five and Six further questions on health behaviour and psychological well-being were asked, while in Waves Seven and Eight the focus shifted to social networks.

The samples

Two samples have been utilised in this research project. The first, the youth sample, consists of young people from each of the eight available waves of the BYP. The second, the follow-on sample consists of those young people who have been interviewed in both the BYP and the BHPS.

The youth sample

The youth sample consists of all those young people who have been interviewed at least once in the BYP, that is, from Table 3.1, those from cohorts A to L inclusive. Observations from Waves Four to 11 were pooled, to increase the effective sample size, to give a total of 7,347 person-wave observations (the total number of observations across all the waves). However, as cohorts have been interviewed more than once, and up to five times, the actual number of individuals in the sample is 2,770, made up as shown in Table 3.2. A small number of person-wave observations were excluded from the sample: those living with two adoptive parents (N=66), those living with a lone father (N=172), and other family types (N=109). It should also be pointed out that information relating to each outcome was not available at all waves, and so the size of the sample also depends on the outcome being analysed.

The young people in the sample were matched with their parents to determine patterns of family structure and parental employment both during their childhood and at the time of interview. Full details of how the sample was constructed are provided in Appendix A. Sample members were born between 1978 and 1990, and were aged between 11 and 15 at the time of the interviews.

The follow-on sample

Chapter 6 considers the impact of parental employment patterns on young people's educational outcomes in terms of achievement and progression into

Table 3.2   The youth sample

N (youths)	Number of times youths have been interviewed					N (youth-wave observations)
	Once	Twice	3 times	4 times	5 times	
2770	744	789	384	392	461	7347

Source: Author's own analysis of BHPS.

Table 3.3   Cohorts of the follow-on sample

Year	Panel Age	BYP 15		BHPS 16/17	N
1994	Wave 4	A			
1995	Wave 5	B		A	129
1996	Wave 6	C		B	135
1997	Wave 7	D		C	112
1998	Wave 8	E		D	115
1999	Wave 9	F		E	144
2000	Wave 10	G		F	139
2001	Wave 11			G	151
				Total	915

Source: Author's own analysis of BHPS.

Table 3.4   Characteristics of the samples

Characteristic		Youth sample %	Follow-on sample %
Gender	Male	50.8	51.4
	Female	49.2	48.6
Age	11	20.6	
	12	20.7	
	13	19.9	
	14	20.0	
	15	18.8	100.0
Family type	Intact	63.3	65.5
	Step	17.7	14.0
	Lone	18.9	20.5
Number of siblings	0	24.6	37.6
	1	43.0	37.6
	2	23.4	17.9
	3+	9.0	6.9
	Mean	1.2	1.0
Mean age of father at childbirth		29.8 years	29.6 years
		N = 5031	N = 661
Mean age of mother at childbirth		26.4 years	26.5 years
		N = 7211	N = 901

Notes: For youth sample, N = 7347, unless otherwise stated. For follow-on sample, N = 915, unless otherwise stated.

Source: Author's own analysis of BHPS data.

non-compulsory education. For these purposes a special follow-on sample was constructed, following fifteen-year-olds in the BYP into the BHPS, as illustrated in Table 3.3.

Responses to questions at age 15, and earlier with regards the intention to leave school at age 16, were linked with achievement of qualifications at the end of compulsory schooling, and participation in post-compulsory education. This information was obtained from the first wave of the BHPS after the young people had completed compulsory education, that is the first BHPS interview for most young people, but the second for those with September to November births. Each individual is included just once, with a total sample size of 915.

Sample characteristics

Table 3.4 provides details of some key characteristics for both samples. Just over half of the young people in each sample were male. The average age of those in the youth sample was just under 13, with an even range distribution from 11 to 15. The young people were born between 1978 and 1990 with the average year of birth being 1985. All those in the follow-on sample were aged 15, being born between 1978 and 1985.

At the time of interview (between 1994 and 2001) around two-thirds of each sample were living in intact families (ie. with both biological parents); around a fifth were living in stepfamilies; and the remainder were residing with a lone mother. In comparison to the population of Great Britain as a whole (Office for National Statistics (ONS) 2002) there are more stepfamilies and fewer lone mother families in the youth and follow-on samples, although this may just reflect the timescale and age distributions of our samples.

A quarter of those in the youth sample lived in households where they were the only child (aged 0–16 years), which reliably compares with the figures for Great Britain as a whole (ONS, 2002). A greater proportion of the follow-on sample were the only child in the household, perhaps because older siblings were likely to have left home and formed their own households.

The mean age of the parents when the members of the samples were born were 30 years for fathers and 26 years for mothers. Again, these compare quite reliably with figures for Great Britain, where in 1981 the mean age of fathers at childbirth was 28.7 years (ONS 2001b) and mothers was 27.0 years (ONS 2006a).

Measures of well-being

This section provides details of the areas of adolescent well-being under analysis in this book, with further details of the specific measures used given in the relevant analysis chapters, 4 to 6. The measures of well-being used are necessarily limited by the specific questions asked in the BYP/BHPS and the answer categories.

Chapter 2 identified several gaps in knowledge relating to the impact of parental employment patterns on the emotional well-being of young people. This is an under-researched but important area, as emotional well-being is vital to the present quality of adolescent's lives, impacting on their health and educational experiences and outcomes, but can also have an important influence on adult life. Chapter 4 discusses how the four key indicators of emotional well-being – feeling troubled, low self-efficacy, low self-esteem, and being unhappy – were established, using responses to a number of questions in the BYP and based on information from the existing literature.

The other main area of investigation under study in this research is that of educational well-being. Although as identified in Chapter 2, there is a wealth of evidence relating to the impact of parental employment patterns on educational attainment, little is known about the impact on young people's attitudes to education, their expectations, or behaviours, such as truanting, bullying and suspension from school. Chapter 5 uses several indicators of these aspects of educational well-being to investigate the impact of parental employment patterns and other factors on young people's educational attitudes and behaviours. Chapter 6 looks at the impact of parental employment on young people's expectation and actuality of leaving school at age 16, together with achievement of GCSE qualifications.

Parental employment and unemployment

The discussion in Chapter 2 identified the need to study the impact of parents' employment patterns at the time that well-being was measured, that is concurrently, together with employment patterns when the young people were growing up. Appendix A details how work-life histories were established for the parents of the young people in the samples.

Measures of parental employment and unemployment

A number of different measures of parental employment patterns were established for the sample members both at the time of interview (when they were aged between 11 and 15) and during their childhoods. Three developmental stages were defined: birth to 12 months; first birthday to fifth birthday; fifth birthday to eleventh birthday. These periods were chosen to consider the impact of parental employment patterns during the primary school years, the pre-school years, and when a child was very young (less than a year old), and to enable direct comparisons with previous research (Ermisch and Francesconi 2001a). Employment details were identified for parents individually and on a household basis. For fathers two categories were used: in employment, and not in employment. For mothers three categories were used to take account of the fact that many women work part-time: in full-time employment, in part-time employment, and not in employment. An overall household parental employment measure was also constructed, which combined the employment status of the mother and the father (where present). The categories for dual-parent families were: father employed/mother employed full-time; father employed/mother employed part-time; father employed/mother not in employment; father not in employment/mother employed; father not in employment/mother not in employment. Three categories were defined for lone mother families: employed full-time; employed part-time; not in employment. Measures were also constructed relating to the number of earners in the household and whether the young person had experience of life in a workless household at any stage. A summary of parental employment patterns in the BHPS, together with how these compare with employment patterns in other surveys is detailed in Appendix B.

Parental employment patterns for the youth and follow-on samples

This section describes the parental employment patterns for the young people in both the youth and the follow-on samples. Table 3.5 shows the employment patterns for fathers of the young people, using two categories: in employment, and not in employment. There are three columns in the table for each sample: the first column gives the number of young people with a father in that employment category, including where the father was not present in the household and where employment details were missing; the second column gives the overall percentages in that category; and the third column provides the percentages in and not in employment, of the valid sample, having excluded those with missing values.

It can be seen that the majority of fathers (around four-fifths) were in employment at each stage of the young people's lives. Missing data was significant for fathers, particularly when the children were very young.

Table 3.6 shows the employment patterns for mothers of the young people in the two samples. For mothers three categories were used to take account of the fact that many women, particularly mothers, are employed on a part-time basis: in full-time employment, in part-time employment, and not in employment.

In line with figures for the population as a whole, mothers are more likely to be in employment the older their child are: around four-fifths of the mothers of young people in each sample had been out of the labour market when their children were in infancy; this reduced to around two-thirds when the children were aged one to five, and a half when they were aged five to eleven. A third of the mothers of the youth sample were currently out of the labour market. More mothers of the follow-on sample were in employment, reflecting that the sample were all aged 15 (as opposed to between 11 and 15) at the time of interview.

An overall household parental employment measure was also constructed, which combined the employment status of the mother and the father (where present). The categories for dual-parent families were: father employed/mother employed full-time; father employed/mother employed part-time; father employed/ mother not in employment; father not in employment/mother employed; father not in employment/mother not in employment. Three categories were defined for lone

Table 3.5 **Fathers' employment patterns for the youth and follow-on samples**

Variable		Youth sample			Follow-on sample		
		N	Overall %	Valid %	N	Overall %	Valid %
Father current employment	Employed	4699	64.0	84.7	615	67.2	84.6
	Not in employment	846	11.5	15.3	112	12.2	15.4
	Father not present	1281	17.4		188	20.5	
	Missing value	521	7.1				
Father employment (child 0-1)	Employed	3869	52.7	92.0	536	58.6	93.2
	Not in employment	337	4.6	8.0	39	4.3	6.8
	Father not present	748	10.2		60	6.6	
	Missing value	2393	32.6		280	30.6	
Father employment (child 1-5)	Employed	3849	52.4	91.3	534	58.4	92.4
	Not in employment	366	5.0	8.7	44	4.8	7.6
	Father not present	1020	13.9		87	9.5	
	Missing value	2112	28.7		250	27.3	
Father employment (child 5-11)	Employed	3580	48.7	89.3	541	59.1	91.5
	Not in employment	431	5.9	10.7	50	5.5	8.5
	Father not present	1613	22.0		147	16.1	
	Missing value	1723	23.5		177	19.3	

Source: Author's own analysis of BHPS data.

Table 3.6 **Mothers' employment patterns for the youth and follow-on samples**

Variable		Youth sample			Follow-on sample		
		N	Overall %	Valid %	N	Overall %	Valid %
Mother current employment	Full-time	2559	34.8	35.3	363	39.7	39.7
	Part-time	2390	32.5	33.0	306	33.4	33.4
	Not in employment	2296	31.3	31.7	246	26.9	26.9
	Missing value	102	1.4				
Mother employment (child 0-1)	Employed full-time	559	7.6	9.6	47	5.1	6.1
	Employed part-time	609	8.3	10.5	74	8.1	9.5
	Not in employment	4634	63.1	79.9	654	71.5	84.4
	Missing value	1545	21.0		140	15.3	
Mother employment (child 1-5)	Employed full-time	845	11.5	14.4	86	9.4	11.1
	Employed part-time	1189	16.2	20.3	169	18.5	21.8
	Not in employment	3818	52.0	65.2	520	56.8	67.1
	Missing value	1495	20.3		140	15.3	
Mother employment (child 5-11)	Employed full-time	1375	18.7	22.1	202	22.1	25.1
	Employed part-time	1842	25.1	29.7	260	28.4	32.3
	Not in employment	2995	40.8	48.2	342	37.4	42.5
	Missing value	1135	15.4		111	12.1	

Source: Author's own analysis of BHPS data.

Table 3.7   Current parental employment patterns for the youth and follow-on samples, lone mother families

Variable	Youth sample			Follow-on sample		
	N	Overall %	Valid %	N	Overall %	Valid %
Employed full-time	421	30.3	33.1	65	34.6	34.6
Employed part-time	292	21.0	23.0	46	24.5	24.5
Not in employment	558	40.1	43.9	77	41.0	41.0
Missing	119	8.6				

Source: Author's own analysis of BHPS data.

mother families: employed full-time; employed part-time; not in employment. Table 3.7 shows current household parental employment patterns for lone mother families. Around a third of the mothers in lone mother families in each sample were in full-time employment at the time of the survey, with a further quarter employed on a part-time basis.

Table 3.8 shows the current household parental employment patterns for dual parent families in both the youth and follow-on samples. Around two-thirds of the young people in dual parent households in each sample lived in households where both parents were currently in employment, with mothers' employment evenly split between full-time and part-time. Almost a fifth (18 per cent) of the youth sample, and slightly less (15 per cent) of the follow-on sample who lived with two parents, lived in a household where the father was in employment and the mother was out of the labour market. Around a tenth of each sample lived in workless dual parent households, and the remainder lived in households where their father was not in the labour market, but their mother was.

Table 3.8   Current parental employment patterns for the youth and follow-on samples, dual parent families

Variable	Youth sample			Follow-on sample		
	N	Overall %	Valid %	N	Overall %	Valid %
Father employed/mother employed full-time	1754	29.4	32.1	267	36.7	36.7
Father employed/mother employed part-time	1812	30.4	33.2	241	33.1	33.1
Father employed/mother not in employment	1072	18.0	19.6	107	14.7	14.7
Father not in employment/ mother employed	327	5.5	6.0	50	6.9	6.9
Father not in employment/ mother not in employment	499	8.4	9.1	62	8.5	8.5
Missing	493	8.3				

Source: Author's own analysis of BHPS data.

Table 3.9   Number of earners in household for the youth and follow-on samples

Variable		N	Youth sample Overall %	Valid %	N	Follow-on sample Overall %	Valid %
Current earners	No earners	1064	14.5	15.8	139	15.2	15.2
	One earner	2118	28.8	31.4	268	29.3	29.3
	Two earners	3567	48.6	52.9	508	55.5	55.5
	Missing value	598	8.1				
Earners (child 0–1)	No earners	509	6.9	12.0	55	6.0	9.5
	One earner	2923	39.8	69.1	434	47.4	75.3
	Two earners	799	10.9	18.9	87	9.5	15.1
	Missing value	3116	42.4		339	37.0	
Earners (child 1–5)	No earners	523	7.1	12.3	58	6.3	10.1
	One earner	2372	32.3	56.0	352	38.5	61.4
	Two earners	1340	18.2	31.6	163	17.8	28.4
	Missing value	3112	42.4		342	37.4	
Earners (child 5–11)	No earners	741	10.1	15.3	70	7.7	11.0
	One earner	1733	23.6	35.9	224	24.5	35.1
	Two earners	2360	32.1	48.8	344	37.6	53.9
	Missing value	2513	34.2		277	30.3	

Source: Author's own analysis of BHPS data.

Table 3.10   Household worklessness for the youth and follow-on samples

Variable		N	Youth sample Overall %	Valid %	N	Follow-on sample Overall %	Valid %
Currently workless household	No	5685	77.4	84.2	776	84.8	84.8
	Yes	1064	14.5	15.8	139	15.2	15.2
	Missing	598	8.1				
Workless household (child 0–1)	No	3722	50.7	88.0	521	56.9	90.5
	Yes	509	6.9	12.0	55	6.0	9.5
	Missing	3116	42.4		339	37.0	
Workless household (child 1–5)	No	3712	50.5	87.7	515	56.3	89.9
	Yes	523	7.1	12.3	58	6.3	10.1
	Missing	3112	42.4		342	37.4	
Workless household (child 5–11)	No	4093	55.7	84.7	568	62.1	89.0
	Yes	741	10.1	15.3	70	7.7	11.0
	Missing	2513	34.2		277	30.3	
Ever workless	No	5323	72.5	75.4	707	77.3	77.3
	Yes	1736	23.6	24.6	208	22.7	22.7
	Missing	288	3.9				

Source: Author's own analysis of BHPS data.

Further parental employment measures were constructed relating to the number of earners in the household and whether the young person had experience of life in a workless household at any stage. Table 3.9 shows the numbers of earners at each stage in both the youth and follow-on samples.

Table 3.10 indicates whether young people in both the youth and follow-on samples had experienced household worklessness at any stage of childhood. Around a sixth of young people in each sample lived in currently workless households, with almost a quarter having experienced household worklessness at some stage whilst they were growing up.

Other variables used in the analysis

Based on findings from the literature (both in the literature review chapter, and the discussions in the three analytical chapters, 4 to 6) various models were specified to investigate the impact of parental employment patterns on young people's emotional and educational well-being. These models included variables relating to various individual characteristics (including age and gender), parental characteristics (including measures of parents emotional well-being and levels of qualifications), and family characteristics (including family type, the levels of family conflict and communication, and various measures of socio-economic circumstances) which might be expected, from the literature, to have an influence on outcomes for children. Table 3.11 summarises the variables used in the analyses.

A number of measures of socio-economic circumstances were used in the analysis in this study. Factors such as housing tenure, access to cars and social class are often used as proxies for factors such as income. Housing tenure has traditionally reflected the economic status and social class of the occupiers, and has regularly been used in research as an indicator of socio-economic circumstances (for example Hobcraft 1998; McCulloch and Joshi 2000; Ermisch et al 2004). Around 70 per cent of the young people in each sample lived in owner-occupied housing, although home-ownership was far higher in couple families than in lone mother families (75 per cent compared with 46 per cent in the youth sample). In 1998–2000 16 per cent of households in Great Britain where the head of household was aged 35–44 did not have access to a car (ONS 2002), and the figures for our two samples are comparable.

An indicator of low household income was constructed for use in the analysis, based on an income threshold of less than half median income after housing costs, using 1994 figures held constant in real terms. Corresponding population figures from the Family Resources Survey indicated that the proportion of children living in families with a household income below this level fluctuated between 19 per cent and 23 per cent for the years 1994/5 to 2000/1 (Department for Work and Pensions (DWP) 2006b) and the figures for both the youth and follow-on samples fall within this range.

Table 3.11   Other variables used in the analysis

Characteristic		Youth sample			Follow-on sample		
		N	Overall %	Valid %	N	Overall %	Valid %
Housing tenure	Owner-occupied	5097	69.4	69.6	673	73.6	73.6
	Rented	2228	30.3	30.4	242	26.4	26.4
	Missing value	22	0.3		0	0.0	
At least one car	Yes	6209	84.5	84.5	777	84.9	84.9
	No	1138	15.5	15.5	138	15.1	15.1
	Missing value	0	0.0		0	0.0	
Equivalent income less than 50% of median after housing costs	Not low income	5654	77.0	77.2	734	80.2	80.2
	Low income	1674	22.8	22.8	181	19.8	19.8
	Missing value	19	0.3		0	0.0	
Family occupational social class	Managerial/ professional	2050	27.9	28.8	280	30.6	30.7
	Non-manual	1559	21.2	21.9	196	21.4	21.5
	Manual/unskilled	2447	33.3	34.4	296	32.3	32.5
	No-one in employment	1064	14.5	14.9	139	15.2	15.3
	Missing value	227	3.1		4	0.4	
Father qualifications	Degree or higher	643	8.8	12.3	89	9.7	13.1
	A level/HND	1054	20.5	28.8	204	22.3	30.0
	O level/GCSE	1699	23.1	32.5	196	21.4	28.8
	None	1367	18.7	26.4	192	21.0	28.2
	Father not present	1281	17.4		188	20.5	
	Missing value	844	11.5		46	5.0	
Mother qualifications	Degree or higher	565	7.7	7.9	80	8.7	8.8
	A level/HND	1441	19.6	20.1	178	19.5	19.7
	O level/GCSE	3226	43.6	44.7	367	40.1	40.6
	None	1954	26.6	27.3	279	30.5	30.9
	Missing value	187	2.5		11	1.2	
Father emotional well-being (GHQ)	Good	4200	57.2	81.4	555	60.7	82.5
	Poor	959	13.1	18.6	118	12.9	17.5
	Father not present	1281	17.4		188	20.5	
	Missing value	907	12.3		54	1.2	
Mother emotional well-being (GHQ)	Good	5142	70.0	72.5	652	71.3	72.9
	Poor	2946	26.5	27.5	242	26.4	27.1
	Missing value	259	3.5		21	2.3	
Family conflict	Low	5208	70.9	71.1	587	64.2	64.2
	High	2117	28.8	28.9	328	35.8	35.8
	Missing value	22	0.3		0		
Family communication	Good	4813	65.5	65.7	587	64.2	64.2
	Poor	2515	34.2	34.3	327	35.7	35.8
	Missing value	19	0.3		1	0.1	

Notes: For youth sample, N = 7347. For follow-on sample, N = 915.

Source: Author's own analysis of BHPS data.

Parental occupational social class is another useful indicator of household socio-economic circumstances, and this variable was constructed by taking the higher of the parents' social classes, based on four categories. Again these figures compare with those for the population as a whole (ONS 2001a).

In 1999/2000 29 per cent of men (aged 16–64) and 34 per cent of women (aged 16–59) had no qualifications (Labour Force Survey (ONS 2001a)). These figures are higher than the proportions of mothers and fathers in our samples with no qualifications, reflecting that younger people are more likely to have achieved academic qualifications.

Parental emotional well-being was included in the analysis, based upon the General Health Questionnaire (GHQ-12) (more details of which are provided in Chapter 4). Around a quarter of mothers in our samples had a GHQ-12 score greater than three, often used as a threshold to detect symptoms of psychological distress. The proportion of men with poor emotional well-being on this basis was less than a fifth. These figures are higher than those for the population as a whole, at 14 per cent of men and 20 per cent of women, although other research has identified that parents are more likely to have a high GHQ score than non-parents (Payne 1999).

Measures of family conflict and family communication were devised for use in this research project, as they have been found to have an important influence on young people's outcomes in previous research (Sweeting et al 1998). An indicator of family conflict was devised by combining the responses to questions asked of the young people in the youth survey about how often they argued with their parents, as shown in Table 3.12. An indicator of family communication was devised by combining the responses to questions about how often young people talked to their parents about things that mattered to them, again shown in Table 3.12. By these measures, around a third of the young people in each sample experienced high family conflict or poor family communication.

This section has outlined the construction of a number of variables used in the analysis in this study, and summarised these variables for both the youth and follow-on samples.

Statistical methods

A range of statistical methods were used in this research. Univariate analyses of parental employment patterns, and other individual, parental and family characteristics used in the later analyses have been presented, including the use of frequency tables, and measures of central tendency and dispersion.

Each of the three analytical chapters provides details of the indicators of well-being used in that chapter, together with how they were constructed (usually through the combination of responses to a number of questions), and a summary of both the original variables and the constructed indicators.

Bivariate and multivariate logistic regressions were then carried out for each indicator of well-being (the dependent variable). Bivariate logistic regressions

Table 3.12   Indicators of family conflict and family communication

Variables	Question		%	Indicator
ARGUEF	How often do you quarrel with your father?	Most days	10.3	
		More than once a wk	18.9	**Family conflict**
		Less than once a wk	23.0	Score of 2.5 or less
		Hardly ever	47.8	
ARGUEM	How often do you quarrel with your mother?	Most days	7.2	(Based on mean of scores, or single score if lone parent family, where most days scores 1 and hardly ever scores 4)
		More than once a wk	12.7	
		Less than once a wk	22.1	
		Hardly ever	58.0	
TALKF	How often do you talk to your father about things that matter to you?	Most days	13.0	
		More than once a wk	16.1	**Family communication**
		Less than once a wk	23.6	Score of 3.5 or more
		Hardly ever	47.2	
TALKM	How often do you talk to your mother about things that matter to you?	Most days	30.1	(Based on mean of scores, or single score if lone parent family, where most days scores 1 and hardly ever scores 4)
		More than once a wk	23.3	
		Less than once a wk	19.6	
		Hardly ever	26.9	

Source: Author's own analysis of BHPS data.

enable the investigation of the relationship between the dependent variable and single explanatory variables. Crosstabulations, together with measures of association and significance were then used to explore the basic relationships between the experience of different parental and family employment types and well-being.

A series of multivariate regressions were then carried out for each indicator of well-being, based on the bivariate results together with evidence from the literature. A forwards stepwise approach was adopted, entering parental employment patterns first, followed by a number of control variables. Models of best fit were established which accounted for the optimal amount of variance in the dependent variable. In some cases, the inclusion or exclusion of parental employment variables in the models was checked by forcing entry, and comparing the percentage of variance explained by the different models. Results are presented as odds ratios, for example the change in the odds of a young person having low self-esteem if their mother is in part-time employment as opposed to full-time employment (see Tabachnick and Fidell 1996, for more details on these methods). The proportion of the variance in the dependent variable explained by each explanatory variable is also presented.

Summary and conclusions

This chapter has outlined the methodological strategy adopted in this research project, and details of the research techniques used. Key aspects of the research design have been discussed, relating to the use of secondary analysis of data from the British Household Panel Survey and it's associated Youth Panel to investigate any relationships between parental employment patterns and young people's well-being. A sample of young people was drawn from the eight available waves of the BYP, and a second, smaller sample which combined data from the BYP and the BHPS was also established for the analysis of particular outcomes. Measures of young people's well-being, parental employment, and other variables included in the analysis have been discussed and described. Chapters 4 to 6 present the analysis of the three areas of young people's well-being: emotional well-being (Chapter 4); educational well-being – attitudes and behaviours (Chapter 5); and educational well-being – attainment and progression (Chapter 6).

Chapter 4
Emotional Well-being

Introduction

Emotional well-being is a broad area, which encompasses a number of complementary components. In relation to young people, emotional well-being includes the degree to which young people report that they feel happy and/or experience worry or satisfaction in their lives, together with both the extent and experience of clinically measured mental disorders. Emotional well-being is vital to the present quality of young adolescents' lives, and can impact on their experience and enjoyment of life, together with health, and educational experiences and outcomes. Childhood and adolescent experience can have an important influence on adult life, and as today's adolescents are the parents, teachers, and leaders of the future, young people's emotional well-being also has important implications for the future.

An understanding of the influences on emotional well-being is essential, and a number of factors have been identified. This chapter focuses on the impact of parental employment patterns on young people's emotional well-being, but also asks what other factors are important. The evidence surrounding the meanings, prevalence and nature of the emotional well-being of children and young people is critically reviewed. The chapter then examines the support for links between mental or emotional well-being, and parental employment patterns, together with personal, familial and other factors, to include family structure, parents' educational qualifications and own emotional well-being, the quality of family relationships, and young people's age and gender. In light of the evidence reviewed, data from the youth survey of the British Household Panel Survey (BHPS) is then analysed and discussed. As outlined in the literature review, a forms of capital approach is adopted to explore and explain the relationships between parental employment patterns, and other factors, and young people's emotional well-being.

What is emotional well-being?

Locating an exact definition of emotional well-being is difficult, if not impossible, not least because the terminology employed varies between different health, education and social work professionals (see Morley and Wilson 2001), and between academics (see Hird 2003). Taking a broad view, emotional well-being could be considered to encompass four main components: the mental health component, defined by the incidence of mental health problems and disorders;

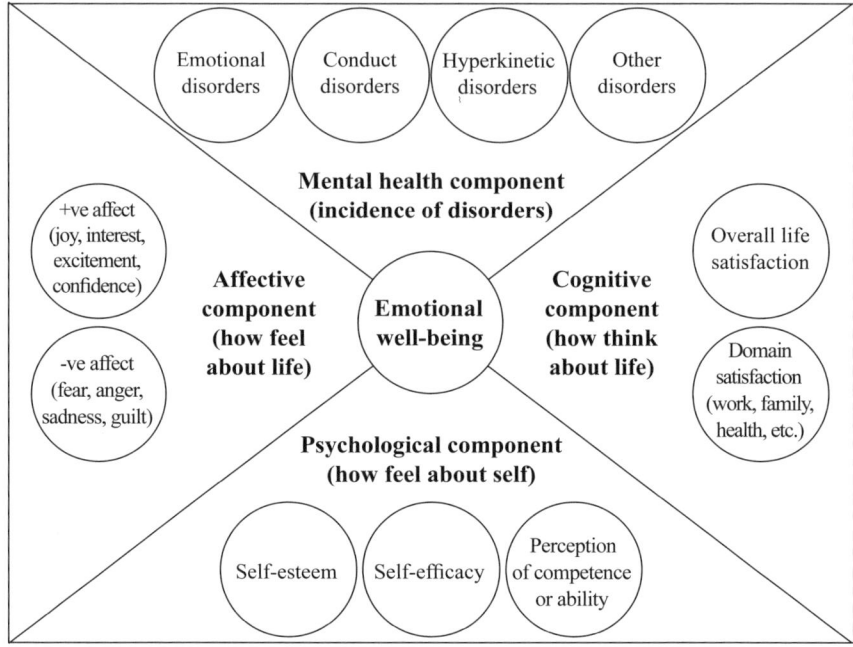

Figure 4.1   Model of emotional well-being
Source: Author's own model.

the cognitive component, that is how an individual thinks about their life; the affective component, how an individual feels about their life; and the psychological component, how an individual feels about their self. This model is illustrated in Figure 4.1.

Mental health has been defined as 'the ability to develop psychologically, socially, emotionally, intellectually and spiritually' (Edwards 2003, 4), although in research terms such an all-embracing definition is inherently difficult to both conceptualise and quantify. According to the Mental Health Foundation (http://www.mentalhealth.org.uk) the term *mental health problem* covers a very wide spectrum, from the worries and grief we all experience as part of everyday life, to the most bleak, suicidal depression or complete loss of touch with reality. When mental health problems are persistent, severe or complex, and interfere with a person's day-to-day functioning, they are often defined as mental disorders. Mental health disorders can be divided into two main types: internalising and externalising disorders (Cowie et al 2004). Internalising disorders are those disorders in which the affected person internalises their difficulties and becomes anxious or depressed or develops physical complaints or an eating disorder. Young people with externalising disorders, such as conduct disorders and attention deficit hyperactivity disorder (ADHD) have behaviour problems visible to those around them.

The prevalence of clinically defined mental disorders, such as depression and schizophrenia, is a useful way of objectively defining emotional or mental well-being, although the prevalence rates and accuracy will depend on the choice of concepts and how these are operationalised, something which will be discussed in more detail in the next section. In addition, although useful as a measure of mental and emotional well-being, prevalence rates of mental disorders take no account of what individuals think and feel, both about their lives and themselves, and do not embrace the more emotive aspects of mental health and well-being, such as satisfaction, self-esteem and confidence. Some researchers, such as Diener et al (1999), argue that objective indicators, such as the incidence of mental health disorders, do not define quality of life, as individuals react differently to the same circumstances, and evaluate conditions based on their unique expectations, values and previous experiences, hence the subjective element is essential. Thus for example, although a young person may be clinically diagnosed as having a hyperkinetic or depressive disorder, with correct treatment they may well experience a good quality of life. Likewise an individual may experience high levels of emotional distress or worry without being clinically diagnosed with a mental disorder.

These more subjective aspects of emotional well-being are much debated, and variously defined, categorised and measured. Figure 4.1 shows a possible model of the various aspects of emotional well-being, and the discussion now turns to the three subjective components.

The affective component of emotional well-being (how you feel about your life) is based on both positive and negative affect, although there is contradictory evidence as to whether these two dimensions form independent factors and should be measured separately, or whether they are interdependent (see Diener 2000; Hird 2003). Ben-Zur (2003) suggests 'positive affect reflects the co-occurrence of positive emotional states, such as joy, interest, excitement, confidence and alertness. Negative affect, in contrast, describes subjective distress and dissatisfaction and is composed of negative emotional states such as anger, fear, sadness, guilt, contempt, and disgust' (68). In short, affect is thought of as how happy or unhappy you are (Prince and Prince 2001).

The cognitive component of emotional well-being (how you think about your life) involves making judgments of one's life – either satisfaction with life as a whole, or satisfactions with life domains such as work, family, leisure, health and finances (Diener et al 1999; Prince and Prince 2001). The domains of life literature (discussed in some detail by Rojas 2004) states that a person's life can be approached as a general construct of many specific domains, and that life satisfaction can be understood as the result of satisfaction in the domains of life. This approach has its limitations, in that the enumeration and demarcation of the domains of life is arbitrary, and usually chosen by the investigators, not by the individuals (Prince and Prince 2001), and that overall well-being is not simply the sum of the satisfaction with various domains (Perri 6 2002). Some researchers argue that domain satisfaction provides useful information about with which aspects of life an individual may be happy or unhappy, but cannot be summed to give an overall impression of life satisfaction, and that it is possible, and necessary to assess overall satisfaction with life, as well as with life domains.

The psychological well-being component of emotional well-being relates to individuals feelings about themselves, such as self-esteem, self-worth, and perceptions of competence or ability. There are huge debates around the individual constituents of psychological well-being, although Ryff's (1989) widely used multidimensional model includes self-acceptance, positive relations with others, environmental mastery (the extent to which an individual is successful and well-adapted), autonomy, purpose in life, and personal growth. Emotional regulation and coping, together with feelings about self are concepts included by other researchers, including Bridges et al (2001). As there are a plethora of well-established scales used to measure subjective well-being, further discussion of the constituent components is included in the next section.

This brief review of what emotional well-being can be considered to encompass is by no means exhaustive. Overall, this broad field can be broken down into several components, indicated in Figure 4.1. The mental health component, cognitive component, psychological component and affective component mesh together to constitute emotional well-being.

Why is young people's emotional well-being important?

Young people's emotional health and well-being is important, both for the impact that it has on their present quality of life, and also for the implications it has for their future social and emotional development, academic experience and achievement. Although adolescence is a time of growth, change and opportunity, moving from childhood to adulthood can bring times of insecurity, self-doubt, frustration, uselessness and isolation. Bergman and Scott (2001) discuss two possible explanations for changes in adolescents' experience of self, in terms of identity transition, self-esteem, and self-efficacy. Society as a whole, including parents, teachers and peers, have specific expectations and place demands on adolescents, which are different from expectations and demands placed upon children, and thus, result in a new identity being formed. The second potential explanation offered takes into account the developing capacity to think in more abstract terms, and refer more to beliefs and ideologies than during childhood. Thus 'adolescents' self-concept emerges both as a reflexive adaptation of social demands and as a result of psychological and physiological development (185).

It is important to understand adolescent's emotional well-being in its own right, in terms of their experience and enjoyment of life. But emotional well-being is also related to health-risk behaviours, educational experience and achievement, and social well-being. Using a variety of different measures, evidence from the research suggests that poor emotional well-being amongst young people is associated with a range of health-threatening behaviours, such as smoking, drinking, illegal drug use, violence, self-harm, and suicide (Balding et al 1998; Clarke et al 2000; Meltzer et al 2000; Green et al 2005). These relationships are also found in the adult population (O'Brien et al 2002). Young people with a mental disorder were also more likely to have special educational needs, to have truanted, and to have been excluded from school than those without a mental disorder (Cowie et al 2004; Green et al 2005), and other research (see Weare and Gray 2003, for a summary) has suggested that work to promote social and emotional well-being in schools can also lead to greater education success, improvements in behaviour, improved learning, and greater social cohesion. In line with the acknowledged relationship in adults (Brugha et al 1993; O'Brien et al 2002) young people with mental disorders were more likely than other young people to have weak social networks, and find it difficult to make and keep friends (Green et al 2005).

There is also clear evidence from life-course research that childhood and adolescent experiences have a pronounced influence on adult life. Research suggests that poor emotional well-being in adolescence increases the risk of mental health problems in adulthood (for example Hobcraft 1998; Sacker et al 1999; Buchanan et al 2002; Sigle-Rushton 2004; Hobcraft and Sigle-Rushton 2005). Associations between various measures of poor adolescent emotional well-being and other adult outcomes or behaviours (including unemployment, receipt of benefits, homelessness, lack of secure relationships, early childbearing, marital breakdown, smoking, drug misuse, alcoholism, poor physical health) have also been found in the literature (Kuh et al 1997; Buchanan et al 2000; Flouri and Buchanan 2002; Collishaw et al 2004).

The policy impact of the present Labour government on the health and well-being of children and young people is profound and far-reaching, with a variety of cross-departmental strategies in place. Promoting social and emotional development is a key aim of the government's Every Child Matters strategy, which encompasses services for children aged 0–19, and the recent Child Poverty Review (HM Treasury 2004b) reaffirmed the importance of promoting child and adolescent mental health. In September 2004, the Children's National Service Framework included the mental health and psychological well-being of children and young people as one of its 11 standards (Department of Health/Department for Education and Skills, 2004). The Sure Start programme, part of the government's policy to prevent social exclusion, started in 1999, and is targeted at pre-school children and their families in disadvantaged areas. One of the key objectives of Sure Start is to improve social and emotional development, health, and the ability to learn (see Glass 1999), which ties in with the overall focus on children's health and well-being.

As Alexander 2002, writes 'the protection and promotion of children and young people's mental health is an investment for life' (1). Emotional well-being in adolescence has implications not only for present quality of life, but for later mental and emotional well-being, and for a wide variety of outcomes in other areas of life, in both adolescence and adulthood. The government clearly recognises the importance of child and adolescent emotional well-being, as the promotion of social and emotional development is a key aim of the government, and is supported by a range of policy initiatives.

How is emotional well-being measured?

Just as there are a variety of different ways of defining emotional well-being, so there are a number of ways of measuring the various elements of this concept. Accordingly, there are a number of sources of information on children and young people's mental and emotional health and well-being, using a variety of different measures.

As many child mental health problems go untreated, prevalence estimates rely on information collected from the child and others who know the child (e.g. parents, teachers), and explicit diagnostic criteria. The epidemiological literature reveals a range of methodological approaches, and a parallel range of prevalence estimates (see Roberts et al 1998, who reviewed 52 separate studies, for a full discussion). In terms of data collection, the Rutter interview schedules or questionnaires, or some variation of them, are commonly used (Rutter et al 1970), although a number of other questionnaires also exist including the more recently developed Development and Well-being Assessment (DAWBA) (Goodman et al, 2000a). The way that the information collected is interpreted and used to clinically diagnose mental disorders is the second stage in measuring the prevalence of disorders, and again a number of strategies exist. The Diagnostic and Statistical Manual of Mental Disorders (DSM) and its successors (the first edition (DSM-I) was published in 1952 by the American Psychiatric Association, and has since been updated in 1968 (DSM-II), 1987 (DSM-III), 1994 (DSM-IV), and 2000 (DSM-IV-TR)) is the standard classification of mental disorders used by mental health professionals in the United States. The International Classification of Diseases, now in it's tenth revision (ICD-10), is endorsed by the World Health Organisation as the international standard diagnostic classification for all general epidemiological and many health management purposes (World Health Organisation 1994). The main categories of mental disorders in young people classified by the ICD-10 are: emotional disorders (including anxiety disorders and depression); conduct disorders; hyperkinetic disorders; and other less common disorders.

The first large-scale national survey of the mental health of children (aged 5 to 16) in the UK was carried out by the Office for National Statistics in 1999 (Meltzer et al 2000), and repeated in 2004 (Green et al 2005). Based on a clinical evaluation of data taken from parents, teachers and the children themselves, using the DAWBA (Goodman et al 2000a), these surveys used the International Classification of Diseases (ICD-10) (World Health Organisation 1994) to present an objective picture of the prevalence of clinically measured mental disorders amongst young people.

Although objective in nature, measuring the prevalence rates of mental health disorders amongst children and young people is not entirely straightforward.

We have seen that as well as a number of data collection instruments there are a number of different ways of diagnosing mental disorders based on the information collected. This lack of consistency complicates the comparison of prevalence rates across time, and as data may be taken from several sources, such as parents, teachers, and the young person themselves, there may also be problems of inconsistency and inaccuracy of responses.

The measurement of subjective well-being, however defined, is also beset with complications, as different studies adopt different measurement instruments. The most commonly used tools for assessing young people's subjective well-being are the General Health Questionnaire (GHQ), the Strengths and Difficulties Questionnaire (SDQ), and the Health-Related Behaviour Questionnaire (HRBQ), each of which is discussed below, together with a brief review some of the studies based on these measures.

The General Health Questionnaire was first introduced in 1972 (Goldberg 1972), and is an extensively researched and well-validated instrument for the identification and measurement of psychological problems (see Campbell et al 2003). It has also been endorsed as being appropriate for use among adolescents (Banks 1983; Radavanovic and Eric 1983). The questionnaire consists of a series of statements about aspects of well-being (for example general levels of happiness, worries, tension or sleep loss) to which respondents indicate on a four-point scale the extent to which each has been present or absent over the recent past compared to their usual experience, and comes in a range of versions based on the number of items used. The GHQ-12 (consisting of 12 items) (Goldberg and Williams 1988) is a popular version of the questionnaire, often used as a measure of psychological strain when included as part of a larger social survey, for example the annual Health Survey for England (HSE) and the BHPS.

There is much debate around how to score and interpret GHQ-12 responses, and a variety of methods have been used. As a uni-dimensional measure of well-being, GHQ-12 responses can be scored in a bi-modal fashion (0-0-1-1) and then summed, giving a scale running from 0 (least distressed) to 12 (most distressed). It has been shown that the most appropriate and efficient threshold to detect symptoms of psychological distress (caseness) is four or more (Goldberg et al 1998), and this has been used in a number of studies (including Ermisch et al 2004; Sproston and Primatesta 2003), although other research (Ely et al 2000; West and Sweeting 2003) uses a cut-off of 2/3 to indicate GHQ caseness (Banks 1983; Goldberg and Williams 1988). Alternatively Likert scoring has been employed (0-1-2-3) to give a range of scores from 0 to 36, and mean GHQ scores used in analyses (West and Sweeting 2003). This scoring method might be considered more appropriate, as the 0–12 scale has been criticised as leading to an under-identification of respondents with existing psychological problems (Newman et al 1988).

Although so far, the GHQ-12 has been considered to be a uni-dimensional measure of well-being, many studies have sought to isolate a number of factors, relating to different aspects of well-being. Two-factor (for example, Andrick and van Schonbroek 1989; Gureje 1991; Politi et al 1994) and three-factor models (for example, Worsely and Gribbin 1977; Graetz 1991; Martin 1999) have been derived from the GHQ-12, although the different studies are quite heterogeneous, often very specific in terms of their subject population, and have utilised different methods of both scoring and analysing the GHQ. While the factor structures vary between the studies, there is some consistency in the factor names used, with the most commonly identified factors being anxiety and depression, feelings of incompetence, somatic complaints, sleeping difficulties, and social function (or dysfunction).

The GHQ-12 is included in the annual Health Survey of England, and asked of all respondents aged 13 and over. It also forms part of the BHPS questionnaire for adult respondents (see Taylor et al 2001), with the youth questionnaire, for respondents aged 11–15, containing a different set of questions on subjective well-being, loosely based on the GHQ.

The Health-Related Behaviour Questionnaire (HRBQ) was developed by the Schools Health Education Unit at Exeter (see Balding 1983) and provides an evaluation of current patterns and time-trends in the health-related behaviour of primary and secondary school pupils, based on self-reported data. It should be noted that the survey does not cover a nationally representative sample of schools, as individual schools across the country opt to participate each year, therefore caution should be applied when interpreting the findings of the survey. That said, 685,000 pupils between the ages of 8 and 18, from more that 5,500 schools have been involved in the survey since the questionnaire's launch in 1977. The results of the HRBQ have been published annually since 1986, most recently as Balding 2005. The HRBQ includes a large range of questions on topics including food choices and weight control; bullying; alcohol, smoking and drugs; exercise and sport; problems, worries, life satisfaction and self-esteem. Of particular note, self-esteem scores are derived from responses to seven statements taken from a self-esteem enquiry method developed by Lawrence (1981). In addition to the annual reports, a more detailed study focussing on young people's worries and concerns (Balding et al 1998) considered the relationships between worrying, other characteristics and behaviours.

The Strengths and Difficulties Questionnaire (SDQ) is a brief behavioural screening questionnaire that can be administered to the parents and teachers of four to 16 year-olds and also to 11–16 year-olds themselves (Goodman 1997; Goodman 1999). The questionnaire consists of 25 questions, with five questions in each of the following domains: pro-social behaviour, hyperactivity, emotional problems, conduct (behavioural) problems, and peer problems, and the question wordings focus on a child's emotional and behavioural strengths as well as difficulties. Each question has three possible answers, which are assigned a score of zero (not true), one (somewhat true) or two (certainly true). Scores for individual domains, such as hyperactivity, range from zero to ten with higher scores indicating a higher level of problems within that domain. For pro-social behaviour, the scale is reversed so lower scores indicate more difficulties. A Total SDQ Score (or Total Deviance Score), with a maximum score of 40, can be calculated by summing the four domain scores (excluding pro-social behaviour). An extended version of the SDQ (Goodman 1999) is also available and includes an impact supplement which asks if the respondent thinks the young person has a problem, and if so, enquires further about chronicity, distress, social impairment and burden for others. The SDQ is included in the British surveys of the mental health of children and young people (Meltzer et al 2000; Green et al 2005); the annual Health Surveys of England (Prescott-Clark and Primatesta 1998; Sproston and Primatesta 2003); and the Avon Longitudinal Survey of Parents and Children (Golding et al 2001). The 1958 National Child Development Study (NCDS) (Fogelman 1983) and the 1970 British Cohort Study (BCS) (Butler et al 1986) assessed young people's emotional well-being at several ages during childhood using questions from the Rutter A scale (Rutter et al 1970; Elander and Rutter 1996), which formed the basis for the development of the SDQ. This measures children's behaviour on three scales: aggression, anxiety and restlessness. GHQ-12 and the Malaise Inventory (Rutter al 1970; Rodgers et al 1999) were used in the adult surveys of these cohorts. The latest cohort study, The Millennium Cohort has used the SDQ at age three (parent-completed), and intends to continue using this in subsequent surveys (see Dex and Joshi 2005).

Other surveys and studies have developed their own measures of subjective well-being, focussing either on one particular aspect (such as Rosenberg's self-esteem scale (1965)) or on a broad measure of well-being through the use of a variety of scales (such as Kerr et al 2001). The international Health Behaviour Survey of School-Aged Children (HBSC) carried out by the World Health Organisation (WHO) includes questions on self-rated health, subjective health complaints, and life satisfaction, and has been carried out every four years since 1982. The 2001–02 survey involved over 17,000 young people aged 11–15 across a total of 36 countries (see Ravens-Sieberer et al 2004).

When conducting secondary analysis of existing data, researchers are limited by the questions that were asked of respondents and the resulting data collected. For the purposes of this research, data from the youth survey of the BHPS have been used, where a series of questions on subjective well-being were asked. Whilst these were loosely based on the GHQ, question wordings differ slightly, thus limiting the direct comparison with other datasets.

This section has considered some of the complexities involved in measuring emotional well-being. Estimates of the prevalence of mental health disorders amongst young people depend upon the choice of data collection tools and the way in which the collected data is interpreted, and a range of instruments exist. The measurement of subjective well-being amongst young people is also complex, and some of the most commonly used tools have been discussed: the GHQ, the SDQ, and the HRBQ. Whilst these instruments assess general levels of subjective well-being, other tools which assess a single element, such as self-esteem also exist. Secondary analysis of data relating to subjective well-being is constrained by the questions asked and the resulting data collected. The wide variety of measurement instruments employed restricts the comparison with other datasets and findings. In addition, like all subjective measures, these assessments of subjective well-being

Table 4.1   Measures and prevalence of young people's emotional well-being

Survey	Measure	Year	Sample size	Age Group		%
British Child Mental Health Survey	Prevalence of mental disorders (DAWBA/ ICD-10)	1999[1]	4609	11–15	Emotional disorders	6
					(Anxiety disorders	5
					(Depression	2
					Conduct disorders	6
					Hyperkinetic Disorders	1
					Less Common disorders*	1
					Any disorder*	11
		2004[2]	4051	11–16	Emotional disorders	5
					(Anxiety disorders	4
					(Depression	1
					Conduct disorders	7
					Hyperkinetic Disorders	1
					Less Common disorders*	1
					Any disorder *	12
Health Survey of England	Strengths and Difficulties (SDQ) high scores	1997[3]	3752	4–15	Emotional symptoms	12
					Conduct problems	15
					Hyperactivity	13
					Peer problems	14
					Pro-social behaviour	4
					Total SDQ score	10
		2002[4]	6800	4–15	Emotional symptoms	11
					Conduct problems	14
					Hyperactivity	14
					Peer problems	13
					Pro-social behaviour	4
					Total SDQ score	10
	General Health Questionnaire (GHQ) score	1995/97	1643	13–15	0 (low)	61
					1-3 (medium)	31
					4+ (high)	10
		2002	2376	13–15	0 (low)	59
					1-3 (medium)	30
					4+ (high)	10

[1]Meltzer et al, 2000.
[2]Green et al, 2005.
[3]Prescott-Clark and Primatesta, 1998.
[4]Sposton and Primatesta, 2003.
*The classification of some disorders, including autism, changed between the two surveys, therefore the figures for hyperkinetic and all disorders are not strictly comparable.

reflect the format and wording of the questions asked, the context in which they were asked, and the way the response categories were formulated and coded.

Rates of emotional well-being and ill-health in the UK

It is useful here to briefly consider the overall prevalence of mental disorders and ill-health amongst children and young people, and how the different measures compare. Bearing in mind that the different measures come from different surveys, in different years, with different aged young people, overall all three measures listed in Table 4.1 suggest that around one in ten young people have poor emotional or mental health (any disorder on the prevalence measure; high score on the total SDQ; high score on the GHQ).

As well as providing a measure of the presence of any disorder/problem, both the SDQ and prevalence measure identify different categories of disorders/problems. Caution needs to be applied when comparing these as they employ different rules, have some different categories, and are calculated for different age-groups. However, both define emotional disorders/problems and conduct disorders/problems, so how do the figures for these categories compare? Overall, the SDQ identifies roughly twice as many young people with both emotional and conduct problems as the prevalence measure does. Further work has been conducted on how accurate the SDQ is at identifying mental disorders, by comparing the answers for the SDQ and prevalence measures in a community sample (Goodman et al 2000b). This found that overall the SDQ (when completed by the child, parent and a teacher) correctly identified individuals with a psychiatric disorder in 63 per cent of cases. However, there were differences between the different types of disorder, in that over 70 per cent of individuals with conduct, hyperactivity, depressive, and some anxiety disorders were identified, but under 50 per cent of individuals with specific phobias, separation anxiety and eating disorders were. Similar work was undertaken in an Australian clinic setting, and found that there was a high level of agreement between SDQ generated diagnoses and diagnosis made by clinicians (Mathai et al 2004). As the HRBQ includes a large number of measures of emotional and mental health and well-being, these are not included in Table 4.1. Some of the measures are discussed later in the chapter.

Influences on young people's emotional well-being

Having considered the importance of young people's emotional well-being, and some of the possible consequences of poor mental health, we now turn to look at some of the influences on adolescents' emotional well-being. Is there support in the literature for a link between children's emotional well-being and parental employment patterns? What other personal, familial and external factors matter? This review of the existing evidence will form the basis of the analysis of data from the youth panel of the BHPS, providing avenues of enquiry and hypothesis.

Parental employment

Looking specifically at evidence relating to the impact of parental employment patterns on children's emotional well-being, we find that the overall picture is complex, with different studies using different measures of emotional well-being and parental employment, at different points in time, with differing aged children,

Table 4.2   Summary of the evidence: Parental employment

Factor	Impact on emotional well-being	Measure of well-being	Reference
Current parental employment			
Workless household	-ve	Incidence of mental health disorders	Meltzer et al, 2000; Green et al, 2005
	-ve	Anxiety	Joshi and Verropoulou, 2000
Father unemployed	-ve	SDQ score	McMunn et al, 2001
	-ve (girls) +ve (boys)	Happy	Clarke et al, 2000
Mother employed part-time (compared to employed full-time or not in employment)	+ve	SDQ score	McMunn et al, 2001
Mother employed	+ve	Anxiety	Joshi and Verroupoulou, 2001
Earlier parental employment			
Workless household during childhood (especially when aged 11–15)	-ve	Psychological distress (GHQ) when aged 16–27	Ermisch et al, 2004
Father more employment when child aged 1–5	+ve	Psychological distress	Ermisch and Francesconi, 2001a
Mother employed when child aged 0–5 (compared with not in employment)	+ve	Anxiety	Joshi and Verroupoulou, 2000
Mother employed fulltime (child aged 0–5)	-ve	Psychological distress	Ermisch and Francesconi, 2001a
Mother employed part-time (child aged 1–5)	+ve		
Mother employed full-time (child aged 6–10)	+ve		

and including different control variables in their analyses. A distinction also needs to be drawn between the impact of current parental employment and parental employment when children were growing up on emotional well-being both during adolescence and young adulthood. Table 4.2 summarises the existing evidence from a number of studies. One finding which is consistent across studies and different measures of emotional well-being is the impact of parental worklessness. Living in a workless household, either during childhood or adolescence, was associated with poorer emotional well-being (increased mental disorders, increased anxiety, and increased psychological distress) during adolescence and early adulthood (Joshi and Verropoulou 2000; Meltzer et al 2000; Ermisch et al 2004; Green et al 2005). However there is little evidence of the mechanism by which this relationship operates.

Parental worklessness reduces the financial capital available within a family, through a reduction in household income. This in turn impacts upon how much parents are able to invest in their children, in terms of books and educational support, toys and material objects, the absence of which may increase young people's stress and anxiety. The relationship between unemployment and mental disorder among adults is well documented (see Meltzer et al 1995), and the observed relationship for children is in line with this. What is not clear however is whether family unemployment has a direct negative impact on the presence of a mental disorder in children, or whether any relationship is due to the impact of parental mental disorder, which itself is associated with unemployment. The impact of parental emotional well-being on children's emotional well-being is considered later in this chapter.

Unfortunately neither family income nor parents own emotional well-being were controlled for in any of the above studies. If income was included as a control variable and a statistically significant relationship was still observed between parental worklessness and children's poorer emotional well-being, then there would be evidence to suggest that it is not just through the increased income from employment that children benefit. Likewise, if parents' own emotional well-being were controlled for, it would be possible to determine whether worklessness has a direct impact on children's well-being, or whether this was an indirect impact via the lowering parents' own emotional well-being.

If we consider the existing evidence relating to the impact of fathers' and mothers' employment, when taken separately, we find mixed results. McMunn et al (2001) found that children with an unemployed father were almost two-and-a-half times more likely to have a high SDQ score, indicating poorer emotional well-being, than those with a father in employment. That this relationship lost significance when socio-economic controls were included again points to the positive effect of improved family socio-economic circumstances, or financial capital, as a result of paternal employment. However, work undertaken using data from the youth panel of the BHPS found no significant relationship between paternal employment status and being sad or with losing sleep through worrying (Clarke et al 2000). With regards feeling happy or satisfied, girls whose father was working were less unhappy, although the opposite was true for boys, that they were very slightly less likely to be unhappy if they had an unemployed father. This unexpected finding was not investigated further by Clarke et al, and may be due to some other variable not included in the analysis, or suggest that girls are more sensitive to their father's employment status than boys, who may just enjoy spending more time with their unemployed father. This would need further investigation. Likewise, the finding that girls have higher (worse) image scores when there is no father employed, but boys do not, needs further verification. However, these findings would suggest that there are distinct gender differences in the impact of fathers' employment on young people's emotional well-being.

Paternal employment during childhood has also been found to have a significant effect on later psychological well-being. Longer periods of employment by fathers when their children were aged one to five reduced the chances that children suffered high levels of psychological distress as young adults. One possible explanation would be that employed fathers had fewer financial worries when their children were growing up, which again suggests a financial capital mechanism of influence (Ermisch and Francesconi 2001a).

In terms of the impact of maternal employment on young people's emotional well-being the evidence is complex and at times inconsistent. Clarke et al (2000) found no relationship between mothers' current employment status and four measures of emotional well-being – sad, worry, image and happy – whether or not socio-economic factors were controlled for. McMunn et al (2001), found that children with a mother currently in part-time employment were less likely to have high SDQ scores, compared with those with a mother in full-time employment or not in the labour market, but the relationship lost statistical significance when socio-economic factors were controlled for. This suggests that as was proposed with fathers' employment, maternal employment may hold benefits for children's emotional well-being through the associated increase in income (financial capital) that comes with it. That part-time maternal employment was 'better' for children's SDQ scores than full-time employment indicates that there is a balance or trade-off involved between increased family income and decreased family time, suggesting that mothers provide important nurturing and role model support to their children (social and cultural capital).

Other research also provides evidence of the protective effect of maternal employment, particularly part-time employment, for children and young people's emotional well-being. Joshi and Verropoulou (2000) used second-generation NCDS data to investigate the effects of both early and current maternal employment on children's emotional well-being. Using standard scales (including the Rutter A scale), mothers were asked to report if their children displayed anxious (including being worried or unhappy) behaviour. There was a positive association between mothers' current employment and non-anxiety, and this was greater where the mothers were in part-time employment. In addition, children whose mothers had been employed at any time between infancy and compulsory school age displayed lower levels of anxiety at the time of interview in 1991 (when they were aged five to 17) than those whose mothers had not been in employment. Household income was not controlled for in this study, but housing tenure was used as a proxy for long-term poverty. Research by Ermisch and Francesconi (2001a) distinguished between the impact of full-time and part-time maternal employment on children's later emotional well-being, using various samples of young people born between 1970 and 1981 and aged between 16 and 27, drawn from the first seven waves of the BHPS. They used a measure of psychological distress experienced by the young people based on the GHQ-12. They found an adverse effect on young adult's psychological well-being associated with mothers' full-time working when children were preschoolers, but that more full-time working when a child was aged six to ten was associated with lower risk of later psychological distress, as were periods of part-time employment when the child was aged one to five. Again, this suggests that there is a fine balance between the financial rewards of paid employment and the benefits that brings to children, and the impact of maternal employment when children are young on the time they spend with their mother. Of course, it is important to stress that no information was collected on the quantity or quality of time that children spent with their parents, or they type or quality of childcare used.

The evidence considered in this section in general suggests that parental employment improves the emotional well-being of children and young people, and that this operates through a mechanism of improved income and socio-economic circumstances (financial capital). Living in a workless household, either during childhood or adolescence, was associated with poorer emotional well-being (increased mental disorders, increased anxiety, and increased psychological distress) during adolescence and early adulthood, and similar results were found when considering the impact of life with an unemployed father. The impact of maternal employment is more complicated, and the benefits to young people's emotional well-being depend upon whether full-time or part-time employment is involved. Part-time maternal employment appears to offer greater protection against poor emotional well-being than either full-time maternal employment or non-employment. This suggests that although the impact on family financial capital may be significant, a balance or trade-off is involved between increased family income and decreased family time, with maternal provision of nurturing protection (social capital) potentially restricted by full-time employment. This nurturing element of mothering (Arendall 2000) is difficult to quantify, but may be influenced by the mother's own emotional well-being and the quality of family relationships, neither of which were controlled for or investigated in any of the research detailed above. This key omission is considered in the current research. In addition, does the quality of the relationships between parents and their children, or parents' own emotional well-being have an impact on the way in which their employment patterns influence their children's emotional well-being?

Having considered the evidence from the literature relating to the impact of parental employment on children's emotional well-being, and highlighted some of the gaps and inconsistencies, we turn to look now at some of the other factors which are important, and need to be considered in any future work.

Socio-economic factors

In addition to the impact of parental patterns of employment on children's emotional well-being, evidence also exists relating to the impact of a range of socio-economic indicators (related to financial capital) including household income, social class, receipt of benefits, and tenure. Many of the relationships between children's emotional well-being and socio-economic factors are however only investigated at a bivariate level, with no other variables controlled for, which limits the true meaning and value of these findings. Table 4.3 presents a summary of the evidence relating to the impact of socio-economic factors on young people's emotional well-being.

Looking first at the relationship with income, differences were found depending on which measures of children's emotional well-being was used. Prevalence rates of mental disorders were found to increase as household income decreased (Meltzer et al 2000; Green et al 2005), and a greater proportion of children in families with lower incomes had high SDQ scores (Prescott-Clark and Primatesta

Table 4.3   Summary of the evidence: Socio-economic factors

Factor	Impact on emotional well-being	Measure of well-being	Reference
Income			
Lower income	-ve	Incidence of mental health disorders	Meltzer et al, 2000; Green et al, 2005
	-ve	SDQ score	Prescott-Clark and Primatesta, 1998; Sproston and Primatesta, 2003
	+ve	Worry	Bergman and Scott, 2001
Receiving means-tested benefits or lacking assets	-ve	Self-image	Clarke et al, 2001
Social Class			
Semi-routine or routine occupational groups	-ve	Incidence of mental health disorders	Green et al, 2005
(compared to higher professional groups)	-ve	SDQ score	Prescott-Clark and Primatesta, 1998; McMunn et al, 2001; Sproston and Primatesta, 2003
	-ve	Self-esteem	Glendinning et al, 2000
Tenure			
Rented accommodation (compared to owner-occupied)	-ve	Incidence of mental health disorders	Green et al, 2005
	-ve	SDQ score	McMunn et al, 2001
	-ve	Self-esteem	Bergman and Scott, 2001
	-ve (girls)	Worried	Clarke et al, 2000
	-ve (boys)	Unhappiness	

1998; Sproston and Primatesta 2003). However, in these last two studies no significant relationship emerged between income and young people's GHQ scores, which may suggest that the different measures are indeed tapping into different aspects of children's emotional well-being. In addition, using BHPS data, there was an absence of a link between income and children's emotional well-being, in terms of being sad, losing sleep through worrying, or being happy (Clarke et al 2000), although receiving means-tested benefits and lacking assets were both associated with worse self-image scores, particularly for girls. Bergman and Scott (2001) also used data from the BHPS, although they derived different measures of emotional well-being and used different statistical methods, finding no link between income and emotional well-being, with one exception; children from the poorest households reported the least past worries. Although this may seem unexpected, they suggest that children from higher income households may feel more pressure to succeed, and thus worry more. This suggestion could be explored further.

The findings relating to the association between children's emotional well-being and parental social class in many ways mirror those of income, which would be expected. In 2004, children in families in semi-routine or routine occupational groups were about three times as likely to have a mental disorder as children in families in a higher professional group (13 per cent and 15 per cent compared with 4 per cent) (Green et al, 2005). Similar results were found for the proportions of children with high SDQ scores (Prescott-Clark and Primatesta 1998; McMunn et al 2001; Sproston and Primatesta 2003), but interestingly, not for high scores on the GHQ (Prescott-Clark and Primatesta 1998; Sproston and Primatesta 2003), or the separate measures of worrying, self-efficacy, being unhappy, or self-esteem (Bergman and Scott 2001). Conversely, Glendinning et al 2000, found a class gradient for self-esteem, but not for feelings of depression, although their sample was restricted to young people from rural parts of Northern Scotland and mid-Sweden, which may account for the differences between this and other work. The only observed study which investigated further the relationship between social class and children's emotional well-being was that by McMunn et al (2001), who found that the relationship lost statistical significance when mothers' own GHQ, qualifications and working status were controlled for, suggesting spurious links between income and one or more of these variables. The impact of parental characteristics is discussed later.

Housing tenure is another useful socio-economic indicator and shows the expected relationship with the prevalence of mental disorders. Children living in rented accommodation, whether social or private sector, were twice as likely to have a mental disorder as those in owned accommodation (17 per cent and 14 per cent compared with 7 per cent) (Green et al 2005). Likewise children were more likely to have a high SDQ score if they lived in rented accommodation, as compared to those whose parents were owners or buyers (McMunn et al 2001). The association between emotional well-being and tenure was less clear when using other, individual measures, with a weak but significant association with self-esteem (Bergman and Scott 2001), girls being more worried and boys more unhappy when living in rented compared with owned housing (Clarke et al 2000), and no significant association between living in social housing and levels of anxiety (Joshi and Verropoulou 2000).

There is then some evidence to support a link between children's emotional well-being and socio-economic circumstances, although this is patchy and seems to apply only to certain measures of well-being. Taking socio-economic circumstances into account is important in future work, although care must be taken when interpreting any association. In particular other variables, such as employment status, and as we shall consider later, parents' own emotional well-being, need to be controlled for, in order to determine whether any impact of socio-economic circumstances on young people's emotional well-being is really down to some spurious connection with other factors.

Family factors

The relationships between children's emotional well-being and a number of factors relating to both family structure and the quality, or cohesiveness of family life have also been explored by a number of studies, with a summary of the

Table 4.4   Summary of the evidence: Family factors

Factor	Impact on emotional well-being	Measure of well-being	Reference
Family structure			
Lone parent family	-ve	Incidence of mental health disorders	Meltzer et al, 2000; Green et al, 2005
	-ve	SDQ score	Prescott-Clark and Primatesta, 1998
	-ve (boys)	GHQ score	
	-ve	Past worries Unhappiness Self-esteem	Bergman and Scott, 2001
	-ve	Self-image	Clarke et al, 2000
	-ve	SDQ score	Dunn et al, 1998
Stepfamily	-ve	Incidence of mental health disorders	Meltzer et al, 2000; Green et al, 2005
	-ve	Self-esteem	Sweeting and West, 1995
	-ve	SDQ score	Dunn et al, 1998
Time in non-intact family during childhood	-ve	Psychological distress	Ermisch et al, 2004
Family life			
Poor family communication	-ve	Incidence of mental health disorders	Meltzer et al, 2000
Low levels of family support	-ve		
Better/more positive parental relationships	+ve	SDQ and GHQ score	Dunn et al, 1998; Ely et al, 2000
More family conflict	-ve	GHQ score	Sweeting and West, 1995
	-ve	Self-esteem	
	-ve	Depressed mood	Donnelley, 1999
Less family time	-ve	GHQ score	Ely et al, 2000
Incohesive/unsupportive family	-ve	Self-esteem Depression Anxiety	Glendinning et al, 2000; Donnelley, 1999

evidence presented in Table 4.4. Looking first at family structure, the findings are quite complex, and there are differences for those living in lone parent families, and stepfamilies or reconstituted families, compared with those living with both biological parents.

Children living in lone parent families had higher rates of mental disorder (Meltzer et al 2000; Green et al 2005), and were at greater risk of high SDQ scores, and for boys but not girls, high GHQ scores (Prescott-Clark and Primatesta 1998). Bergman and Scott (2001) also found that children, again especially boys, from lone parent families were more likely to report past worries, greater unhappiness and have lower self-esteem, whilst Clarke et al (2000) found that children from lone parent families, again particularly boys, had lower self-image.

Children living in stepfamilies (also referred to as reconstituted families) were for some, but not all, measures of emotional well-being at the same increased risk as those living in lone parent families. The prevalence of mental disorders was higher amongst children in stepfamilies (Meltzer et al 2000; Green et al 2005), and for girls there was a greater chance of low self-esteem (Sweeting and West 1995). Ermisch et al (2004) also found that having spent some time in a non-intact family during childhood was associated with an increased risk of psychological distress as a young adult.

Some of the above findings came from simple bivariate analyses, providing little clue to how the impact of family structure on emotional well-being operates. However, there have been suggestions that it is not family type per se that lowers emotional well-being, but that differences in outcomes may simply reflect the (sometimes observed, other times unobservable) characteristics, such as lower parental educational attainment, emotional well-being and financial problems, associated with life in a lone parent or stepfamily. For example, Dunn et al (1998) found that living in a stepfamily or lone parent family was associated with greater likelihood of having a high SDQ score, but that this relationship lost significance when the psychological status of the mother, the mother-child relationship and socio-economic factors were simultaneously taken in account. McMunn et al (2001) found a similar affect on the relationship between family type and SDQ scores when just socio-economic factors were controlled for. This all means that when considering the impact of family type of children's emotional well-being it is important to take other factors into account.

Other research suggests that there is in fact a stronger link between children's mental health and family life or culture, than with family structure. Children in families with poor communication and low levels of support were much more likely to have a mental disorder than children in other families (Meltzer et al 2000). Other measures of family cohesiveness and relationships were also connected with children's emotional well-being: better or more positive parental relationships were associated with better SDQ and GHQ scores (Dunn et al 1998; Ely et al 2000); young people who reported more conflict with their parents were more likely to have a high GHQ score and lower self-esteem (Sweeting and West 1995), and greater levels of depressed mood (Donnelley 1999); young people spending more time with their families were less likely to have a high GHQ score (Ely et al 2000); and young people who perceived their families as being incohesive and as offering little support tended to have lower levels of self-esteem, and higher levels of depression and anxiety (Donnelley 1999; Glendinning et al 2000).

That the associations observed above between young people's emotional well-being and family type, income and social class might operate through family time and relationships has been investigated (Sweeting and West 1995; Sweeting et al 1998; Ely et al 2000). They not only found a strong relationship between family structure and income, with lone parent families being disadvantaged compared to reconstituted families who in turn are more disadvantaged than intact families, but that there was a similar association between family structure and family time, and between family structure and the quality of family relationships. In addition, there was greater family centredness (family time) and less conflict in non-manual households, and correspondingly in families in the least deprived income tertile.

Table 4.5   Summary of the evidence: Parental factors

Factor	Impact on emotional well-being	Measure of well-being	Reference
Parents' emotional well-being			
Depressed parent	-ve	Emotional and conduct disorders	Ross and Roberts, 1999
Depressed parent	-ve	Behavioural problems	Cummings et al, 2000
Mother with high GHQ score	-ve (girls)	GHQ score	Prescott-Clark and Primatesta, 1998
Mother or father with high GHQ score	-ve	GHQ score	McMunn et al, 2001
	-ve	SDQ score	Prescott-Clark and Primatesta, 1998
Depressed mother	-ve	SDQ score	Dunn et al, 1998
Parental qualifications			
Mother no qualifications	-ve	SDQ score	Prescott-Clark and Primatesta, 1998

Thus the apparent detrimental effect on children's emotional well-being of poor socio-economic circumstances and family structure may be operating through the impact that these circumstances have on family time and relationships. Unfortunately, parental employment patterns were not taken into account, as this may have an impact on both family time and relationships.

Parents' emotional well-being

The general psychological well-being of parents during childhood and associated patterns of parenting is important. Depressed mothers may be less likely to provide stimulation to their babies by talking and looking at them, or to provide positive emotional interactions (see Table 4.5).

Children of depressed parents have been shown to be two to five times more likely to develop behaviour problems than children of non-depressed parents (Cummings et al 2000), and are more likely to have problems relating to others, to have emotional and conduct disorders, and to have problems with substance abuse in later life (Ross and Roberts 1999). There is also evidence that girls, but not boys, whose mothers have a high GHQ score are far more likely to have a high GHQ score themselves, but there is no association with fathers' GHQ scores for either girls or boys. Children's SDQ scores also show a strong significant relationship with both mothers' and less strongly with fathers' GHQ scores, with the relationships being stronger for girls than boys (Prescott-Clark and Primatesta 1998). This finding was substantiated by Dunn et al (1998) who found that children of mothers with high levels of depressive symptomatology had higher total SDQ scores than children of other mothers, and by McMunn et al (2001) who found that children whose mother or father had a high GHQ score were twice as likely to have a high SDQ score themselves. This work illustrated the overwhelming importance of parental psychological well-being for children, even after controlling for both socio-economic circumstances and family structure. In addition, as mothers with

Table 4.6   Summary of the evidence: Children's own characteristics

Factor	Impact on emotional well-being	Measure of well-being	Reference
Age			
Older child	-ve	Incidence of mental health disorders	Meltzer et al, 2000; Green et al, 2005
	-ve	Depression	Glendinning et al, 2000
	-ve	Worrying	Schools Health Education Unit (SHEU), 2004
	+ve	Self-esteem	
	+ve	Satisfaction with life	
Gender			
Boys	-ve	Incidence of mental disorders (particularly conduct and hyperkinetic)	Meltzer et al, 2000; Green et al, 2005
	+ve	GHQ score	Prescott-Clark and Primatesta, 1998; Sproston and Primatesta, 2003
	-ve	SDQ score	Prescott-Clark and Primatesta, 1998; Sproston and Primatesta, 2003
	+ve	Self-esteem	Clarke et al, 2000; Glendining et al, 2000; Bergmam and Scott, 2001; SHEU, 2004.
	+ve	Satisfaction with life	
	+ve	Sadness	
	+ve	Unhappiness	
	+ve	Worry	
	-ve	Self-efficacy	

high GHQ scores were more likely to be in receipt of benefits (McMunn et al 2001) or have limited financial resources (Dunn et al 1998), parental emotional well-being may well go some way to mediating the relationship between benefit receipt and children's emotional well-being.

Parental qualifications

The proportion of children with high SDQ scores has been shown to increase as the level of mothers' educational attainment declines; 16 per cent of girls and 22 per cent of boys whose mothers had no qualifications had high SDQ scores, compared with 5 per cent of boys and negligible girls whose mothers had higher education qualifications (Prescott-Clark and Primatesta 1998). This was corroborated by McMunn et al (2001) who also suggested that as qualifications are linked with employment status and socio-economic circumstances, need to be taken into account in future research (see Table 4.5).

Children's own characteristics

Finally we turn to look at the impact that children's own characteristics, specifically age and gender, have been found to have on their emotional well-being (Table 4.6). Although most of the studies reported here considered samples of children and young people of a broader age-range than that in the current research, it is useful to consider age-related differences. One of the most consistent findings is that older children are more likely to experience mental health problems than younger children in terms of the prevalence of mental disorder (Meltzer et al 2000; Green et al 2005), feelings of depression (Glendinning et al 2000), and worrying, although older young people had higher levels of self-esteem and of feelings satisfied with life (SHEU 2004).

In terms of gender, overall boys were more likely to have a mental disorder than girls, with particularly higher rates of conduct and hyperkinetic disorders (Meltzer et al 2000; Green et al 2005). Looking at more subjective measures however different patterns are found: girls were more likely than boys to have high GHQ scores (Prescott-Clark and Primatesta 1998; Sproston and Primatesta 2003), but less likely to have high overall SDQ score (McMunn et al 2001). Boys reported higher self-esteem, greater levels of satisfaction with life, less feelings of depression, sadness, unhappiness and worry, and lower self-efficacy (Clarke et al 2000; Glendinning et al 2000; Bergmam and Scott 2001; SHEU 2004).

Summary

This section has considered the existing evidence relating to the impact that parental employment patterns, and other family, parent and child factors have on children's emotional well-being. The effect of parental employment is complex. Spending some time as a child in a household with no earners was associated with poorer emotional well-being during adolescence and young adulthood, as was concurrent family worklessness. Maternal employment, particularly part-time employment, during childhood appeared to offer protection against poorer emotional outcomes later in life, although the impact of full-time maternal employment when children were pre-school age was less clear. Living with an unemployed father was clearly associated with poorer concurrent emotional well-being among adolescents, and maternal employment, again in some cases particularly part-time employment, appeared to have a positive impact, although this was not found with all measures of emotional well-being.

Socio-economic factors, including family income, social class, and housing tenure, were also seen to have an important impact on children's emotional well-being, and in some cases accounted for the apparent differences related to parental employment. Living in a lone parent or stepfamily tended to be detrimental, although again links were found between family type and family income. Not always considered were factors relating to parents' own psychological well-being and the quality of family relationships, which proved to be closely affiliated with children's emotional well-being in certain research. As these factors were also linked with family structure, and perhaps parents' employment status, it could be suggested that it is actually parents' own psychological well-being and the quality of family relationships, which have a crucial impact on children's well-being. The next section uses data from the youth survey of the BHPS to explore some of the issues raised so far in this chapter, investigating any connection between young people's emotional well-being and parental employment patterns. The influence of other factors, such as socio-economic circumstances, individual, parental and familial characteristics is also considered, together with some of the mechanisms by which these relationships operate.

Young people's emotional well-being and the BHPS

We have seen then that the relationship between parental employment patterns and children's emotional well-being is complex, and that other individual, familial and parental factors are also important. Data from the youth survey of the BHPS is used in this section to consider the following research questions: whether differences in children's emotional well-being are observed by parental employment status, and if so whether these are accounted for through the inclusion of socio-economic factors? Are there differences for children living in different family types, and does parents' own psychological well-being, and the quality of family relationships matter? Does the inclusion of these factors account for the apparent differences due to parental employment patterns? And can these influences and relationships be explained in terms of capitals – financial, social and cultural?

The youth survey of the BHPS covers a wide range of topics, and includes a number of questions relating to emotional well-being. These have been used to derive four indicators, as can be seen in Table 4.7. The BHPS does not measure the incidence of mental health disorders, and therefore all the indicators of emotional well-being used are subjective measures.

The first indicator, troubled, combines responses to the questions about feeling unhappy or depressed, and losing sleep worrying about things. As the majority of young people were unhappy for less than 3 days in the previous month, and didn't lose sleep on any night in the previous week, it was decided to consider all responses above these thresholds as contributing to feeling troubled. Overall, 36 per cent of the young people in the sample felt troubled, that is felt sad or depressed for four or more days in the previous month, and/or lost sleep worrying for one or more nights in the previous week. Sensitivity analysis confirmed this threshold to be appropriate, as combining different responses led to a much higher or lower percentage of young people being classed as troubled, which made the results hard to interpret, and in many cases not statistically significant. This indicator can be located in the affective component of the model of emotional well-being discussed earlier in this chapter, and illustrated in Figure 4.1, representing how individuals feel about their lives.

The second indicator is a measure of low self-efficacy, which combines questions about individuals' perceptions of themselves having a number of good qualities and being a likeable person. Overall, 11 per cent of the sample disagreed or strongly disagreed with one or both of these statements, indicating a low level of self-efficacy.

Table 4.7   Emotional well-being indicators in the BHPS youth survey

Variables	Question			Indicator
SAD	In the past month, how many days have you felt unhappy or depressed? (N=6829)	**Days**	**%**	
		None	32.9	
		1–3	46.9	Troubled
		4–10	14.7	Sad for 4+ days in the past
		11+	5.4	month and/or lost sleep
WORRY	In the past week, how many nights have you lost sleep worrying about things? (N=6827)	**Days**	**%**	worrying one or more nights during last week 36.0%
		None	72.7	
		1–2	21.9	
		3–5	4.0	
		6–7	1.4	
GOODQUAL	I feel I have a number of good qualities. (N=6785)		**%**	
		Strongly agree	26.2	
		Agree	66.3	Low self-efficacy
		Disagree	6.2	Disagreed or strongly
		Strongly disagree	1.3	disagreed with goodqual
LIKEABLE	I am a likeable person. (N=6777)	Strongly agree	23.0	and/or likeable. 11.2%
		Agree	71.4	
		Disagree	4.4	
		Strongly disagree	1.3	
USELESS	I certainly feel useless at times. (N=6796)		**%**	
		Strongly agree	5.0	
		Agree	31.6	
		Disagree	39.1	
		Strongly disagree	24.3	Low self-esteem
FAILURE	All in all, I am inclined to feel I am a failure. (N=6786)	Strongly agree	2.3	Agreed or strongly agreed
		Agree	7.6	with useless and/or failure
		Disagree	34.8	and/or nogood.
		Strongly disagree	55.2	44.7%
NOGOOD	At times I feel I am no good at all. (N=6799)	Strongly agree	3.8	
		Agree	24.7	
		Disagree	39.2	
		Strongly disagree	32.4	
	How do you feel about your:	**Mean**	**SD**	
FEELFAM	Your family? (N=6822)	1.66	1.07	
FEELFR	Your friends? (N=6815)	1.80	0.99	Unhappy
FEELAPP	Your appearance? (6805)	2.66	1.34	Overall score of 14 or more.
FEELLIFE	Your life as a whole (6806)	2.15	1.27	22.2%
FEELSCH	Your school work? (N=6815)	2.68	1.29	
	Overall (range 5-35)	10.95	4.06	

[1] On a scale of 1-7 using smiley faces where 1 = very happy and 7 = not happy at all.
Source: Author's own analysis of BHPS data.

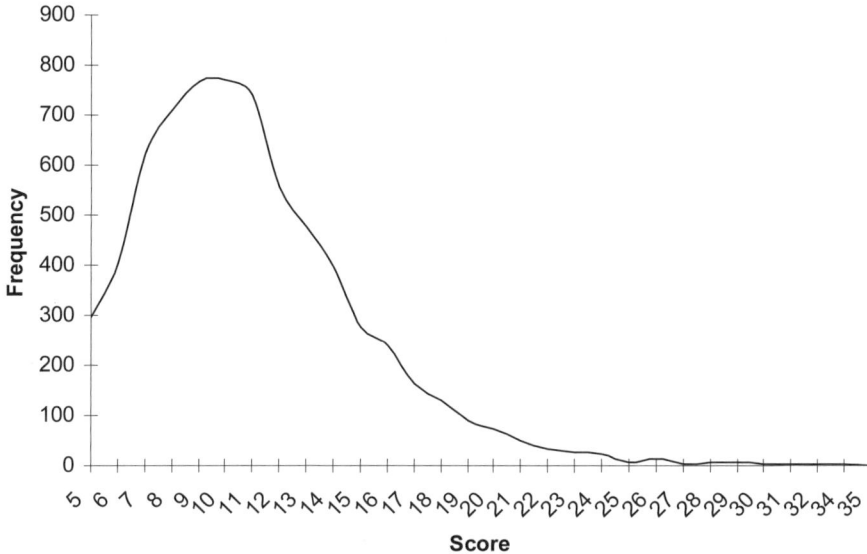

Figure 4.2 **A graph to show the distribution of scores on the happiness scale variable**

Low self-esteem is represented by the combination of responses to questions about feeling useless, feeling a failure, and sometimes feeling no good at all. Overall, 45 per cent of the young people agreed or strongly agreed with at least one of these statements. Both self-esteem and self-efficacy are constituents of the psychological component of the model of emotional well-being, relating to how individuals feel about themselves. Although the constituent variables of self-esteem and self-efficacy have sometimes been combined into a single measure (for example, Clarke et al 2000), exploratory factor analysis was carried out, which found that the use of 2 separate indicators (or factors) were justifiable.

The fourth indicator of emotional well-being is happiness, or satisfaction with life. Individuals were asked how they felt about four specific areas (their family, friends, appearance, and schoolwork) and about their lives as a whole. This indicator fits into the cognitive sector of the model of emotional well-being, that is how individuals think about their lives. They were asked to rate each aspect on a scale of one to seven, where one represented very happy and seven represented not happy at all. These scores were then added together to give an overall happiness score with a range from 5 to 35. The distribution for this overall happiness variable is shown in Figure 4.2.

It can be seen that the distribution is positively skewed, that is more young people had low scores than high scores. A dichotomous indicator was created using a threshold of 14 to indicate unhappiness, and on this basis, 22 per cent of the young people were unhappy. Although the unhappiness scale variable could

Table 4.8   Correlations between the 4 indicators of emotional well-being

	Unhappy	**Troubled**	**Low self-efficacy**	**Low self-esteem**
Unhappy		0.27***	0.27***	0.30***
Troubled	0.27***		0.16***	0.32***
Low self-efficacy	0.27***	0.16***		0.21***
Low self-esteem	0.30***	0.32***	0.21***	

Statistical significance: *=p<0.05, **=p<0.01, ***=p<0.001.
Source: Author's own analysis of BHPS data.

have been used in the analysis, the use of a dichotomous indicator was justified on the grounds that the other indicators used in this chapter were dichotomous, and that this would simplify the evaluation of results from the regression analyses. Sensitivity analysis was carried out to ensure that the use of a dichotomous indicator did not affect the overall results.

Table 4.8 shows a matrix of correlations for the 4 indicators of emotional well-being used in the analysis. All the correlations are fairly weak, ranging between 0.16 and 0.32, which supports the use of these 4 distinct measures of emotional well-being. If any of the indicators had been highly correlated it would have been more appropriate to combine them into one factor.

Parental employment patterns

As we saw earlier the existing evidence is mixed with regards to the impact of parental employment patterns on young people's emotional well-being. Living in a currently workless household or with an unemployed father was associated with poorer emotional well-being, using a variety of indicators, although the impact of maternal employment patterns is less clear-cut. In some cases any maternal employment appears to offer some protection against poorer levels of emotional well-being, but in others it is only part-time employment which affords this protection. A variety of research has also considered the impact of parental employment patterns when young people were growing up on their later emotional well-being. Again, worklessness or experience of life with an unemployed father can have a detrimental effect on a young persons later emotional well-being, although the evidence relating to the impact of early maternal employment is mixed and often contradictory.

This section uses the data from the youth survey of the BHPS to explore the relationships observed in previous research, and to investigate whether any associations exist between the four measures of emotional well-being outlined above and parental employment patterns. A series of logistic regressions were carried out to assess the impact of each measure of parental employment on each indicator of emotional well-being separately, and the results are shown in Table 4.9.

Table 4.9 **Logistic regressions for the odds of being troubled, being unhappy, having low self-efficacy and low self-esteem: Parental employment patterns**

Variable		N	Bivariate odds			
			Troubled	Unhappy	Low self-efficacy	Low self-esteem
Father current employment	Employed	4527	1.00	1.00 (0.1%)	1.00	1.00 (0.3%)
	Not in employment	780	1.07	1.23*	1.19	1.28***
Mother current employment	Full-time	2334	1.00 (0.3%)	1.00 (0.3%)	1.00 (0.5%)	1.00 (0.5%)
	Part-time	2238	0.93	0.83**	0.89	0.88*
	Not in employment	1996	0.80***	1.09	1.29**	1.19**
Father employment (child 0–1)	Employed	3751	1.00	1.00	1.00	1.00
	Not in employment	319	0.81	0.94	1.01	1.10
Father employment (child 1–5)	Employed	3742	1.00 (0.2%)	1.00	1.00	1.00
	Not in employment	339	0.77*	0.94	1.01	1.02
Father employment (child 5–11)	Employed	3476	1.00	1.00	1.00	1.00
	Not in employment	393	0.90	0.82	0.88	1.06
Mother employment (child 0–1)	Employed full-time	508	1.00	1.00	1.00	1.00 (0.2%)
	Employed part-time	594	0.99	0.93	1.21	1.31*
	Not in employment	4358	1.02	1.04	1.03	1.32**
Mother employment (child 1–5)	Employed full-time	795	1.00	1.00	1.00	1.00 (0.3%)
	Employed part-time	1159	1.06	1.04	1.18	1.25*
	Not in employment	3530	1.04	1.01	1.15	1.30***
Mother employment (child 5–11)	Employed full-time	1299	1.00 (0.2%)	1.00	1.00	1.00 (0.4%)
	Employed part-time	1783	0.84*	0.91	0.81	0.95
	Not in employment	2317	0.82**	1.02	1.14	1.20**
Current earners	No earners	823	1.00	1.00 (0.6%)	1.00 (0.4%)	1.00 (0.6%)
	One earner	1839	1.02	0.85	0.82	0.77**
	Two earners	3434	1.11	0.68***	0.69***	0.68***
Earners (child 0–1)	No earners	469	1.00	1.00	1.00 (0.4%)	1.00 (0.2%)
	One earner	2857	1.21	0.88	0.66**	0.85
	Two earners	782	1.16	0.87	0.75	0.76*
Earners (child 1–5)	No earners	497	1.00	1.00 (0.2%)	1.00 (0.2%)	1.00
	One earner	2327	1.11	0.79*	0.73*	0.84
	Two earners	1314	1.09	0.90	0.79	0.82
Earners (child 5–11)	No earners	725	1.00	1.00	1.00 (0.8%)	1.00 (0.2%)
	One earner	1699	0.95	0.87	0.80	0.91
	Two earners	2298	1.05	0.85	0.59***	0.80**

Statistical significance: *=p<0.05, **=p<0.01, ***=p<0.001.

Note: Single observations only with substantive significance shown in brackets.

Source: Author's own analysis of BHPS data.

Troubled Parental employment patterns, past and current, were found to have very little impact on the likelihood that young people felt troubled or worried. Fathers' current employment patterns had no significant impact on young people feeling troubled, but having a mother not in employment, as opposed to employed on a full-time basis was associated with a slightly lower likelihood of feeling troubled. This only accounted was a very tiny proportion of the variance (0.3 per cent) in whether young people felt troubled, and thus although statistically significant, represents a very small influence. Fathers' employment patterns when young people were aged 0–1 and 5–11 had no significant impact on whether they felt troubled as adolescents, but young people who had a father out of the labour market when they were aged 1–5 were actually less likely to feel troubled later in life, although this slightly surprising finding only accounts for a very small proportion of the variance in this indicator of emotional well-being.

Mothers' employment when the young people were aged 0–1 and 1–5 had no significant impact on their propensity to feel troubled, but those whose mothers were employed part-time or were not in the labour market when they were aged 5–11 were less likely to feel troubled as an adolescent than those whose mothers were employed on a full-time basis. This might suggest that when children are younger having a mother at home affords some protection against poorer emotional well-being in adolescence, but as they get older this is balanced by the benefit to household income and the associated effect of emotional well-being of having a mother in paid employment. This is investigated further later in this chapter, when multiple regression techniques are used to study the impact of parental employment patterns on young people's emotional well-being whilst controlling for other factors, including household income.

When we look at the combined impact of maternal and paternal employment, by considering the number of earners in a household both at the current time and when the young people were growing up, we find that there are no statistically significant associations with young people feeling troubled.

Unhappy   When we look at the impact of parental employment patterns on young people's happiness, we find that only current patterns make a significant impact. Young people whose fathers were not currently in the labour market were more likely to be unhappy than those with an employed father, and those whose mothers were employed part-time as opposed to full-time were less likely to be unhappy. Having a mother who was not currently in the labour market had no significant impact upon young people's happiness, nor did parental patterns of employment when the young people were growing up. In line with these findings, young people were less likely to be unhappy if they were currently living in a dual-earner household, compared with a no-earner household. Again, this suggests that parental employment benefits young people with regards their emotional well-being through an increase in financial capital available within the family, but that part-time maternal employment carries more benefit that full-time employment, perhaps through a mechanism of nurturing or emotional support.

Low self-efficacy   Low self-efficacy, not feeling that you have a number of good qualities or are a likeable person, is influenced more by the number of earners in the household than it is by paternal and maternal employment patterns when measured separately, and this is true of employment patterns at all stages of childhood.

Having lived in a one-earner household in infancy or during the pre-school years was beneficial for young people's self-efficacy in adolescence compared with living in a workless household, but those who had two working parents were no better off. This suggests that during these early years it is important to have both a working role model and the nurturing support of a parent at home. When children are in primary school (aged 5–11) living in a dual-earner household appeared to be most beneficial for young people's self-efficacy, as it does also in terms of current parental employment patterns. Indeed having a mother currently out of the labour market is associated with a higher chance of having low self-efficacy.

Low self-esteem Young people's self-esteem was the only indicator of emotional well-being which was significantly influenced by both maternal and paternal current employment patterns. Having a mother or father currently out of the labour market was associated with a higher chance that young people had low self-esteem, whereas having a mother employed part-time as opposed to full-time was linked with a lower chance of low self-esteem, which again might reflect the balance between financial and social capital introduced into a family through maternal employment. To confuse the picture, a slightly different pattern is seen when we look at past patterns of maternal employment. Compared with having a mother in full-time employment, young people had a greater chance of having low self-esteem if their mother had not been in paid employment at any stage when they were growing up, or if they had been in part-time employment at ages 0–1 or 1–5. Consistent with these results, living in a household with no current earners either currently or in the past was associated with a higher chance of young people having a low level of self-esteem. Although all the relationships reported attain statistical significance, that is it is unlikely that such an association would be found by chance, substantively the findings are very small. Less than 1 per cent of the variance in emotional well-being is explained by any of the different measures of parental employment.

Summary In summary then, having a father currently in employment appears to offer young people some protection against being unhappy and having low self-esteem, but has no impact on feeling troubled or on low self-efficacy. The odds ratios indicate that young people whose fathers were not currently in the labour market were one-and-a-quarter times as likely to be unhappy or have low self-esteem than those whose fathers were in employment. These findings point towards the importance of paternal employment for young people's emotional well-being, although we do not know what mechanism this advantage operates through. Later in the chapter, using multivariate regression, we consider whether the advantage accorded to young people's emotional well-being through paternal employment operates through increasing the financial capital available within the family.

The impact of maternal employment is more complicated. Having a mother currently employed part-time as opposed to full-time was associated with around 20 per cent lower odds of being unhappy and having lower self-esteem. Having a mother out of the labour market increased the odds by about a quarter that young people had low self-esteem, and by around a fifth that they had low self-efficacy, but actually decreased the odds that they felt troubled. These results suggest the trade-off between the benefits of increased family income (financial capital) as a result of maternal employment, and the nurturing support (social capital) that mothers who are not in full-time employment appear to provide.

A measure of current parental employment based on the number of earners in the household also reflects these findings, except in the case of feeling troubled where no significant impact is found. Living in a household with two earners, and in the case of low self-esteem with one earner, offered protection against poor emotional well-being, compared to those who lived in a workless household, again suggesting the importance of financial capital.

Parental employment patterns when the young people were growing up only had a significant impact upon feeling troubled and having low self-esteem. Young people whose father had been out of the labour market when they were aged 1–5 were less likely to feel troubled as an adolescent. They were also less likely to feel troubled if their mother had been in part-time employment or not in employment when they were aged 5–11. In the case of self-esteem, young people whose mothers had not been employed full-time when they were aged 0–1 or 1–5 were more likely to have low self-esteem, whereas only having had a mother out of the labour market when aged 5–11 was associated with lower self-esteem. If we look at the impact of the number of earners in the household at the various stages of childhood, we see that living with one-earner, and in some cases, two earners, appears to offer some protection against poor emotional well-being outcomes, compared with those living in a workless household.

Here we have considered the impact of parental employment patterns on young people's emotional well-being. Although some statistically significant results have been found, substantively these are very small. In other words, only a tiny proportion of the variance in the indicators of emotional well-being can be explained by parental employment patterns. The next section considers whether other factors can shed more light on the influences on young people's emotional well-being, or the mechanisms by which advantage stemming from parental employment operates.

Other factors

The four indicators of young people's emotional well-being were regressed against a number of family, parental, and individual factors. Table 4.10 presents the results, indicating statistically significant findings, and for those that are significant, the percentage of the variance in emotional well-being that can be explained by that factor.

Troubled Looking first at the odds of a young person feeling troubled, the most important finding is the influence of high levels of family conflict. Perhaps

Table 4.10 Logistic regressions for the odds of being troubled, being unhappy, having low self-efficacy and low self-esteem: Other variables

Variable		N	Bivariate odds			
			Troubled	Unhappy	Low self-efficacy	Low self-esteem
Equivalent income less than 50% of average after housing costs	No	5306	1.00	1.00	1.00	1.00 (0.1%)
	Yes	1343	0.90	1.13	1.18	1.16*
Family social class	Man/pro	1957	1.00 (0.2%)	1.00	1.00 (0.9%)	1.00
	Non-man	1432	0.92	0.87	0.93	0.87
	Man/unskilled	2255	0.85*	1.07	1.48***	1.09
At least one car	Yes	5782	1.00 (0.1%)	1.00	1.00 (0.4%)	1.00
	No	879	0.85*	1.07	1.51***	1.15
Tenure	Owned	4826	1.00	1.00 (0.3%)	1.00 (1.3%)	1.00 (0.5%)
	Rented	1823	0.91	1.25***	1.72***	1.30***
Family type	Intact	4551	1.00 (0.2%)	1.00 (0.8%)	1.00 (0.5%)	1.00 (0.4%)
	Step	1247	1.22**	1.33***	1.47***	1.26***
	Lone	863	1.13	1.57***	1.12	1.30***
High family conflict	No	4743	1.00 (5.4%)	1.00 (5.3%)	1.00 (2.3%)	1.00 (2.8%)
	Yes	1898	2.49***	2.60***	2.05***	1.92***
Poor family communication	No	4404	1.00	1.00 (3.2%)	1.00 (1.5%)	1.00 (0.3%)
	Yes	2241	0.94	2.05***	1.75***	1.23***
Father GHQ+4	No	4016	1.00 (0.5%)	1.00 (0.5%)	1.00 (0.4%)	1.00 (0.1%)
	Yes	921	1.37***	1.39***	1.41***	1.19*
Mother GHQ+4	No	4704	1.00 (1.1%)	1.00 (0.5%)	1.00 (0.3%)	1.00 (0.4%)
	Yes	1719	1.50***	1.36***	1.30**	1.30***
Father qualifications	Degree or higher	605	1.00 (0.2%)	1.00	1.00 (1.0%)	1.00 (0.7%)
	A level/HND	1453	0.81*	0.84	1.13	0.85
	O level/GCSE	1640	0.80*	0.91	1.39	0.92
	None	1301	0.90	0.96	1.88***	1.23*
Mother qualifications	Degree or higher	510	1.00 (0.2%)	1.00 (0.4%)	1.00 (0.8%)	1.00 (0.3%)
	A level/HND	1337	0.91	0.70**	1.27	0.98
	O level/GCSE	2913	0.81*	0.74**	1.41*	1.04
	None	1727	0.81*	0.91	1.98***	1.26*
Child gender	Male	3411	1.00 (3.0%)	1.00 (0.3%)	1.00 (0.2%)	1.00 (3.1%)
	Female	3250	1.86***	1.25***	1.24**	1.86***
Child age	11	1349	1.00 (0.8%)	1.00 (2.0%)	1.00	1.00 (0.4%)
	12	1391	0.92	1.22*	1.08	0.85*
	13	1339	0.99	1.58***	1.00	0.74***
	14	1329	1.21*	1.83***	0.95	0.82**
	15	1253	1.43***	2.19***	0.90	0.78**

Statistical significance: *=p<0.05, **=p<0.01, ***=p<0.001.
Note: Single observations only with substantive significance shown in brackets.
Source: Author's own analysis of BHPS data.

unsurprisingly, those living in families with a high level of family conflict were two-and-a-half times more likely to feel troubled, and this accounts for 5 per cent of the variance in this measure of emotional well-being. Gender is also important, with girls almost twice as likely to feel troubled as boys, accounting for 3 per cent of the variance in this measure of emotional well-being.

Young people whose mother had a GHQ score of 4 or above were one-and-a-half times as likely to feel troubled as other young people, accounting for 1 per cent of the variance in feeling troubled. The influence of other variables on the odds of young people feeling troubled attained statistical significance, although each accounted for less than 1 per cent of the variance in this measure of emotional well-being. Young people were less likely to be troubled if they came from manual or unskilled households (compared with managerial and professional households); if their family did not have at least one car; and if either of their parents had less than degree-level qualifications; but more likely to be troubled if they lived in a stepfamily; if their father had a GHQ score of four or above; and if they were older.

Unhappy   In terms of happiness, again the most important influence found was that of family conflict. Those in high conflict families were over two-and-a-half times as likely to be unhappy as other young people, and this accounted for 5 per cent of the variance in unhappiness. Poor family communication was also associated with the odds that young people feel unhappy, and accounted for 3 per cent of the variance in unhappiness. Young people in families with low levels of communication were just over twice as likely to be unhappy as those who experienced good family communication. Age was also important, with older youths more likely to be unhappy, accounting for 2 per cent of the variance in young people's unhappiness. Again, other variables had a statistically significant association with unhappiness, but accounted for very little of the variance. Young people were more likely to be unhappy if they lived in rented accommodation; if they lived in a stepfamily or a lone parent family; if either their mother or father had a high GHQ score; if their mother had less than degree-level qualifications (although there is no relationship with fathers' level of qualifications); and if they were a girl.

Low self-efficacy   Family conflict was also an important influence on young people's self-efficacy, accounting for 2 per cent of the variance in this measure of emotional well-being. Young people living in households with high levels of family conflict had higher odds of having low self-efficacy. Likewise, poor communication in a family was also associated with low self-efficacy, and this accounted for around 1 per cent of the variance in this measure of emotional well-being. Low self-efficacy was the only measure of emotional well-being for which tenure explained more than 1 per cent of the variance, with young people living in rented accommodation more likely to have low self-efficacy than those in owner-occupied accommodation. Young people whose father had no qualifications were almost twice as likely as those whose father had a degree to have low self-efficacy, explaining 1 per cent of the variance in this measure of emotional well-being. Family social class, family type, car ownership, parents' GHQ scores, mothers' qualifications, and gender were also associated with young people's self-efficacy, although these factors each accounted for less than 1 per cent of the variance in young people's self-efficacy.

Low self-esteem Girls, and those living in families with high levels of conflict were around twice as likely as other young people to have low self-esteem, but these were the only two variables to account for more than 1 per cent of the variance in this measure of emotional well-being. Young people were also more likely to have low self-esteem if they lived in a low-income household; if they lived in a stepfamily or a lone parent family; if they experienced low levels of family communication; if either their father or mother had a high GHQ score; if either their father or mother had no academic qualifications; and if they were younger.

Summary In summary then, we have seen that living in a family with a high level of conflict had the most significant detrimental effect on all four indicators of emotional well-being, a finding which is consistent with previous research (Sweeting and West, 1995; Donnelley, 1999). Family communication was also substantively important in the case of happiness and self-efficacy, and less so for self-esteem. These findings are significant as they reflect the importance of different types of family capital on young people's emotional well-being. As was suggested above, parental employment contributes more than financial capital to the family, and particularly in terms of maternal employment there appears to be a balance between financial capital and nurturing support, or social capital stemming from employment. The only socio-economic variable to account for more than 1 per cent of the variance in emotional well-being was housing tenure, and then only for self-efficacy. The weakness of the influence of socio-economic variables is surprising, considering the evidence from other work, although this could be influenced by the actual measures of emotional well-being used. Although family type had a statistically significant association with all four indicators of emotional well-being, it accounted for less than 1 per cent of the variance in any of them. Similarly parents' own GHQ scores and qualifications had only a limited association with the 4 indicators. Although girls were more likely to have poorer emotional well-being on all four indicators of emotional well-being, only for feeling troubled and low self-esteem did gender account for more than 1 per cent of the variance. Similarly age had a substantive association only with unhappiness.

Multivariate analysis

We have seen then that although statistically significant, the association between parental employment and young people's emotional well-being is substantively very small. In the previous section we saw that other factors, particularly the quality of family relationships, in terms of conflict and communication, had a more important association with emotional well-being than measures of parental employment patterns. Could it be that any observed impact of parental employment on emotional well-being operates through a mechanism associated with socio-economic factors, or factors relating to the quality of family life? In terms of capitals, does parental employment influence young people's emotional well-being through the effect on financial capital, or are there more significant influences, such as social, and cultural capital. These factors, particularly those relating to the quality of family life, have rarely been controlled for in previous work.

All the relationships considered so far have been bivariate, that is the association of single variables with the four indicators of emotional well-being. We now turn to multivariate logistic regressions, to consider the impact of one variable, whilst holding a number of other variables constant. This takes into account that some of the explanatory variables may interact. We do this for each indicator of young people's emotional well-being in turn.

Troubled   A series of forwards multiple regressions were carried out, starting with those variables that had a significant impact on feeling troubled in the bivariate analyses. Seven variables emerged in the best fitting model, shown in Table 4.11.

The model correctly predicted 67 per cent of cases, a 3 per cent increase on step 0 (with no explanatory variables in the equation). However, the Nagelkerke R^2 value was 0.01, which indicates that the variables included in the model explained just 1 per cent of the variance in whether young people felt troubled. That the proportion of variance explained is so low is important, as this indicates that the factors included in the model, including maternal employment, have a negligible impact upon whether young people feel troubled, and that there must be a number of other factors, not included in this model, which have a more important influence.

It can be seen from the model in Table 4.11 that even when a number of other important variables were controlled for, young people living with a mother not in the labour market were around 20 per cent less likely to feel troubled than those whose mothers are employed on a full-time basis. This suggests that mothers who are not employed on a full-time basis are able to offer their children some degree of protection (social capital) against poor emotional well-being. However, the impact of other variables, particularly family conflict was far greater. Young people living in families with high levels of conflict were over twice as likely to feel troubled, and those whose mothers had a high GHQ score were one-and-a-half times as likely to feel troubled as other young people. Fathers' emotional well-being did not play a significant part in this model, which suggests that young people garner more of their emotional support and feelings from their mother. These findings suggest that the impact of family conflict and poor maternal emotional well-being on young people's emotional well-being operates over and above the effect of parental employment patterns. Girls were more likely to feel troubled, as were older youths, and those living in lone parent or stepfamilies. As the model controls for the level of family conflict it can be concluded that the impact of family type

Table 4.11 Logistic regression for feeling troubled: Model of best fit

Variables entered		Odds ratios
Mother current employment	Full-time	1.00
	Part-time	0.92
	Not in employment	0.79***
High family conflict	No	1.00
	Yes	2.33***
Mother GHQ+4	No	1.00
	Yes	1.52***
Child gender	Male	1.00
	Female	1.84***
Child age	11	1.00
	12	0.92
	13	0.97
	14	1.19*
	15	1.30***
At least one car	Yes	1.00
	No	0.76***
Family type	Intact	1.00
	Step	1.28***
	Lone	1.17*

Statistical significance: *=$p<0.05$, **=$p<0.01$, ***=$p<0.001$
% correctly predicted = 66.8%
Nagelkerke R^2 = 0.010
N = 6404
Source: Author's own analysis of BHPS data.

on young people's emotional well-being does not operate through a mechanism of family conflict. That young people living in a household without at least one car were around 25 per cent less likely to feel troubled than other young people might operate in the opposite direction to that expected. However, perhaps young people from wealthier backgrounds feel more pressure to succeed, and thus worry more.

Unhappy In the bivariate analyses, mothers' current employment had a significant, if substantively small association with young people's unhappiness, with those whose mothers were employed part-time less likely to be unhappy than those working full-time, again suggesting the nurturing effect of having a mother not in full-time employment. However, when investigated further it was found that this relationship was far more important for young people living with a lone mother, and lost its statistical significance amongst those in dual parent families (see Table 4.12). Young people in lone mother families were around half as likely to be unhappy if their mother was in part-time employment as compared to full-time employment, and this accounted for almost 2 per cent of the variance in

Table 4.12   Logistic regression for unhappiness and mothers' current employment (lone mother and dual parent families separately)

Variable		Dual parent families	Lone mother families
Mother current employment	Full-time	1.00	1.00
	Part-time	0.90	0.51***
	Not in employment	1.15	0.73
Nagelkerke R²		0.002	0.018
N		5706	862

Source: Author's own analysis of BHPS data.

Table 4.13   Logistic regression for unhappiness: Model of best fit (lone mother families only)

Variables entered		Odds ratios
Current mother employment	Full-time	1.00
	Part-time	0.43***
	Not in employment	0.58*
Mother employment (child 0–1)	Full-time	1.00
	Part-time	1.02
	Not in employment	1.51
Mother employment (child 1–5)	Full-time	1.00
	Part-time	2.41**
	Not in employment	1.04
Mother employment (child 5–11)	Full-time	1.00
	Part-time	0.71
	Not in employment	1.36
High family conflict	No	1.00
	Yes	2.13***
Poor family communication	No	1.00
	Yes	2.27***
Child gender	Male	1.00
	Female	1.54**

% correctly predicted = 73.8%
Nagelkerke R^2 = 0.14
N = 749
Source: Author's own analysis of BHPS data.

unhappiness amongst this subset of young people. Further analysis was therefore carried out for lone parent and dual parent families separately.

For those in lone mother families, the model of best fit is shown in Table 4.13. The level of conflict and communication within a family had a significant impact on whether young people were unhappy, with those experiencing a high level of conflict or low levels of communication over twice as likely to be unhappy as other young people. As we saw for feeling troubled, girls were more likely to be unhappy than boys. As in the bivariate analysis, young people with a mother in current part-time employment were around half as likely to be unhappy as those whose mothers were employed on a full-time basis, again suggesting the social capital benefit of part-time maternal employment. When other factors were taken into account, young people with a mother not in employment were also around half as likely to be unhappy as those whose mothers worked full-time. In terms of the impact of maternal employment patterns when the young people were growing up, the inclusion of these variables contributed to the variance in unhappiness controlled for by the model, which stands at 14 per cent. However, only the association with part-time maternal employment when the young people were aged 1–5 reached statistical significance, with these young people almost two-and-a-half times as likely as those whose mothers were employed full-time during this period to be unhappy in adolescence. This finding is counter-intuitive, as previous results have indicated that non full-time maternal employment is more beneficial to young people's emotional well-being.

A similar process was carried out to obtain the model of best fit for unhappiness amongst young people in dual parent families, which is shown in Table 4.14.

Table 4.14   Logistic regression for unhappiness: Model of best fit (dual parent families only)

Variables entered		Odds ratios
Current earners	No earners	1.00
	One earner	0.95
	Two earners	0.77**
High family conflict	No	1.00
	Yes	2.51***
Poor family communication	No	1.00
	Yes	1.90***
Mother GHQ+4	No	1.00
	Yes	1.36***
Child gender	Male	1.00
	Female	1.16**
Child age	11	1.00
	12	1.15
	13	1.46***
	14	1.67***
	15	1.85***

% correctly predicted = 78.8%

Nagelkerke R^2 = 0.101

N = 5082

Source: Author's own analysis of BHPS data.

Table 4.15   Logistic regression for low self-efficacy and mothers' current employment (lone mother and dual parent families separately)

Odds ratios	Dual parent families	Lone mother families
Full-time	1.00	1.00
Part-time	0.88	0.95
Not in employment	1.29**	1.29
Nagelkerke R²	0.005	0.004
N	5706	862

Source: Author's own analysis of BHPS data.

Table 4.16   Logistic regression for low self-efficacy: Model of best fit (lone mother families only)

Variables entered		Odds ratios
Mother current employment	Full-time	1.00
	Part-time	0.65
	Not in employment	0.98
Mother employment (child 0–1)	Full-time	1.00
	Part-time	0.82
	Not in employment	0.60
Mother employment (child 1–5)	Full-time	1.00
	Part-time	1.80
	Not in employment	1.30
Mother employment (child 5–11)	Full-time	1.00
	Part-time	0.31**
	Not in employment	0.81
High family conflict	No	1.00
	Yes	1.89**
Poor family communication	No	1.00
	Yes	1.74*
At least one car	Yes	1.00
	No	2.02**

% correctly predicted = 88.7%
Nagelkerke R² = 0.097
N = 749
Source: Author's own analysis of BHPS data.

Here, the number of earners in the household (none, one or two) explained slightly more of the variance in unhappiness than when mother and father current employment patterns were considered specifically. Young people living in dual earner households were around 25 per cent less likely to be unhappy as those living in households without an earner. As has been seen with the other indicators of emotional well-being, young people experiencing high levels of family conflict or poor family communication were between two and two-and-a-half times more likely to be unhappy than other young people. Those whose mother had a high GHQ score were around a third more likely to be unhappy, and girls and older youths were also more likely to be unhappy than other young people.

Low self-efficacy The impact of maternal employment on young people's self-efficacy varied depending upon whether they live in lone mother or dual parent families (Table 4.15). In dual parent families, having a mother who was not currently in the labour market was associated with a greater risk of young people having low self-efficacy, as compared to those whose mothers were in full-time employment. In lone mother families, there was no statistically significant association between maternal employment and young people's self-efficacy. Thus further analysis was undertaken separately for those in lone mother and dual parent families.

In lone mother families a model of best fit was determined which accounted for around 10 per cent of the variance in young people's self-efficacy (Table 4.16).

Maternal employment patterns both currently and when the young people were growing up were included in the model, but only part-time maternal employment when young people were aged 5–11 had a statistically significant impact on their later self-efficacy, significantly reducing the odds of low self-efficacy. Young people living in households without at least one car were around twice as likely as other young people to have low self-efficacy, as were those who experienced high levels of family conflict or poor family communication. In dual parent families, parental employment patterns, both currently and when the young people were growing up, had no statistically significant association with young people's self-efficacy, but the exclusion of these variables reduced the proportion of the variance in self-efficacy accounted for by the model (see Table 4.17).

High levels of family conflict and poor family communication put young people at greater risk of low self-efficacy, as did living in rented accommodation. Young people in stepfamilies were over twice as likely as those in intact families to have low self-efficacy. Mother and father GHQ scores added to the model, but young people were only at a significant increased risk of low self-efficacy if their father had a high GHQ score. As has been seen with other indicators of emotional well-being, girls were more likely to have low self-efficacy than boys.

Low self-esteem As with young people's unhappiness, the impact of maternal employment on young people's self-esteem varied depending upon whether they lived in lone mother or dual parent families (see Table 4.18).

In dual parent families, having a mother not currently in the labour market was associated with a greater risk of young people having low self-esteem, as compared to those whose mothers were in full-time employment. This only accounted for less than 1 per cent of the variance in self-esteem. However, in lone mother families, maternal employment accounted for 2 per cent of the variance in self-esteem, with those young people whose mothers were in part-time employment

Table 4.17   Logistic regression for low self-efficacy: Model of best fit (dual parent families only)

Variables entered		Odds ratios
Current earners	No earners	1.00
	One earners	1.18
	Two earners	0.89
Earners (child 0–1)	No earners	1.00
	One earners	1.23
	Two earners	1.43
Earners (child 1–5)	No earners	1.00
	One earners	0.99
	Two earners	1.36
Earners (child 5–11)	No earners	1.00
	One earners	1.43
	Two earners	1.02
High family conflict	No	1.00
	Yes	1.85***
Poor family communication	No	1.00
	Yes	1.50***
Tenure	Owned	1.00
	Rented	1.77***
Family type	Intact	1.00
	Step	2.32***
Father GHQ+4	No	1.00
	Yes	1.41*
Mother GHQ+4	No	1.00
	Yes	1.15
Child gender	Male	1.00
	Female	1.32*

% correctly predicted = 90.2%
Nagelkerke R^2 = 0.069
N = 3206
Source: Author's own analysis of BHPS data.

Table 4.18   Logistic regression for low self-esteem and mothers' current employment (lone mother and dual parent families separately)

Odds ratios	Dual parent families	Lone mother families
Full-time	1.00	1.00
Part-time	0.94	0.56***
Not in employment	1.26***	0.78
Nagelkerke R^2	0.005	0.015
N	5706	862

Source: Author's own analysis of BHPS data.

Table 4.19   Logistic regression for low self-esteem: Model of best fit (lone mother families only)

Variables entered		Odds ratios
Mother current employment	Full-time	1.00
	Part-time	0.51***
	Not in employment	0.58**
Mother employment (0–1)	Full-time	1.00
	Part-time	1.37
	Not in employment	1.21
Mother employment (1–5)	Full-time	1.00
	Part-time	1.51
	Not in employment	1.46
Mother employment (5–11)	Full-time	1.00
	Part-time	0.54**
	Not in employment	1.10
High family conflict	No	1.00
	Yes	2.56***
Child gender	Male	1.00
	Female	1.90***
Mother GHQ+4	No	1.00
	Yes	1.40*

% correctly predicted = 62.4%
Nagelkerke R^2 = 0.127
N = 745
Source: Author's own analysis of BHPS data.

less likely to have low self-esteem than those whose mothers worked on a full-time basis. These findings suggest that in terms of self-esteem, some maternal employment is important, but that part-time maternal employment may be most beneficial. Further analysis was undertaken separately for those in lone mother and dual parent families.

The model of best fit for lone mother families, which correctly predicted 62 per cent of cases, an improvement of 12 per cent, is shown in Table 4.19. The model explained around 13 per cent of the variance in young people's self-esteem.

From the table we can see that young people whose mothers were currently employed part-time or who were not in the labour market were almost half as likely as other young people to have low self-esteem. This suggests that even though maternal employment is likely to increase household income, it is important for young people's self-esteem to have a mother who is not in full-time employment, which again points to the nurturing role of mothers in protecting their children against poor emotional well-being. Maternal employment patterns when the young people were aged 0–1 and 1–5 had no statistically significant impact upon their self-esteem as adolescents, but the exclusion of these variables from the model did impact upon the proportion of variance in self-esteem that is explained. Having had a mother employed part-time when aged 5–11 was associated with young people being half as likely to have low self-esteem compared with those whose mothers were employed on a full-time basis, a similar effect to that of current part-time maternal employment. Young people whose mother had a high GHQ score were around 40 per cent more likely to have low self-esteem than other young people. Again, high levels of family conflict were associated with a higher chance of having low self-esteem, around two-and-a-half times that for other young people, but family communication (not included in the final model) had no statistically significant impact on self-esteem. Girls were more likely to have low self-esteem, but age (again, not included in the final model) had no statistically significant impact.

The model of best fit for low self-esteem amongst those in dual parent families is shown in Table 4.20. This model only explained 9 per cent of the variance in self-esteem, but contained more variables than other models considered so far, suggesting weaker prediction of self-esteem than some of the other measures of emotional well-being. Those living in households with either one or two current earners were around half as likely as those in workless households to have low self-esteem, which indicates that some level of parental employment protects against young people having low self-esteem. Patterns of employment when the young people were growing up had no statistically significant association with self-esteem in adolescence, but as has been seen elsewhere, exclusion of these variables reduced the predictive power of the model. Girls were again almost twice as likely as boys to have low self-esteem, as were those who experienced high levels of family conflict. Young people whose mothers have a high GHQ score were around a third more likely to have low self-esteem as other young people.

Fathers', but not mothers', qualifications had a significant impact upon young people's self-esteem, with parental qualifications lower than degree level being associated with a lower likelihood of low self-esteem. Young people living in households which did not own at least one car were around a third less likely to have low self-esteem than other young people, again suggesting that those from wealthier families may feel under more pressure to succeed, which impacts upon their emotional well-being. Age was once again included in the model, although the relationship with self-esteem was opposite to that found for feeling troubled and unhappiness, with older youths being less likely to have low self-esteem.

Summary   In this section we have considered the best fitting multiple regression models to explain four indicators of young people's emotional well-being – troubled, unhappy, low self-esteem and low self-efficacy. For three of these indicators (all except self-efficacy) current parental employment patterns have a positive association, although the observed relationships are substantively small. The results tentatively point towards the nurturing role of mothers in protecting their children against poor emotional well-being, which seems to be in operation when the young person's mother is either out of the labour market or in part-time

Table 4.20   Logistic regression for low self-esteem: Model of best fit (dual parent families only)

Variables entered		Odds ratios
Current earners	No earners	1.00
	One earner	0.50***
	Two earners	0.51***
Earners (child 0–1)	No earners	1.00
	One earner	0.82
	Two earners	0.71
Earners (child 1–5)	No earners	1.00
	One earner	1.18
	Two earners	1.25
Earners (child 5–11)	No earners	1.00
	One earner	1.18
	Two earners	0.95
At least one car	Yes	1.00
	No	0.68**
High family conflict	No	1.00
	Yes	1.82***
Mother GHQ+4	No	1.00
	Yes	1.36***
Father qualifications	Degree or higher	1.00
	A level/HND	0.71***
	O level/GCSE	0.70***
	None	0.96
Child gender	Male	1.00
	Female	1.89***
Child age	11	1.00
	12	0.81
	13	0.67***
	14	0.79*
	15	0.74**

% correctly predicted = 62.0%
Nagelkerke R^2 = 0.086
N = 3235
Source: Author's own analysis of BHPS data.

employment, compared to full-time employment, although there are differences for those in lone mother and dual parent families for some of the indicators of well-being. Young people were less likely to be troubled if they lived with a mother who was not in the labour market. Young people whose lone mother was in full-time employment were more likely to be unhappy and have low self-esteem than those whose mother was either employed part-time or not in employment.

But for those in dual parent families it is the number of earners in the household that appears to affect their emotional well-being, with life in a workless household having a detrimental effect on young people's happiness and self-esteem.

Other factors have a greater impact on young people's emotional well-being than parental employment patterns. Living in a family with high levels of conflict is associated with poorer self-esteem and self-efficacy and with being more troubled and unhappy. Although this finding might be expected, it occurs even when family type and employment patterns are controlled for, suggesting that this is not the mechanism through which these factors influence emotional well-being. Mothers' own measures of emotional well-being (GHQ score) appears to be another important influence on young people's self-esteem and self-efficacy, and their feelings of unhappiness and trouble, again pointing to the contribution that mothers make to their children's emotional well-being.

Discussion and conclusions

Young people's emotional health and well-being is important, both for the impact that it has on their present quality of life, and also for the implications it has for their future social and emotional development, academic experience and achievement. This chapter began with a discussion of the different aspects of emotional well-being – the mental health component, the cognitive component, the psychological component and the affective component. It then went on to consider some of the ways in which emotional well-being can be defined and measured.

Critical analysis of the existing evidence relating to the impact of parental employment patterns on young people's emotional well-being concluded that in general parental employment improves the emotional well-being of children and young people, and that this operates through a mechanism of improved income and socio-economic circumstances (financial capital). Part-time maternal employment appeared to offer greater protection against poor emotional well-being than either full-time maternal employment or non-employment. This suggests that although the impact on family financial capital may be significant, a balance or trade-off is involved between increased family income and decreased family time, with maternal provision of nurturing protection (social capital) potentially restricted by full-time employment. Other factors, such as socio-economic circumstances and family structure were found to have a greater influence on young people's emotional well-being than parental employment patterns. Other factors, such as the quality of family relationships and parents' own measures of emotional well-being were rarely included in studies.

Some of these relationships were then explored using data from the youth panel of the BHPS. Living in a currently workless household was associated with greater unhappiness, lower self-esteem and lower self-efficacy amongst young people, and statistical significant but substantively very small associations were observed between the four indicators of young people's emotional well-being and various measures of parental employment, when analysed individually. Multiple regressions were then conducted and models of best fit obtained for each indicator of emotional well-being.

Parental employment does appear to matter for young people's emotional well-being, and there are distinct differences between the impact in lone and dual parent families. Young people were less likely to be troubled if they lived with a mother who was not in the labour market. Young people whose lone mother was in full-time employment were more likely to be unhappy and have low self-esteem than those whose mother was either employed part-time or not in employment. But for those in dual parent families it is the number of earners in the household that appears to affect their emotional well-being, with life in a workless household having a detrimental effect on young people's happiness and self-esteem.

Other factors have a greater impact on young people's emotional well-being than parental employment patterns. Living in a family with high levels of conflict is associated with poorer self-esteem and self-efficacy and with being more troubled and unhappy. Although this finding might be expected, it occurs even when family type and employment patterns are controlled for, suggesting that this is not the mechanism through which these factors influence emotional well-being. Mothers' own measures of emotional well-being (GHQ score) appears to be another important influence on young people's self-esteem and self-efficacy, and their feelings of unhappiness and trouble, again pointing to the contribution that mothers make to their children's emotional well-being.

In conclusion then, parental employment patterns, particularly whether a young person's mother is in paid employment, do appear to have an impact on emotional well-being. But other factors, such as the quality of family relationships, and mothers' own emotional well-being have more significant influence on this important aspect of young people's lives.

Chapter 5
Educational Well-being:
Behaviour and Attitudes

Introduction

Education was a key political priority of the incoming Labour government of 1997, and has remained so during their time in parliament. At the top of the agenda was the issue of school standards and performance, with the setting of national targets for improving student performance, reinforcement of the inspection framework for schools, and the introduction of a plethora of funding initiatives (such as Education Action Zones) aimed at raising performance (Department for Education and Employment (DfEE) 1997). How well children do in school is seen as crucial to their success in later life in terms of both employment opportunities and other factors, such as health and likelihood of criminal activity (Riley and Rustique-Forrester 2002; Department for Work and Pensions 2003), thus improving educational outcomes across the board, but particularly amongst those from lower socio-economic backgrounds is seen as an important strategy in breaking the cycle of disadvantage. Issues of school behaviour and exclusion are also part of the wider government agenda on social inclusion, and one of the first reports of the newly established Social Exclusion Unit (SEU) considered truancy and school exclusion (SEU 1998).

Understanding the factors that influence children's attendance at school, their attitudes, behaviour and achievement is crucial to improving both behaviour and standards. This chapter reviews the existing evidence surrounding bullying, truancy, and school exclusion, reflecting on the scale and nature of these issues, and considering the individual, family, school and societal characteristics which may have an influence.

Parental employment, and conversely unemployment, has both positive and negative effects on individual and family levels of economic, social and cultural capital, which is reflected in educational outcomes. It is suggested that parental employment patterns influence children's educational outcomes in a number of ways: through the impact on household income; through the provision of a role model to children; and through the impact on young people's expectations and aspirations.

Later in this chapter, data from the youth survey of the British Household Panel Survey (BHPS) is used to investigate links between young people's educational outcomes and parental employment patterns, together with personal, familial and other factors, using a forms of capital approach (Bourdieu 1983) to explain any associations. The next chapter (Chapter 6) considers educational achievement and progression, and a discussion of the relationship between all the educational outcomes considered – truancy, exclusion, worrying about bullying, attitude to education, staying on post-16 and the achievement of qualifications – is included in that chapter.

Bullying

Bullying in schools has been an important issue for governments and policy makers for nearly two decades. In the late 1980s, for example, a public enquiry was launched into unruly behaviour in schools. The resulting Elton Report (Department of Education and Science (DES) 1989) highlighted the issue of bullying, and suggested that a positive school ethos provides the essential factor in facilitating academic success and positive pupil relations. Research conducted in Sheffield during the early 1990s indicated that bullying is far more prevalent in some schools than others, and that some schools appear to be more effective than others at introducing and sustaining anti-bullying work (Smith and Sharp 1994). This research formed the basis for the government's first major attempt to provide schools with evidence-based research on effective anti-bullying strategies, through the production of an anti-bullying pack (Department for Education (DfE) 1994), which was subsequently evaluated (Smith and Madsen 1997), revised (Department for Education and Skills (DfES) 2002), and evaluated again (Smith and Samara 2003). The National Healthy School Standard (DfEEa 1999) also recommended the development of anti-bullying initiatives as part of a whole-school approach to raising educational standards, improving the health of children and young people, and reducing social exclusion, and schools are now required by law to have policies in place to counter bullying (School Standards and Framework Act 1998).

Definitions of bullying

The definition of bullying has been the subject of considerable academic debate. An appreciation of the diverse ways in which bullying is defined is important, because how bullying is understood necessarily influences the aims and context of anti-bullying initiatives. Olweus (1993) worked from a child-centred perspective to establish a definition of bullying as the repeated or long-term exposure of the victim to verbal or physical attack, or social ostracism, perpetrated by a single student or group of students. The power dynamics of bullying have also been highlighted, and Smith and Sharp (1994) assert that 'bullying can be described as the systematic abuse of power' (2). Different forms of bullying behaviour have been identified, such as indirect or direct, involving individuals or groups, and as verbal and physical (Rigby 1996; DfES 2002a; Oliver and Candappa 2003). It is generally agreed that verbal abuse is the most common form of bullying followed by various forms of physically aggressive behaviour, although within this broad pattern there are important differences, based on age, gender, sexuality and ethnicity (see Smith 1999; Oliver and Candappa 2003).

Incidence of bullying

Bullying certainly is a significant problem – for the ninth year running bullying has been the biggest single reason for children to call Childline, and now accounts for one in four calls to the helpline, with over 32,000 calls about bullying between April 2004 and March 2005 (Oliver and Candappa 2003; Childline 2005). But there are considerable difficulties involved in accurately estimating the prevalence of bullying in schools. For example, studies vary in their definitions of bullying, timescales for measuring the incidence of bullying are not always made clear (for example, over the last week, or year), and often samples are not sufficiently representative or cover different age ranges. Despite these problems many surveys have sought to assess the incidence of bullying, either by asking teachers or parents about their assessment of bullying, or asking pupils about their own experiences of bullying or being bullied, or by asking less direct questions about pupils' fear of bullying, or perceptions of bullying in their school.

Teachers have been found to generally estimate that around 5–10 per cent of children are consistently bullied, and 5 per cent are bullies (Smith and Sharp 1994), whilst parent surveys suggest that around 35 per cent of children have been bullied, and 8 per cent have ever been accused of bullying (Adelman et al 2003). Estimates from pupil reports are higher, suggesting that around half of children have experienced bullying at some time (Smith and Shu 2000) with rates being lower amongst secondary school pupils (Oliver and Candappa 2003). Using a more precise definition of regular bullying, Todd et al (2004) found that one in ten (10 per cent) of 11-year-old pupils reported being bullied, compared with approximately one in twenty (5.6 per cent) of the 15-year-olds. Again with the caveat of differing definition and frequency, it is generally found that there are more children who report being bullied than there are self-reported bullies. Between 3 per cent and 5 per cent of pupils admit to having bullied others at least two or three times a month (Smith and Shu 2000; Todd et al 2004), although with no specification of frequency another study reported rates of 17 per cent amongst primary school pupils, and 10 per cent amongst secondary school pupils (Oliver and Candappa 2003). In addition to the identified age differences, admission of bullying tends to be higher amongst boys (35 per cent) than girls (26 per cent) (Katz et al 2001). In response to less direct questions, around a quarter of pupils thought that bullying was a 'big problem' in their school (Oliver and Candappa 2003; Park et al 2004). Other surveys suggest that between a quarter and a third of all young people, with higher rates for girls than boys, worry about bullying or sometimes feel afraid of going to school because of bullying (Balding 1996; National Society for the Protection of Cruelty to Children (NSPCC) 2004; Schools Health Education Unit 2004; Magadi and Middleton 2005).

Consequences of bullying

Numerous studies of the short- and long-term consequences have been carried out, in many parts of the world. Although they have mainly focussed on the effects on bullying's victims, they have also given some attention to the possible social consequences for those who bully others (see Rigby 2003a for a review). Bullying not only has wide contemporaneous effects for the victims and perpetrators, in terms of their health and emotional well-being, and their behaviour and success at school, but also has longer-term consequences for their lives.

In terms of general health, both bullies and victims are less likely to report good or excellent health, and more likely to report subjective health complaints, than their peers (Holliday 2000; Alexander et al 2004a; Ravens-Sieberer et al 2004). Bullying has also been found to have pronounced and often long-lasting effects on children's emotional well-being. Children who habitually bully are significantly more likely than others to experience high levels of depression (Farrington 1993; Salmon et al 1998; Rigby 2003a), report more psychological complaints, and report that they are unhappy (Alexander et al 2004a). Other research has found that bullies are equally or less anxious than their peers (Olweus 1994; Salmon et al 1998). The psychological well-being of victims of bullying tends to be similar, or worse than that of bullies. Victimised children tend to have high levels of psychological distress, be more depressed, anxious and insecure, have lower self-esteem and self-efficacy, and feel lonely and more depressed than children who are not victimised (Boulton and Underwood 1992; Olweus 1994; Craig 1998; Salmon et al 1998; Hawker and Boulton 2000; Ma et al 2001; Rigby 2003a; Morgan et al 2006). Likewise, those individuals who worried about bullying tended to indicate lower levels of self-esteem, and satisfaction with life (Balding 1996; Balding et al 1998). Children who are both bullies and victims are seen as especially prone to mental illness (Rigby 2003b). Some of the effects of bullying on victims' emotional well-being have been seen to be long lasting, with reports of depression, loneliness, lack of trust, and low self-esteem persisting into adulthood (Boulton and Underwood 1992; Elliott and Kilpatrick 1994; Ma et al 2001). In a survey of adults who were bullied as children, men tended to feel angry and frustrated by the bullying, whilst women were more likely to feel depressed, scared and vulnerable, and express difficulties in making friends (Kidscape 1999).

Extreme responses to bullying include self-harm, running away, considering or committing suicide, and killing bullies (Boulton and Underwood 1992; Ma et al 2001; Elliott 2002; Hawton et al 2002). A survey of over 800 victims of bullying found that nearly half (46 per cent) had contemplated suicide, and 20 per cent had attempted suicide because of the bullying, some more than once (Kidscape 1999). Bullies were more likely to report risk behaviours in adolescence than their peers, including smoking, drunkenness, and cannabis use (Alexander et al 2004a). Being involved in bullying has also been associated with a range of problem behaviours in adulthood, such as criminality, alcohol misuse and violence (Olweus 1993; Bowers et al 1994; Olweus 1994; Rutter 1995; Utting 1997; Farrington 1998;

Ferero et al 1999; Elliott 2002). Both bullies and victims have been observed as having problems with personal relationships in adulthood, and men who had been identified as bullies at school are more likely than others to have children who behave aggressively (Gilmartin 1987; Farrington 1993).

Although there is some inconsistency, being a victim of bullying has been found to have a negative impact on other educational outcomes, including attendance, attainment, progression and attitudes to school, both directly and indirectly through the impact on emotional well-being. In some studies, bullying was found to be associated with increased absenteeism and truancy (Sharp 1995; Ma et al 2001; Boulton and Underwood 1992; Smith et al 2004), although others found no significant link (Wolke et al 2001; Glew et al 2005). In a more general sense, bullying was recognised by parents, teachers and pupils as a major cause of truancy and disaffection (Children's Society 2002; Malcolm et al 2003; DFES 2005a), and was considered by parents/carers to be an acceptable reason for keeping a child off school (Dalziel and Henthorne 2005). Interestingly, in one study significantly fewer bullies reported skipping school compared with their peers (Alexander et al 2004b). Having negative feelings about school, teachers, and other pupils has been associated with being a victim of bullying (Katz et al 2001; Smith et al 2004; Glew et al 2005), and bullies were also less likely to have a positive view of their school atmosphere, teachers and other pupils than their peers (Alexander et al 2004b).

The majority of research that explores the link between bullying and academic achievement has found a damaging effect of victimisation on pupils' attainment. It is generally accepted that being bullied leads to difficulties in concentrating on schoolwork, and a decline in academic performance and achievement (Sharp 1995; Children's Society 2002; Boulton and Underwood 1992; Ma et al 2001; DfES 2005a; Glew et al 2005; Beran et al 2005). Glew et al (2005) also found that academic achievement was lower for bullies than for those who were neither bullies nor victims. The only research findings which go against those reported above, that bullying has a detrimental impact on pupil's academic attainment, come from research by Woods and Wolke (2004), who found levels of achievement to be similar between victims and non-victims. They also suggested that children who are bullied might try to cope with negative feelings by actually increasing their academic effort (focussing more on schoolwork) as a method of escaping the victimisation.

Longer-term negative impacts of bullying on victims' employment prospects have also been identified. A survey of over 1000 adults (Kidscape 1999) found that those who had been bullied often cited this as a reason for leaving school at age 16, and that it had affected their plans for further education. An association between being a victim of bullying and unemployment or low wages in adulthood has been highlighted in a number of studies, although the explanations for this vary, including the negative effect on education achievement, on attitude to education, and on self-esteem, all of which are related to unemployment, or low wages (Farrington 1993; Elliot and Kilpatrick 1994; Varhama and Björkqvist 2005; Waddell 2006).

Influences on bullying

Having considered some of the potential consequences of bullying behaviour, for both victim and bully, we turn to look at the individual, parental, and family factors which may have an influence on whether young people are bullies or victims of bullying. Is there any evidence from the literature to support an association between parental employment patterns and bullying or victimisation amongst children and young people? Do family socio-economic circumstances, family structure and quality of family relationships matter? Using a forms of capital approach (Bourdieu 1983) to the resources available within families, the influence of a number of factors is discussed.

Parental employment and socio-economic factors   Parental employment patterns affect the financial (or economic), social and cultural capital available within families, and thus might influence young people's educational behaviours. A young person living in a workless household may be more susceptible to bullying as a result of their poor socio-economic circumstances or lack of consumer goods, such as expensive trainers or electronic gadgets. However, no evidence was found which related parental employment patterns to children's bullying or victimisation, although the relevance of socio-economic circumstances has often been considered. Higher rates of victimisation were found amongst children and young people from lower socio-economic backgrounds, those entitled to free school meals, those living in bad housing, and those who were categorised as severely poor (Glover et al 1998; Adelman et al 2003; Shelter 2004; Glew et al 2005). More generally, bullying was found to be more prevalent in socially and culturally disadvantages areas (Stephenson and Smith 1989; Cutright 1995). In terms of worrying about bullying, the pattern is less clear, with different studies finding that those in the lower socio-economic classes worry more about bullying (NSPCC 2004), those in persistent and severe poverty worry less about being bullied (Magadi and Middleton 2005), and that there are no significant differences in relation to bullying and demographic and socio-economic variables (Glew et al 2005; Morgan et al 2006). These conflicting findings suggest that the impact of socio-economic circumstances on bullying and fear of bullying may depend on other factors, such as the choice of measures, and the size and age structure of the sample in question. To the extent that low income, poor housing or poverty are negatively associated with being bullied or worrying about bullying, it could be expected that living in a workless household could have the same detrimental effect, and this is worth investigating.

Family factors   The impact of family structure, and to a greater extent, family relationships, on bullying and fear of bullying has been considered in a large number of studies. Children living in lone mother families were consistently more likely to both be accused of bullying, and be victims of bullying (Bowers et al 1992; Berdondini and Smith 1996; Middleton 2002). The quality of relationships both with and between parents appear to be important predictors of both bullying and victimisation. Young people who experienced lower levels of support at home, or who were less likely to turn to their parents for help were more likely to fear bullying (Balding 1996), whilst those who reported that their families lacked positive effective communication or cohesion, or that their parents were conflicting or controlling were more likely to be victims of bullying (Bowers et al 1992; Rigby 1994; Baldry and Farrington 2005; Morgan et al 2006). Similarly, bullies were significantly more likely to indicate lower levels of family cohesion and support, and higher levels of conflict, harshness and punitiveness (Bowers et al 1992; Bowers et al 1994; Rigby 1994; Berdondini and Smith 1996; Ahmed and Braithwaite 2004; Baldry and Farrington 2005). These family factors clearly have an important influence on both bullying and victimisation, and need to be considered in future work.

Children's own characteristics   Gender differences are apparent in both bullying and victimisation. Several studies have indicated that boys are more likely than girls to bully others (Olweus 1994; Smith and Sharp 1994; Salmon et al 1998; Baldry 2004; Todd et al 2004), and that boys are more likely to bully girls than vice versa (Olweus 1993). It is generally agreed that boys are more likely to be physically aggressive than girls, and that girls are more likely to engage in verbal abuse, social ostracism, and gossip (Baldry 2004; Smith 1999; Besag 1989). Boys and girls tend to report a similar proportion of victimisation (Oliver and Candappa 2003; Todd et al 2004), though some studies indicate that boys are more often victimised by their peers than girls (Whitney and Smith 1993), or vice versa (Baldry and Farrington 1998). In terms of worrying about bullying, boys were consistently less likely than girls to sometimes, often, or very often fear going to school because of bullying (Balding 1996; SHEU 2004), although among Year 5 students, boys were slightly more likely to think that bullying was 'a big problem' in their school. There were no apparent gender differences amongst Year 8 pupils (Oliver and Cadappa 2003). Although bullying occurs at all age levels, its prevalence tends to decrease with age, as does the proportion of young people who are afraid of going to school because of bullying (SHEU 2004; Todd et al 2004). Age and gender are thus important influences on both bullying and victimisation.

Summary

This section has reviewed the prevalence, consequences and correlates of bullying, victimisation, and the fear of bullying. Although no evidence has been located specifically regarding the impact of parental employment patterns on bullying, that lower socio-economic circumstances are associated with higher rates of bullying and victimisation might suggest a link between bullying and living in a workless household. Other factors that emerged as important include age, gender, family type and relationships. Later in this chapter, data from the youth panel of the BHPS is used to examine any potential relationship between worrying about bullying and parental employment patterns, together with a number of other factors.

Truancy

Promoting regular school attendance is a key component in the government's strategy to raise educational standards. It is also an important factor in reducing wider problems associated with social exclusion, as demonstrated by the fact that it was one of the first areas addressed by the Social Exclusion Unit established by the Prime Minister (SEU 1998). In a sense, truancy is a voluntary form of exclusion on the part of the young person, with frequent truanting the clearest expression of disaffection with the education provided.

Each time a pupil does not attend school, their parent or carer is required to provide an explanation to the school, which then decides whether the reason for absence is acceptable (authorised) or not acceptable (unauthorised). Around 90 per cent of absence is authorised, for example where pupils are unwell or where the school agrees to an absence on a family holiday during term-time. Unauthorised absence is often known as truancy, and is the form of absence with which government, education workers and schools have been most concerned (National Audit Office (NAO) 2005). Schools differ in the degree to which they accept reasons for absence as legitimate, and have been criticised by Local Education Authorities (LEAs) for 'being over ready to accept the reasons given for absence, and authorising too many absences because they were under pressure to reduce unauthorised absence' (Malcolm et al 2003, 6), thus perhaps understating the problem of truancy. But truancy means different things to different people, and while many might associate truancy with pupils taking time off school without their parents'/carers' knowledge, this is not always the case. The Audit Commission (1999) estimated that at least 40,000 of the 400,000 pupils absent from school each day were 'truanting or being kept off school by their parents/carers without permission', while an Office for Standards in Education (OFSTED) report (2001) suggested that 'truancy is not synonymous with unauthorised absence' (2). In other words, unauthorised absence may sometimes be condoned by parents, such as holidays taken during term time which have not been authorised by the school.

Incidence of truancy

The Department for Education and Skills (DfES) has been publishing annual attendance statistics to monitor progress since 1992–93, and set a Public Service Agreement (PSA) target for school absence to reduce the 2003 level of school absence by 8 per cent (from 6.83 per cent to 6.28 per cent) by 2008. In 2004/05 secondary schools reported that 1.23 per cent of school time was lost to unauthorised absence, with a further 6.58 per cent of school time lost to authorised absence. Over 750,000 secondary school pupils – around a quarter of all pupils – took at least one half day off without authority, with the average time missed per absent pupil being 7 days (DfES 2005b). Figure 5.1 shows that although the percentage of school time lost to authorised absence has been gradually falling over the last

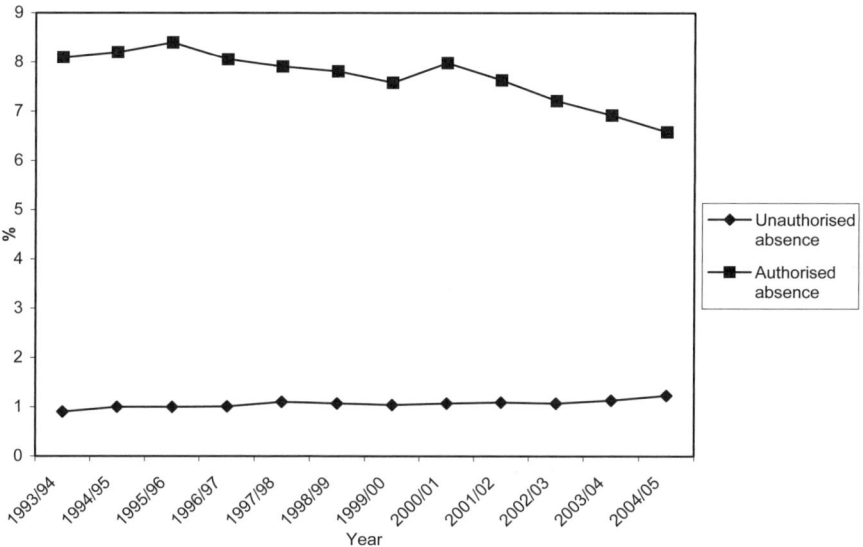

Figure 5.1   Percentage of half days missed by secondary school pupils, 1993/4–2004/5

Source: (1993/94–1997/98) DFEE, 1998b; (1996/97–2004/05) DFES, 2005, Trends in Education and Skills Online, http://www.dfes.gov.uk/trends/index.cfm.

few years, the percentage of half days lost to unauthorised absence has remained stubbornly constant at around 1 per cent.

These figures do not take account of absences taking place after pupils have registered, and anonymised surveys of pupils suggest the true incidence of truancy may be much higher than that reported in the official statistics (e.g. Graham and Bowling 1995; Casey and Smith 1995). Information from the Youth Cohort study (YCS – a cohort based survey begun in 1989) suggests that in 2004 around a third (29 per cent) of Year 11 pupils reported occasional truanting, with 4 per cent being persistent truants (DfES 2005d). Figure 5.2 shows the trend in self-reported truancy in the YCS since 1989.

It can be seen that although the proportion of young people reporting occasional truancy has fallen over time, with a corresponding rise in the proportion reporting that they had not truanted at all, persistent truancy has remained virtually constant, reported by around 5 per cent of individuals.

Consequences of truancy

The consequences of truancy for individuals are broad and long-lasting, with the long-term economic consequences for society equally large. Links have been made

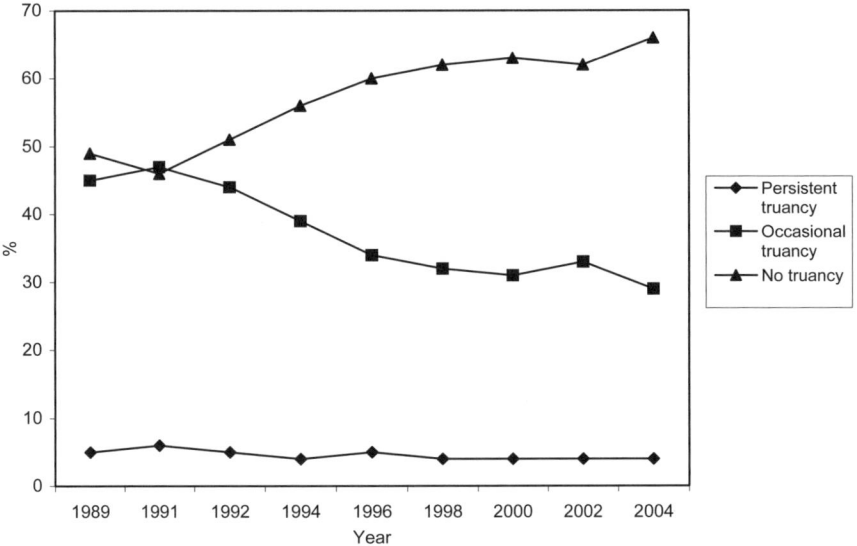

Figure 5.2   Self-reported Year 11 truancy, 1989–2004 (percentages)
Source: Youth Cohort Study (DFES, 2005d).

between truancy and educational underachievement and drop-out, unemployment, homelessness, problems with relationships, and crime.

The associations between truancy and educational attainment are well documented (see Bosworth 1994; Sparkes 1999). Persistent, and to a lesser extent occasional truants tend to obtain significantly lower examination scores. Data from the YCS indicated that in 2004, only 10 per cent of those who reported persistent truancy in year 11 attained 5 or more GCSEs Grade A*–C, compared with 41 per cent of those who reported occasional truancy and 62 per cent of those who reported that they had not truanted at all in year 11. The proportions obtaining no GCSEs were 29 per cent of persistent truants, 4 per cent of occasional truants and 2 per cent of those who reported no truancy (DfES 2005d).

Related to educational attainment, persistent and occasional truants are also less likely to stay on in full-time education at age 16, and more likely to be not in education, employment or training (NEET). Figure 5.3 shows that in 2004, just a quarter (25 per cent) of persistent Year 11 truants stayed on in full-time education at 16, compared with three-fifths (61 per cent) of occasional truants and four-fifths (79 per cent) of those who reported no truancy. Persistent and occasional truants were far more likely to be NEET than non-truants (DfES 2005d).

Looking at the relationship between truancy and NEET from the opposite angle, Rennison et al 2005, found that NEET young people self-reported much higher rates of persistent truancy during Years 10 and 11 (15.4 per cent) than young people in general (3.3 per cent) and, in particular, than young people

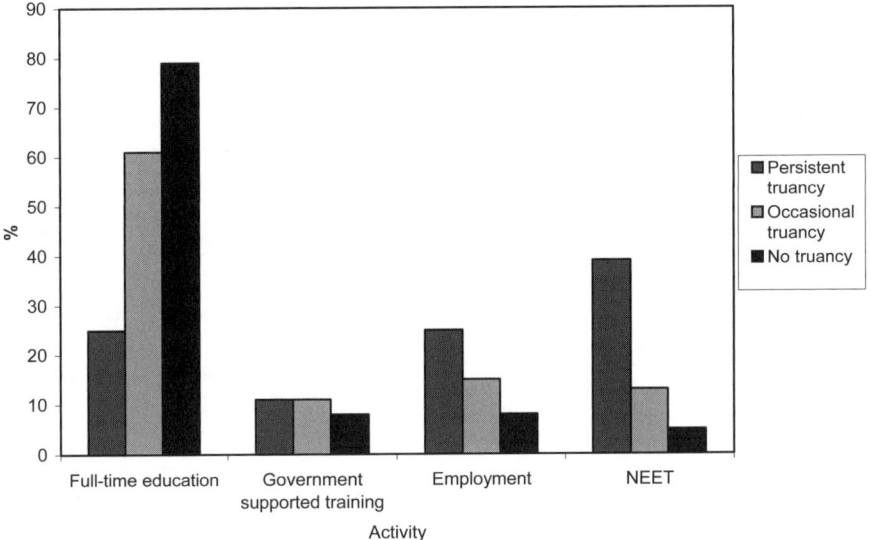

Figure 5.3   Main activity at age 16 by Year 11 truancy, 2004
Source: Youth Cohort Study (DFES, 2005d).

who continued their education after Year 11 (1.2 per cent). Conversely, less than one-third (31.6 per cent) of young people in the NEET group had never truanted compared to 64.1 per cent of young people overall.

According to Hibbert et al (1990) at the age of 23, truants have lower status occupations, less stable career patterns and are up to twice as likely to be unemployed as non-truants. When in work, former truants' income is no lower, but if the number of children in the household is taken into account they are considerably less well-off. These differences remained statistically significant after controlling for the effects of social background, educational ability, poor attendance due to other reasons (e.g. sickness) and qualifications on leaving school.

Early research (Gray et al 1980) suggested that the difficulties encountered by truants, particularly in the labour market were a result of their depressed examination performance and lack of qualifications at the end of their schooling; and that thereafter their problems were no greater than others with similarly poor qualifications. However, other research has demonstrated that truancy is a predictor of employment problems over and above those experienced by others who share the disadvantaged background and low attainment which typify the truant (Hibbert et al 1990).

A relationship between truancy and both juvenile and adult crime is well established (see Utting 1997; Collins 1998; Reid 1999). The Audit Commission (1996) found that around a quarter of individuals appearing in the youth court had truanted significantly, and a Metropolitan Police study discovered that 5 per cent of offences were committed by children in school hours (cited in DFES/Home Office 2002). Other, more general surveys of young people have also showed that those who play truant are more likely to offend than those who do not (Graham and Bowling 1995), with the most recent MORI survey suggesting that whilst a quarter (26 per cent) of all young people (aged 11 to 16) in mainstream education reported having truanted for at least one day, this ranged from 18 per cent for those who had not committed an offence to 45 per cent for those who had (Youth Justice Board (YJB) 2004). However, while there is a clear link between truancy and delinquency, attributing cause and effect remains an area of debate (Graham and Bowling 1995). Truancy and offending often begin at a similar time: in the Youth Lifestyle Survey, the average age of first playing truant and of starting to offend for boys was 13.6 years. Truancy and offending also began at similar ages for girls; on average, girls started to truant at 13.9 years and to offend at 14.1 years (Flood-Page et al 2000).

In addition to the links with educational underachievement and crime, truancy has also been associated with an increased likelihood of having tried solvents, illicit and hard drugs (Swadi 1989), becoming a teenage parent (SEU 1998), and with unemployment (Casey and Smith 1995), depression, heavy smoking, and martial breakdown in early adulthood (Hibbert et al 1990).

This section has considered some of the consequences of truancy, with links being made between truancy and educational underachievement and drop-out, unemployment, homelessness, problems with relationships, and crime.

Influences on truancy

Many studies have explored the characteristics of truants, and undertaken to assess the factors associated with a greater likelihood of truanting, including individual, parental and family characteristics, together with factors relating to school.

Parental employment and socio-economic factors   Of key concern to the current research is the potential impact that parental employment patterns may have on young people's truanting behaviour. Parental employment patterns influence individual and family levels of economic, social and cultural capital. Living in a workless household may increase a young person's likelihood of truanting, because of the absence of an employed role model and the lowering of expectations and aspirations. Conversely, living in a dual parent household where both parents are engaged in full-time employment could sometimes lead to truancy, as there is less parental monitoring of school attendance.

Although few studies have considered the impact of parental employment on truancy directly, several have used various measures of family socio-economic circumstances. Where analyses have included parental employment it has generally been found that rates of truancy are higher amongst young people living in households where neither parent was in employment (Casey and Smith 1995), and in schools servicing communities with high levels of unemployment (OFSTED

2001). Considering maternal and paternal employment patterns separately, one study found that a mother's labour force participation does not appear to affect truancy in either direction, but that truancy rates increase where the father is not working (Dustmann et al 1997).

In terms of the relationship between socio-economic circumstances and truancy, several different measures have been used, although a fairly consistent pattern has been established. Although household income itself generally had no significant impact on levels of truancy (Dustmann et al 1997; Dearden et al 2000), individuals living in local authority housing were more likely to report playing truant than those living in other forms of accommodation (Bosworth 1994; Casey and Smith 1995). Likewise, there was a marked relationship between parents' social class and truancy, with the highest rates amongst children of low-skilled workers, and the lowest among children of people employed in professional or managerial jobs (Casey and Smith 1995).

In more general terms schools serving more affluent communities generally had better attendance (OFSTED 2001), and high levels of unemployment or economic deprivation within communities can be seen to devalue education, leading to 'a sense of resignation about future prospects' (Kinder et al 1995, 11). The sense in which negative attitudes towards the value of education pass down and across the generations was something also identified by Malcolm et al (2003).

Family factors   With regards to the association between family structure and truancy rates, a recent survey suggested that truancy rates were higher amongst young people in lone parent households (YJB 2004), and Youth Cohort Study data also supports this relationship (Bosworth 1994; Casey and Smith 1995). Further work suggests that living in a lone parent family was a risk factor for boys, but not for girls (SEU 1998).

An interesting connection has been found between truancy and the number of siblings in a household. Boys were more likely to truant when there were older siblings in the household, but the presence of younger siblings had no effect. For girls the presence of older siblings had no effect whereas there was a weak but significant effect where young siblings were present (Dustmann et al 1997).

Other parental and family factors, such as levels of parental academic qualifications, attitudes to education and the levels of support and communication within a household could also have an important impact of levels of truancy. Several studies have noted that although a fairly weak relationship, the parents of truants were more likely to have lower levels of qualifications themselves (Bosworth 1994; Casey and Smith 1995; Dustmann et al 1997). Research among South African young people found that learners whose parents expected them to do well at school, or who were highly involved with the school or more interested in their schoolwork, were less likely to skip school (Moseki 2004). Where parents attributed little value to education, or where there were significant domestic problems within the home, truancy levels tended to be higher, as education may not be seen as a priority (Kinder et al 1995). In the sense that parental employment can contribute to parents' expectations, and the levels of support, communication, and conflict with families, living in a household without an adult in employment, or with parents who have low levels of education themselves may result in young people having low aspirations for their own future, leading to poor attendance.

Children's own characteristics There have generally been no significant differences found between truancy rates amongst girls and boys (O'Keefe 1993; Bosworth 1994; SEU 1998), although some studies suggest that truancy is higher amongst boys (Moseki 2004). Truancy tends to increase with age (SEU 1998; YJB 2004).

The influence of several other factors on levels of truancy has also been investigated. Analysis of YCS data from 1990 suggested that young black people reported higher rates of truancy than those belonging to other ethnic groups (Casey and Smith 1995), and small regional differences have also been seen (Casey and Smith 1995; YJB 2004).

There is some evidence that high levels of truancy are associated with poor emotional well-being or having a psychological disorder (Kinder et al 1995; Meltzer et al 2000), with pressure from peers to truant also cited a major cause of truancy (Malcolm et al 2003; Kinder et al 1995).

Although lack of educational achievement was found to be a significant consequence of truancy, a lack of academic ability has also been cited as a potential cause (OFSTED 1995; OFSTED 2001; SEU 1998) with young people playing truant in order to avoid the anxiety associated with difficult schoolwork or a fear of being humiliated because of being a weak reader, for instance (Kinder et al 1996; Moseki 2004). Experience or fear of bullying as a reason for truanting has been highlighted by several sources. Balding (1996) reported that a third of girls and a quarter of boys described being afraid to go to school at some time because of bullying, and in one study, parents often attributed their children's truancy to a fear of being bullied (Berridge et al 2001).

Summary

This section has considered the incidence and consequences of truancy. The evidence relating to the factors associated with truancy, at an individual, parental, and family have also been discussed. Evidence concerning the impact of parental employment patterns on truancy rates amongst young people is patchy, and there is scope for a rigorous analysis of this area.

School exclusion

Although children have always been expelled or suspended from school, it is only since exclusion entered the statute book in the mid-1980s that the attention of researchers, professionals and policy-makers has focused on the issue as an important indicator of educational and social problems. The term 'exclusion' was first introduced in the Education (No 2) Act 1986, and replaced the older expressions of 'suspension' and 'expulsion' (Wright et al 2000). In the same way that truancy can be viewed as a voluntary form of withdrawal from education on the part of a pupil, so exclusion is the ultimate sanction a school can employ against a pupil who is persistently disobedient, disruptive or violent (Pearce and Hillman 1998).

Exclusion from school can have long-term effects and is strongly associated not only with poor academic progress, but also with other wider aspects of social exclusion in the UK such as becoming a teenage parent, being unemployed or homeless later in life, or ending up in prison (Graham and Bowling 1995; Casey and Smith 1995). Children excluded from school are not the only ones to be affected; the wider community can also suffer because of high levels of crime into which many non-attenders are drawn (Young 1999). Exclusion is expensive in terms of the administrative costs and the extra resources needed to support children in special units or alternative educational provision (Parsons 1996; Parsons 1999; Audit Commission 1999) and in terms of the potential long-term social, emotional and occupational consequences.

Exclusion from school may be permanent or fixed-term (up to a maximum of 45 days in any one school year). Since September 2002, all LEAs have been compelled to provide suitable full-time education for all permanently excluded pupils and to make every effort to do so for pupils excluded for a fixed period over 15 school days. Pupils who are excluded from school are not excluded from education and should therefore be provided with continuing education until a permanent school or other placement is found (DFES 2004a). In addition to the formal categories of fixed-term and permanent exclusion, frequent reference has also been made to the issue of 'informal' or 'unofficial' exclusion (Stirling 1992a; SEU 1998; Berridge et al 2001). This refers to cases where schools discourage students from returning to a school, or encourage parents to remove their children. Official guidance emphasises that this is unacceptable practice, although there is evidence that unofficial exclusions continue to take place (DFES 2004a).

Incidence of school exclusion

In 2003/04 there were a total of 9,880 permanent exclusions from primary, secondary and special schools, which represents just 0.13 per cent of the school population (13 pupils in every 10,000). This represented a slight increase on the previous year, but overall the number of permanent exclusions has decreased by almost 20 per cent since 1997/98. In addition 201,780 primary, secondary and special school pupils (2.6 per cent of the school population) served a total of 344,510 fixed period exclusions in 2003/04, with the majority of pupils (65 per cent) excluded only once. The average length of a fixed period exclusion was 3.8 days, and the majority of all fixed period exclusions (86 per cent) lasted one week or less. Around 84 per cent of both permanent and fixed period exclusions applied to secondary school pupils (DFES 2005e).

Consequences of school exclusion

Most research has concentrated on permanent exclusions, due partly to the lack of collated data on fixed-term (and unofficial) exclusions. But what are the consequences of being excluded from school, and what risk factors are associated with higher rates of school exclusions?

As is the case with truancy, exclusion from school has serious consequences, both for the individuals concerned, their families, and society as a whole. Looking first at the impact on educational attainment and progression, it is clear that permanent exclusion from school is often associated with long periods without education, educational under-attainment and reduced employment opportunities (Commission for Racial Equality (CRE) 1996; SEU 1998; Audit Commission 1999; Daniels et al 2003). Analysis of YCS data (DFES 2005d) shows that only 20 per cent of pupils who had been excluded in Years 10 or 11 achieved 5 or more GCSE passes at grade C or above, compared with 58 per cent of those who had not been excluded. The true figure for excluded pupils may actually be even lower, as those excluded from school before Year 10 may be missing from this sample. In another survey only around a quarter of those permanently excluded were known to have passed at least one GCSE two years later (Daniels et al 2003). Young people excluded from school are also more likely to be not in education, employment or training (NEET) in young adulthood, and if in employment there is a tendency for it to be low paid and insecure (DFES 2005d; Daniels et al 2003).

Again similarly to truancy, there is evidence of a link between school exclusion and offending (Graham and Bowling 1995; Audit Commission 1996; SEU 1998; Parsons 1999; Berridge et al 2001). The Youth Justice Board's annual Youth Crime Survey, carried out by MORI, shows that excluded young people are more than twice as likely as those in mainstream education to commit offences. In the 2004 survey, for example, 26 per cent of young people in mainstream school reported having committed an offence in the previous 12 months, while 60 per cent of excluded young people reported having committed an offence over the same period (YJB 2004).

Other observed associations with exclusion from school include substance misuse, and later homelessness. Randall and Brown (1999) found that children who had been excluded from school were 90 times more likely to end up living on the streets than those who stayed on and passed exams, whilst other research evidence suggests that over three quarters (78 per cent) of a sample of children permanently excluded from school had used illegal drugs at some point in their lives, with over one third (38 per cent) having used drugs other than cannabis (Powis et al 1998; see also McAra 2004).

Influences on school exclusion

Having considered some of the potential consequences of being excluded from school, we turn now to look at some of the characteristics of those excluded. How do these individuals differ from their peers, if at all, and what parental, family and school factors are important in predicting whether a young person is at risk of being excluded from school?

Parental employment and socio-economic factors As with other aspects of educational behaviour considered in this chapter, little evidence exists regarding the possible association between parental employment and the propensity of young people to be excluded from school. In one study, a quarter of resident fathers of a sample of young people who had been excluded were unemployed (Daniels et al 2003). Other sources have found that exclusion rates tend to be higher in areas of social deprivation, generally measured by the proportion of the school population entitled to free school meals. In general, schools with high permanent exclusion rates tend to have high proportions of pupils known to be eligible for free school meals, although it is important to note that this is not true for all schools (DfES 2004a). These findings would suggest that it is poor socio-economic circumstances (economic capital) within families which leads to a greater likelihood of being excluded from school. Thus parental employment patterns might influence the likelihood of being excluded through the impact that it has on the economic circumstances of the household.

Family factors Family factors have also been found to be important, with a high proportion of excluded children experiencing disturbed or disrupted home contexts including family break up, bereavement, illness, alcoholism, abuse, and stress (Brodie and Berridge 1996; OFSTED 1996; Parsons 1999). Although based on a very small study within one school, Ashford (1994) found that children of lone parent families and those from reconstituted families were far more likely to be excluded from school than those living with both biological parents. Young people in care were on average 10 per cent more likely to be excluded than their peers (SEU 1998). Exclusion has particularly significant implications for this group of young people, as this frequently triggers a break down in their care placement (Pearce and Hillman 1998).

Children's own characteristics Of the permanent exclusions in 2002/03, around three-quarters involved pupils aged 13–15, and boys were four times more likely to be excluded than girls (OFSTED 2001; DfES 2004a). Although girls made up only around 16 per cent of permanent exclusions, it is important that they are not neglected, and that gender-appropriate services are developed (Smith 1998; Osler et al 2001). Black children, particularly Afro-Caribbean boys are greatly over-represented in the exclusion figures (see Hayden and Dunne 2001; DfES 2004a). Although the reasons for this are little understood, research has highlighted tension and conflict in relations between white teachers and Afro- Caribbean pupils as a plausible explanation (Gillborn and Gipps 1996).

There is some evidence that poor literacy is, in some cases, a causal factor of exclusion from school. An early survey by the Children's Society showed that the majority of those excluded started secondary school with a reading age behind that of their peers, and limited aspirations and opportunities have also been cited (OFSTED 2001). Children with Special Educational Needs (SEN) are also known to be more vulnerable to exclusion, with 0.45 per cent of pupils with SEN pupils excluded, compared with 0.05 per cent of those with no SEN (DfES 2004a). This has been attributed at least in part to the funding systems for special educational needs. Stirling (1992b) suggests that from the school's perspective, the process of exclusion is a speedier and more predictable process than the implementation of the lengthier assessment procedures leading ultimately to a 'statement' of SEN (which results in additional resources to help meet the pupil's needs) under the 1981 Education Act. In addition he suggests that schools may be using the process of exclusion to speed up the allocation of additional SEN funding as in many cases the act of exclusion triggers the statementing process.

Summary

This section has considered the incidence, causes and consequences of permanent exclusion from school. The significant consequences of school exclusion include educational underachievement, unemployment, homelessness, substance misuse and offending. Little evidence exists specifically concerning the impact of parental employment patterns on young people's risk of being excluded from school, although social deprivation, family disruption, and individual characteristics including age, gender and ethnicity are important.

As discussed earlier, living in a household where no adult is in employment can have serious consequences for young people. In terms of educational outcomes, parental unemployment affects the resources that parents have available to invest in their children's upbringing and education. Parental attitudes to education, together with their aspirations for both their own lives and their children's can be negatively affected by unemployment or low-paid work. In turn, low parental expectations can impact upon children's own expectations, which may affect their attitude and commitment to education, and their behaviour within school. Having a positive attitude to education is vital to achieving a good level of education and qualifications, which are important for future prospects.

On the other hand, education is about more than just the achievement of academic qualifications. Attitudes to education are important both for their experience of learning, for future achievement, and for other areas of life. Negative educational behaviours, such as bullying, truanting and exclusion have significant consequences both contemporaneously and in the future.

Young people's educational well-being and the BHPS

We have seen then that the impact of parental employment on young people's educational behaviour and experience is complex, with a lack of consistent existing evidence. More work has been done on the other factors which influence bullying, truancy and exclusion from school, including socio-economic factors, family structure and relationships, and individual factors, such as age and gender. The main gaps identified in the literature relate to the potential influence of parental employment patterns on young people's educational behaviours, and the mechanisms through which these influences might operate. The research presented here seeks to address these gaps in the literature, by using data from the youth survey of the BHPS to explore the impact of parental employment on young people's experiences of and attitudes to education, using several indicators of educational well-being: worrying about being bullied; truanting in the last year; having been suspended or expelled in the last year; and having a negative educational attitude.

The key research questions to be considered here are: whether any differences in children's educational behaviours and attitudes are observed by parental employment status, and if so, whether these can be accounted for through the inclusion of socio-economic factors? What other factors are important in explaining any apparent differences in educational behaviour and attitudes?

Table 5.1 illustrates the 4 indicators of educational well-being used in the analysis presented in this chapter. From Wave Five onwards, young people in the survey were asked how much they worried about being bullied at school, with the possible responses being 'a lot', 'a bit' and 'not at all'. Around a third (36 per cent) of young people reported that they worried about bullying either 'a bit' or 'a lot', and this is comparable to that found by the Schools Health Education Unit (2004), using data from the Health Related Behaviour Questionnaire. Although the focus here is on fear of bullying, as opposed to the actual experience of bullying, this is still useful in terms of the impact that being worried about bullying can have on children and young people's experience of education and learning.

The second indicator of educational well-being used in the analysis was truancy, or unauthorised absence from school. From Wave Seven onwards, young people were asked if they had skipped school without an excuse within the last year. Over four-fifths (83.9 per cent) said that they had not truanted at all in the last year, with 16.1 per cent reporting that they had skipped school at least once without an excuse. This level of reported truancy is lower than the official rates discussed above (DFES 2005b; DFES 2005d), perhaps because it depended on self-report and there may be a tendency for young people to 'forget' about absences. There may also be some flexibility over what might constitute an 'excuse' for being off school – some young people may have considered a shopping trip or holiday as an excuse for skipping school, when this is likely to be recorded as an unauthorised absence by the school.

Young people in the sample were also asked if they had been expelled or suspended in the last year, which in current terminology would include permanent and temporary exclusions, although some measurement error could occur because of the differences. Around 5 per cent of respondents reported that they had been expelled or suspended in the last year, the majority of these being temporary

Table 5.1   Educational well-being indicators in the BHPS youth survey

Variables	Question		%	Indicator
YPBULL	How much do you worry about being bullied at school? (N=6098)	Not at all	64.0	Bullying (N=6098)
		A bit	29.2	Worry about being bullied at school, a bit or a lot.
		A lot	6.8	36.0%
YPTRUN	In the past year, have you skipped school without an excuse? (N=4707)	Never	83.9	Truant (N=4707)
		Once or twice	11.7	Truanted at least once in the last
		Several times	2.7	year.
		Often	1.7	16.1%
YPEXPL	In the past year, have you been suspended or expelled from school? (N=4710)	No	94.9	Expelled (N=4710)
		Yes	5.1	Suspended or expelled in last year. 5.1%
PTCHA	I like most of my teachers (N=4704)	Strongly agree	15.5	
		Agree	56.2	
		Disagree	19.0	
		Strongly disagree	9.2	
PTCHB	Teachers are always getting at me (N=4690)	Strongly disagree	30.4	
		Disagree	49.7	
		Agree	13.8	Attitude (N=4672)
		Strongly agree	6.1	Negative education attitude
POPSC	How much does it mean to you to do well at school? (N=6093)	A great deal	65.9	Overall score of 10+[a]
		Quite a lot	29.2	18.8%
		A bit but not v much	3.8	
		Very little	1.1	
SCHWK	How do you feel about your schoolwork? (N=6815)	Completely happy	16.2	
		Happy	62.6	
		Neither unhappy/happy	13.5	
		Unhappy	7.4	

[a] Where the 4 constituent questions are coded 1-4, with 4 being the most negative attitude.
Source: Author's own analysis of BHPS data.

exclusions (suspensions), and these figures are roughly in line with official exclusion statistics – official statistics on fixed-term exclusions were not recorded before 2002/03, when around 5 per cent of the secondary school population served one or more periods of fixed-term exclusion (DFES 2005b).

An indicator of negative educational attitude was constructed using young people's responses to a number of questions about how they feet about different aspects of school. The correlations between these variables are shown in Table 5.2.

Young people were asked 'How much does it mean to you to do well at school: a great deal, quite a lot, a bit but not very much, or very little?' which reflects the value young people place on school and their commitment to the outcomes of schooling. A measure of attitude to school was also included as one of a series of questions about how happy young people were about different aspects of their

Table 5.2 **Correlations between the four variables which constitute the 'negative education attitude' indicator**

	I like most of my teachers	Teachers get at me	How much it means to do well at school?
Teachers get at me	0.54***		
How much it means to do well at school?	0.34***	0.33***	
Happy with school work?	0.41***	0.41***	0.34***

Statistical significance: *=p<0.05, **=p<0.01, ***=p<0.001.
Source: Author's own analysis of BHPS data.

Table 5.3 **Correlations between the four indicators of educational well-being**

	Worry about bullying	Truanted	Suspended/ expelled
Truanted	-0.04**		
Suspended/expelled	-0.03*	0.23***	
Negative educational attitude	-0.05***	0.33***	0.21***

Source: Author's own analysis of BHPS data.

lives. Young people were also asked about their relationships with teachers. They were asked to respond to the statements 'I like most my teachers' and 'Teachers are always getting at me' on scales of 'strongly agree – agree – disagree – strongly disagree'. Reponses to these four questions were recoded on a scale of 1–4, with 4 being the most negative, then added together to create an overall composite variable with a range between 4 and 16. A score of 10 or more was considered to represent a negative attitude to education, held by 18.8 per cent of young people, and this indicator was used in further analysis.

The correlations between the four indicators of educational attitude and experience (bullying, truant, expelled, attitude) are shown in Table 5.3.

As would be expected, young people who held a negative attitude to education were more likely to have truanted and/or been excluded, and there was also a positive correlation between these two negative behaviours. Although quite small, there was a negative correlation between worrying about bullying and the other 3 indicators, so that those who worried about bullying were less likely to truant, be expelled, and have a negative educational attitude.

Fear of bullying

Earlier discusssion revealed that there was no evidence to relate parental employment patterns to young people's bullying or victimisation, although it was suggested that through the impact on financial capital available within a

Table 5.4   Logistic regressions for the odds of worrying about being bullied: Parental employment patterns

Variable		N	Odds ratios
Father current employment	Employed	4148	1.00
	Not in employment	707	1.10
Mother current employment	Full-time	2120	1.00
	Part-time	2066	1.04
	Not in employment	1820	0.96
Father employment (child 0–1)	Employed	3353	1.00
	Not in employment	294	1.00
Father employment (child 1–5)	Employed	3343	1.00
	Not in employment	310	0.93
Father employment (child 5–11)	Employed	3069	1.00
	Not in employment	362	1.13
Mother employment (child 0–1)	Employed full-time	482	1.00 (0.2%)
	Employed part-time	546	1.12
	Not in employment	3888	1.29*
Mother employment (child 1–5)	Employed full-time	742	1.00 (0.3%)
	Employed part-time	1043	1.24*
	Not in employment	3216	1.32**
Mother employment (child 5–11)	Employed full-time	1136	1.00
	Employed part-time	1619	1.10
	Not in employment	2506	1.02
Current earners	No earners	750	1.00
	One earner	1673	0.88
	Two earners	3151	0.98
Earners (child 0–1)	No earners	445	1.00
	One earner	2515	1.17
	Two earners	733	0.98
Current earners	No earners	750	1.00
	One earner	1673	0.88
	Two earners	3151	0.98
Earners (child 0–1)	No earners	445	1.00
	One earner	2515	1.17
	Two earners	733	0.98
Currently workless household	No	4824	1.00
	Yes	750	1.06
Workless household (child 0–1)	No	3248	1.00
	Yes	445	0.89
Workless household (child 1–5)	No	3256	1.00
	Yes	468	0.93
Workless household (child 5–11)	No	3598	1.00
	Yes	690	1.04
Ever workless	No	4506	1.00
	Yes	1539	1.00

Statistical significance: *=p<0.05, **=p<0.01, ***=p<0.001.
Note: Single observations only with substantive significance shown in brackets.
Source: Author's own analysis of BHPS data.

Table 5.5   Logistic regressions for the odds of worrying about being bullied: Other variables

Variable		N	Odds ratios
Equivalent income less than 50% of median after housing costs	No	4879	1.00
	Yes	1207	1.10
Family social class	Man/pro	1774	1.00
	Non-man	1340	0.91
	Man/unskilled	2050	0.93
At least one car	Yes	5305	1.00 (0.1%)
	No	793	1.18*
Tenure	Owned	4390	1.00 (0.1%)
	Rented	1695	1.14*
Family type	Intact	4111	1.00
	Step	1196	1.04
	Lone	791	0.96
High family conflict	No	4395	1.00 (0.9%)
	Yes	1683	1.46***
Poor family communication	No	3995	1.00 (0.8%)
	Yes	2086	0.71***
Father qualifications	Degree or higher	558	1.0 (0.3%)
	A level/HND	1331	1.11
	O level/GCSE	1526	1.29*
	None	1157	1.31*
Mother qualifications	Degree or higher	483	1.00
	A level/HND	1247	0.92
	O level/GCSE	2690	0.85
	None	1515	0.90
Child gender	Male	3190	1.00 (2.4%)
	Female	2989	1.75***
Child age	11	1258	1.00 (1.6%)
	12	1279	0.90
	13	1233	0.84*
	14	1201	0.66***
	15	1127	0.52***
Negative school attitude	No	3785	1.00 (0.3%)
	Yes	878	0.76**

Statistical significance: *=p<0.05, **=p<0.01, ***=p<0.001.
Note: Single observations only with substantive significance shown in brackets.
Source: Author's own analysis of BHPS data.

family, worklessness might increase a young persons likelihood of being bullied. Likewise, living in a workless household might be expected to increase a young person's fear of being bullied. Table 5.4 shows the bivariate relationships between worrying about being bullied and parental employment patterns for young people in the BHPS, and indicates that there was very little association between parental employment and the likelihood that young people worried about being bullied, and no statistically significant relationships with the number of earners or living in a workless household.

A series of regressions were then carried out to explore any relationship between worrying about bullying and a series of other variables, with the results shown in Table 5.5.

There was a small, but significant relationship between worrying about bullying and having a low household income, and with not having a car, which may suggest that young people are bullied, or worry about being bullied, because they are poor. Those young people experiencing high levels of family conflict were more likely to be worried about bullying, whereas those in families with poor communication were found to be less likely to worry about bullying. This may be due to young people not reporting their worries about bullying because they are used to not talking about their problems with their families. Living with a father with a low level of educational qualifications was associated with being slightly more likely to be worried about bullying, as was gender (girls worrying more than boys), and age (older children worrying less than younger children). As suggested above, a negative relationship was evident between fear of bullying and having a negative educational attitude.

In terms of the proportion of variance in worrying about bullying explained by individual variables, age and gender explained 1.6 per cent and 2.4 per cent respectively, with other variables considered so far each explaining less than 1 per cent of the variance.

Table 5.6 shows that the indicators of poor emotional well-being (introduced in Chapter 4) were more important predictors of whether a young person worried about being bullied, accounting for between 1.5 per cent (low self-efficacy) and 7.2 per cent (low self-esteem) of the variance. Young people who were troubled or who had low self-esteem were at least two-and-a-half times as likely to worry about bullying as those with good emotional well-being.

With these bivariate results in mind step-wise regression methods were used to establish a model of best fit for worrying about being bullied (Table 5.7). As there had been no significant difference in the odds of worrying about bullying by family type, a model of best fit was determined for all the young people together, and the workless household set of parental employment variables used.

All four indicators of emotional well-being entered the model, with poorer emotional well-being associated with higher odds of worrying about bullying. As was found in the bivariate analyses, having a negative attitude to school, or living in a family with poor levels of communication were associated with lower odds of worrying about bullying, but high levels of family conflict were associated with higher odds of worrying about bullying. Age and gender held the same relationship with worrying about bullying; girls worried more than boys, and the odds of worrying about bullying decreased with age. Parental worklessness, either current or at any stage of childhood did not enter the model, and when entry was forced, the relationship between worrying about bullying and worklessness at any age was not statistically significant. The model accounted for 15 per cent of the variance in worrying about bullying, and this did not increase when household worklessness was included in the model.

Table 5.6 **Logistic regressions for the odds of worrying about being bullied: Emotional well-being variables**

Variable		N	Odds ratios
Troubled	No	3939	1.00 (4.9%)
	Yes	2155	2.28***
Unhappy	No	4705	1.00 (1.9%)
	Yes	1329	1.79***
Low self-efficacy	No	5363	1.00 (1.5%)
	Yes	669	1.96***
Low self-esteem	No	3499	1.00 (7.2%)
	Yes	2555	2.68***

Statistical significance: *=p<0.05, **=p<0.01, ***=p<0.001.
Note: Single observations only with substantive significance shown in brackets.
Source: Author's own analysis of BHPS data.

Table 5.7 **Logistic regression for worrying about being bullied: Model of best fit**

Variables entered		Odds ratios
Troubled	No	1.00
	Yes	1.72***
Low self-efficacy	No	1.00
	Yes	1.42**
Low self-esteem	No	1.00
	Yes	2.15***
Unhappy	No	1.00
	Yes	1.35**
Negative school attitude	No	1.00
	Yes	0.58***
High family conflict	No	1.00
	Yes	1.25**
Poor family communication	No	1.00
	Yes	0.66***
Child gender	Male	1.00
	Female	1.44***
Child age	11	1.00
	12	0.97
	13	1.01
	14	0.71**
	15	0.52***

Statistical significance: *=p<0.05, **=p<0.01, ***=p<0.001.
% correctly predicted = 69.1%
Nagelkerke R^2 = 0.148
N = 4542
Source: Author's own analysis of BHPS data.

In summary then, parental employment patterns, however defined and whether currently or during childhood, were found to have no significant impact on whether young people worried about bullying. Indicators of emotional well-being were the most significant predictors of worrying about bullying, with age and gender, family communication and conflict also important.

Truanting

The evidence discussed earlier suggested that where previous research has considered the association between parental employment patterns and rates of truancy, a detrimental effect of household worklessness and living with an unemployed father was found. This section seeks to verify any influence of parental employment patterns on rates of truancy, and to disentangle the mechanism by which any influences operate. Parental employment patterns influence individual and family levels of economic, social and cultural capital. Living in a workless household may increase a young person's likelihood of truanting because of the absence of an employed role model and the lowering of expectations and aspirations. Conversely, living in a dual parent household where both parents are engaged in full-time employment could sometimes lead to truancy, as there may be less parental monitoring of school attendance.

Bivariate analysis   Initial analysis of data from the youth panel of the BHPS discovered that parental employment had different associations with the truanting behaviour of girls and boys, and thus further analysis was carried out for all young people, and for girls and boys separately. Table 5.8 presents the logistic regressions of the odds of truanting for maternal and paternal employment patterns.

Table 5.9 presents the logistic regressions of the odds of truanting controlling for housing tenure, which allows us to identify whether any relationships between truancy and parental employment patterns operate through a mechanism of socio-economic circumstances. Housing tenure is a broader measure of socio-economic circumstances than either social class or income, and although potentially related to neighbourhood characteristics which may influence children in different ways (for example, the impact on children's friendships of living on a housing estate), housing tenure has traditionally reflected the economic status and social class of the occupiers, and has regularly been used in research as an indicator of longer-term material disadvantage (for example Hobcraft 1998; McCulloch and Joshi 2000; Ermisch et al 2004). Boys whose fathers were not currently in employment were more likely to have truanted in the last year, but there was no statistically significant association for girls. A similar pattern was seen for the impact of paternal unemployment at all three stages when the child was growing up (ages 0–1, 1–5, 5–11) on their later truanting behaviour. However, when current housing tenure (either owner-occupied or rented) was controlled for (see Table 5.9), the negative impact for boys of fathers' unemployment, at all ages, lost its significance, suggesting that it is not unemployment per se that has a detrimental effect on

Table 5.8   Logistic regressions for the odds of truanting: Parental employment patterns

Variable		N	Bivariate odds ratios		
			All	Boys	Girls
Father current	Employed	3242	1.00 (0.5%)	1.00 (1.2%)	1.00 (0.1%)
employment	Not in employment	524	1.50**	1.87***	1.21
Mother current	Full-time	1629	1.00 (1.1%)	1.00 (2.2%)	1.00 (0.5%)
employment	Part-time	1582	0.67***	0.64**	0.70*
	Not in employment	1421	1.15	1.40**	0.92
Father	Employed	2482	1.00 (0.8%)	1.00 (1.1%)	1.00 (0.6%)
employment	Not in employment	208	1.95***	2.19**	1.76*
(child 0–1)					
Father	Employed	2459	1.00 (0.6%)	1.00 (1.0%)	1.00 (0.4%)
employment	Not in employment	227	1.76**	2.04**	1.54
(child 1–5)					
Father	Employed	2201	1.00 (0.2%)	1.00 (0.7%)	1.00 (0.0%)
employment	Not in employment	263	1.34	1.74*	1.03
(child 5–11)					
Mother	Employed full-time	397	1.00 (0.1%)	1.00 (0.2%)	1.00 (0.3%)
employment	Employed part-time	406	0.81	0.88	0.76
(child 0–1)	Not in employment	2798	0.90	1.21	0.69
Mother	Employed full-time	580	1.00 (0.8%)	1.00 (1.0%)	1.00 (1.0%)
employment	Employed part-time	746	0.61**	0.78	0.49**
(child 1–5)	Not in employment	2359	1.00	1.34	0.77
Mother	Employed full-time	805	1.00 (0.8%)	1.00 (0.8%)	1.00 (0.7%)
employment	Employed part-time	1178	0.77	0.78	0.76
(child 5–11)	Not in employment	1946	1.19	1.22	1.16

Statistical significance: *=$p<0.05$, **=$p<0.01$, ***=$p<0.001$.
Note: Single observations only with substantive significance shown in brackets.
Source: Author's own analysis of BHPS data.

boys' likelihood of truanting, but the associated economic disadvantage (financial capital) that stems from this unemployment. Girls appeared only to be negatively affected by paternal unemployment when they were aged 0–1, and again this lost statistical significance when housing tenure was controlled for.

The impact of maternal employment on young people's propensity to truant is complex. For boys, having a mother currently out of the labour market, compared to being in full-time employment, was associated with greater odds of truanting, but this lost statistical significance when housing tenure was controlled for, which suggests that as with fathers' unemployment, this operated through a mechanism of economic disadvantage (financial capital). For all young people, having a mother in current part-time employment, as compared to full-time employment was associated with a lower likelihood of having truanted, and this remained significant even when housing tenure was controlled for. A similar effect was seen

Table 5.9 **Logistic regressions for the odds of truanting: Parental employment patterns (controlling for housing tenure)**

Variable		N	Controlling for tenure		
			All	Boys	Girls
Father current	Employed	3242	1.00 (1.8%)	1.00 (3.2%)	1.00 (1.0%)
employment	Not in employment	524	1.19	1.39	1.02
Mother current	Full-time	1629	1.00 (2.7%)	1.00 (4.6%)	1.00 (1.5%)
employment	Part-time	1582	0.65***	0.62**	0.69**
	Not in employment	1421	0.97	1.16	0.80
Father	Employed	2482	1.00 (1.6%)	1.00 (2.4%)	1.00 (1.1%)
employment	Not in employment	208	1.60*	1.56	1.59
(child 0–1)					
Father	Employed	2459	1.00 (1.4%)	1.00 (2.4%)	1.00 (0.8%)
employment	Not in employment	227	1.42	1.47	1.35
(child 1–5)					
Father	Employed	2201	1.00 (1.0%)	1.00 (2.7%)	1.00 (0.1%)
employment	Not in employment	263	1.07	1.15	0.96
(child 5–11)					
Mother	Employed full-time	397	1.00 (2.5%)	1.00 (2.8%)	1.00 (2.7%)
employment	Employed part-time	406	0.83	0.94	0.74
(child 0–1)	Not in employment	2798	0.84	1.15	0.64*
Mother	Employed full-time	580	1.00 (2.9%)	1.00 (3.2%)	1.00 (3.0%)
employment	Employed part-time	746	0.60**	0.79	0.46**
(child 1–5)	Not in employment	2359	0.87	1.78	0.66*
Mother	Employed full-time	805	1.00 (2.6%)	1.00 (3.8%)	1.00 (1.7%)
employment	Employed part-time	1178	0.75*	0.77	0.74
(child 5–11)	Not in employment	1946	1.01	0.98	1.02

Statistical significance: *=p<0.05, **=p<0.01, ***=p<0.001.
Note: Substantive significance shown in brackets.
Source: Author's own analysis of BHPS data.

for girls, but not for boys, in terms of maternal part-time employment when the young people were aged 1–5. That the apparently beneficial effects of maternal part-time employment remained significant even when housing tenure was controlled for suggests that having a mother at home more (if she is working less hours) offers young people some sort of nurturing or protection (social capital) against truanting, perhaps because she is more likely to be able to monitor what her child(ren) are doing.

When parents' employment patterns were considered at the same time, by looking at the impact of household worklessness on truancy, a fairly consistent pattern emerged (Table 5.10). Experience of living in a workless household, either currently or at any stage of childhood, had a detrimental impact on young people's truanting behaviour, and this was true for all young people, and for girls and boys when considered separately (except worklessness at age 1–5 for girls).

Table 5.10   Logistic regressions for the odds of truanting: Workless households

Variable		N	Bivariate odds ratios		
			All	Boys	Girls
Currently workless household	No	3747	1.00 (0.8%)	1.00 (1.1%)	1.00 (0.6%)
	Yes	561	1.69***	1.85***	1.57**
Workless household (child 0–1)	No	2386	1.00 (1.3%)	1.00 (1.6%)	1.00 (1.0%)
	Yes	337	1.96***	2.08***	1.85**
Workless household (child 1–5)	No	2389	1.00 (0.6%)	1.00 (1.3%)	1.00 (0.2%)
	Yes	369	1.61**	1.89**	1.32
Workless household (child 5–11)	No	2654	1.00 (1.2%)	1.00 (2.0%)	1.00 (0.5%)
	Yes	565	1.76***	2.06***	1.46*
Ever workless	No	3473	1.00 (1.3%)	1.00 (1.8%)	1.00 (0.9%)
	Yes	1056	1.72***	1.87***	1.57***

Statistical significance: *=p<0.05, **=p<0.01, ***=p<0.001.
Note: Single observations only with substantive significance shown in brackets.
Source: Author's own analysis of BHPS data.

Table 5.11   Logistic regressions for the odds of truanting: Workless households (controlling for housing tenure)

Variable		N	Controlling for tenure		
			All	Boys	Girls
Currently workless household	No	3747	1.00 (2.2%)	1.00 (3.1%)	1.00 (1.4%)
	Yes	561	1.31*	1.31	1.31
Workless household (child 0–1)	No	2386	1.00 (2.3%)	1.00 (2.5%)	1.00 (2.0%)
	Yes	337	1.50*	1.55	1.47
Workless household (child 1–5)	No	2389	1.00 (2.0%)	1.00 (2.9%)	1.00 (1.3%)
	Yes	369	1.12	1.24	0.96
Workless household (child 5–11)	No	2654	1.00 (1.8%)	1.00 (2.7%)	1.00 (1.1%)
	Yes	565	1.45**	1.65**	1.22
Ever workless	No	3473	1.00 (2.2%)	1.00 (3.2%)	1.00 (1.3%)
	Yes	1056	1.39**	1.40*	1.36*

Statistical significance: *=p<0.05, **=p<0.01, ***=p<0.001.
Note: Substantive significance shown in brackets.
Source: Author's own analysis of BHPS data.

That worklessness during childhood had a negative effect on young people's later truanting behaviour illustrates the residual impact that this experience can have.

There appeared to be some gender differences, and the percentage of variance in truanting accounted for by parental worklessness was consistently higher for boys than for girls, suggesting that boys are more strongly influenced by the experience of living in a workless household.

To investigate whether the impact of worklessness operated through the impact on socio-economic circumstances, the regressions were repeated controlling for housing tenure (Table 5.11). Indeed when housing tenure was controlled for, the impact of worklessness generally lost significance.

When a measure that encompassed whether a young person had ever lived in a workless household was used, there was a statistically significant negative effect on truanting. This remained significant even when housing tenure was controlled for, which suggests that overall there is something about the experience of life in a workless household that effects children, over and above the experience of economic deprivation.

Although statistically the relationships between parental employment patterns and truancy were significant, substantively the effects were quite small, with each measure controlling a maximum of 2.5 per cent of the variance in truanting behaviour. Other factors, relating to the young person, their parents and household had a greater substantive effect on truancy (Table 5.12).

Current household income itself had only a small impact upon girls' likelihood of truanting, but indicators of longer-term deprivation (not having a car, living in rented accommodation, and lower family social class) were associated with being more likely to have truanted in the last year, for both girls and boys. These findings mirror the residual impact of earlier household worklessness.

Truanting was also more likely amongst those in lone or stepfamilies, and where there was high family conflict or poor family communication. These factors appeared to be more important for girls, evidenced by higher odds ratios than for boys. This is contrary to the evidence discussed above (SEU 1998), where family structure had a more significant impact on boys' truanting than on that of girls. Fathers' emotional well-being had only a small effect on girls likelihood of truanting, and although significant for both girls and boys, mothers' emotional well-being had a greater impact for girls than boys. These findings all indicate the importance of family stability for young people's likelihood of truanting.

In line with the evidence presented above (Bosworth 1994; Casey and Smith 1995; Dustmann et al 1997) having a father or mother with no educational qualifications was associated with higher odds of truanting, and this appeared to be slightly more important for boys than for girls. As with other studies (O'Keefe 1993; Bosworth 1994; SEU 1998) there was no statistically significant impact of gender on the likelihood of truancy, although it is clear that the impact of other factors showed gendered differences. Age had a statistically and substantively significant impact on the likelihood of truancy, accounting for 5.8 per cent of the variance in truanting for boys, and 12.8 per cent for girls. Fifteen-year-old girls were over 12 times as likely to truant as 11-year-old girls. Firstborn children, and those with at least one sibling were less likely to truant. Those with a negative educational attitude were 5 times (boys) and 8-and-a-half times (girls) as likely to have truanted as other youths. Again, emotional well-being indicators (see Table 5.13) were important predictors of truanting behaviour.

Table 5.12   Logistic regressions for the odds of truanting: Other variables

Variable		N	All	Boys	Girls
Equivalent income less than 50%	No	3797	1.00 (0.1%)	1.00 (0.0%)	1.00 (0.3%)
of average after housing costs	Yes	900	1.15	0.98	1.34*
Family social class	Man/pro	1341	1.00 (0.9%)	1.00 (1.3%)	1.00 (0.6%)
	Non-man	1078	0.90	0.74	1.10
	Man/unskilled	1579	1.41**	1.37*	1.47*
At least one car	Yes	4122	1.00 (0.9%)	1.00 (0.9%)	1.00 (1.0%)
	No	585	1.75***	1.73***	1.78***
Tenure	Owned	3346	1.00 (1.9%)	1.00 (3.0%)	1.00 (1.0%)
	Rented	1350	1.82***	2.16***	1.54***
Family type	Intact	3114	1.00 (1.1%)	1.00 (0.9%)	1.00 (1.3%)
	Step	992	1.53***	1.52**	1.52**
	Lone	601	1.60***	1.45*	1.77***
High family conflict	No	3426	1.00 (2.8%)	1.00 (2.1%)	1.00 (3.8%)
	Yes	1265	2.11***	1.94***	2.34***
Poor family communication	No	3104	1.00 (2.3%)	1.00 (1.5%)	1.00 (3.4%)
	Yes	1588	1.93***	1.68***	2.23***
Father GHQ+4	No	2862	1.00 (0.1%)	1.00 (0.0%)	1.00 (0.5%)
	Yes	666	1.13	0.89	1.47*
Mother GHQ+4	No	3314	1.00 (0.7%)	1.00 (0.3%)	1.00 (1.2%)
	Yes	1224	1.46***	1.31*	1.63***
Father qualifications	Degree or higher	440	1.00 (0.8%)	1.00 (1.7%)	1.0 (0.7%)
	A level/HND	1051	0.98	0.74	1.49
	O level/GCSE	1227	0.97	0.89	1.18
	None	858	1.50*	1.53*	1.74*
Mother qualifications	Degree or higher	389	1.00 (2.3%)	1.00 (2.8%)	1.00 (2.3%)
	A level/HND	980	0.99	1.30	0.71
	O level/GCSE	2111	0.87	1.25	0.56*
	None	1103	1.82***	2.59***	1.19
Child gender	Male	2376	1.00 (0.0%)		
	Female	2331	0.92		
Child age	11	977	1.00 (9.1%)	1.00 (5.8%)	1.00 (13.8%)
	12	993	1.47*	1.28	1.86*
	13	952	2.65***	1.77**	4.66***
	14	934	3.92***	2.48***	7.28***
	15	851	6.60***	4.20***	12.22***
Only child	No	3628	1.00 (0.6%)	1.00 (0.4%)	1.00 (0.9%)
	Yes	1079	1.45***	1.37*	1.55***
Firstborn	No	2538	1.00 (0.4%)	1.00 (0.8%)	1.00 (0.1%)
	Yes	2014	0.77**	0.69**	0.85
Number of siblings	0	1079	1.00 (0.9%)	1.00 (1.3%)	1.00 (0.9%)
	1	2075	0.67***	0.70**	0.64**
	2	1127	0.63***	0.63**	0.63**
	3+	426	0.94	1.28	0.67
Negative school attitude	No	3790	1.00 (15.0%)	1.00 (12.3%)	1.00 (18.3%)
	Yes	877	6.26***	4.98***	8.26***

Statistical significance: *=p<0.05, **=p<0.01, ***=p<0.001.
Note: Single observations only with substantive significance shown in brackets.
Source: Author's own analysis of BHPS data.

Table 5.13   Logistic regressions for the odds of truanting: Emotional well-being variables

Variable		N	All	Boys	Girls
Troubled	No	3063	1.00 (2.3%)	1.00 (1.2%)	1.00 (4.3%)
	Yes	1638	1.92***	1.61***	2.41***
Unhappy	No	3670	1.00 (5.6%)	1.00 (5.3%)	1.00 (5.9%)
	Yes	989	2.99***	2.93***	3.08***
Low self-efficacy	No	4158	1.00 (1.4%)	1.00 (0.9%)	1.00 (2.1%)
	Yes	503	2.06***	1.80***	2.35***
Low self-esteem	No	2754	1.00 (1.4%)	1.00 (2.3%)	1.00 (0.9%)
	Yes	1922	1.65***	1.89***	1.49**

Statistical significance: *=p<0.05, **=p<0.01, ***=p<0.001.
Note: Single observations only with substantive significance shown in brackets.
Source: Author's own analysis of BHPS data.

Table 5.14   Logistic regression for truanting: Model of best fit (whole sample)

Variables entered		Odds ratios
Ever workless household	No	1.00
	Yes	1.22
Attitude to school	Positive	1.00
	Negative	4.70***
Age	11	1.00
	12	1.30
	13	2.11***
	14	3.54***
	15	6.13***
Mother qualifications	Degree	1.00
	A level	0.90
	O level	0.72
	None	1.37
High family conflict	No	1.00
	Yes	1.39**
Tenure	Owned	1.00
	Rented	1.49***
Troubled	No	1.00
	Yes	1.37**
Poor family communication	No	1.00
	Yes	1.38**
Family type	Intact	1.00
	Step	1.47**
	Lone	1.33*
Unhappy	No	1.00
	Yes	1.31*

Statistical significance: *=p<0.05, **=p<0.01, ***=p<0.001.
Constant = 0.02***
% correctly predicted = 85.8%
Nagelkerke R^2 = 0.279
N=4338
Source: Author's own analysis of BHPS data.

In terms of substantive significance, the binary analyses revealed that having a negative attitude to education was the most important predictor of the likelihood that a young person had truanted in the last year, followed by the young person's age, unhappiness, family conflict and mothers' level of academic qualifications.

Multivariate analysis   With these results in mind, a series of multiple regressions were carried out to obtain models of best fit for truancy, firstly for all youths (Table 5.14), and then because of the apparent differences by family structure, for young people in lone mother families (Table 5.15) and dual parent families (Table 5.16) separately. The model obtained for the whole sample correctly predicted 85.6 per cent of cases, and accounted for 27.9 per cent of the variance in truanting.

As in the bivariate analysis, having a negative attitude to education was an important predictor of truanting. This and the age of the young person were the only variables to at least double the odds of truanting. Although whether a young person had ever lived in a workless household was included in the model, this had no statistically significant relationship with the likelihood of truanting.

Lone mother families   A model of best fit was then established (Table 5.15) for truanting amongst young people in lone mother families only. The model accounted for 31.6 per cent of the variance in truanting and correctly predicted 83.6 per cent of cases.

Having a negative attitude to education and age were still the strongest predictors of truanting, although young people who had experienced life in a

Table 5.15   Logistic regression for truanting: Model of best fit (lone mother families only)

Variables entered		Odds ratios
Ever workless household	No	1.00
	Yes	2.11***
Attitude to school	Positive	1.00
	Negative	6.01***
Age	11	1.00
	12	1.94
	13	2.31
	14	4.75***
	15	9.45***
High family conflict	No	1.00
	Yes	1.86**

Statistical significance: *=p<0.05, **=p<0.01, ***=p<0.001.
Constant = 0.02***
% correctly predicted = 83.6%
Nagelkerke R^2 = 0.316
N=590
Source: Author's own analysis of BHPS data.

Table 5.16   Logistic regression for truanting: Model of best fit using ever workless as parental employment variable (dual parent families only)

Variables entered		Odds ratios
Ever workless	No	1.00
	Yes	1.16
Attitude to school	Positive	1.00
	Negative	4.53***
Age	11	1.00
	12	1.22
	13	2.10***
	14	3.37***
	15	5.58***
Mother qualifications	Degree	1.00
	A level	0.97
	O level	0.81
	None	1.55*
High family conflict	No	1.00
	Yes	1.38**
Tenure	Owned	1.00
	Rented	1.60***
Troubled	No	1.00
	Yes	1.40**
Poor family communication	No	1.00
	Yes	1.38*
Unhappy	No	1.00
	Yes	1.33*

Statistical significance: *=p<0.05, **=p<0.01, ***=p<0.001.
Constant = 0.25***
% correctly predicted = 86.4%
Nagelkerke R^2 = 0.261
N=3766
Source: Author's own analysis of BHPS data.

workless household or high levels of family conflict were around twice as likely to have truanted as other youths. It is interesting to note that no measures of economic status entered the model. If housing tenure was added to the model, it had no significant impact on truanting, and having ever lived in a workless household retained its significance. As suggested above, this might indicate that there is something about the experience of life in a workless household that effects children, over and above the experience of economic deprivation (lack of financial capital). If current worklessness was included in the model, instead of having ever lived in a workless household, it had no significant association with truanting amongst young people in lone mother families, which again indicates the residual impact of earlier worklessness.

When talking about worklessness in a lone mother household, this really refers to the employment status of the mother. Thus an alternative regression (not shown) was conducted entering current maternal employment instead of whether young people had ever lived in a workless household. However defined (full-time/part-time/not in employment or employed/not in employment) and however entered (stepwise or as a block of variables) there was no significant association between current maternal employment and truanting. This corroborates the suggestion that it is something about experiencing the state of worklessness that has a negative impact on truanting behaviour, rather than the lack of parental employment per se.

Dual parent families   Turning then to look at the influences on truancy amongst young people living in dual parent families, a model of best fit (Table 5.16) was achieved which contained 9 variables, explained 26.1 per cent of the variance in truanting and correctly predicted 86.4 per cent of all cases. Although having ever lived in a workless household was included in the model this did not have a statistically significant influence on truanting. Again, having a negative attitude to education and the age of the young person were the only variables to at least double the odds of truanting.

If the variables were entered into the model in a stepwise fashion, having ever lived in a workless household had a significant impact upon truanting until housing tenure entered the model, suggesting that for those in dual parent families, the detrimental impact of having ever lived in a workless household operates through a mechanism of economic deprivation.

A similar model (not shown) was established using current household worklessness as the parental employment variable, and again, this lost statistical significance when household tenure was controlled for.

In the bivariate analysis, having a mother currently in part-time employment, as opposed to full-time employment was associated with a lower likelihood of having truanting in the last year. Therefore a multiple regression was conducted to establish a model which in terms of parental employment just controlled for mothers' current status (Table 5.17).

It can be seen that as in the bivariate analysis, having a mother in part-time employment was consistently associated with lower odds of truanting, even when housing tenure was controlled for. Having a negative attitude to education, and age were still the most important predictors of truanting, although mothers' level of qualifications, family conflict and communication, and the young person's emotional well-being (in terms of feeling troubled and unhappy) also had a significant impact on truanting.

Summary   The analysis conducted with regards the impact of parental employment status on young people's likelihood of truanting has shown several

Table 5.17   Logistic regression for truanting: Model of best fit using mothers' current employment as parental employment variable (dual parent families only)

Variables entered		Odds ratios
Mother current employment	Full-time	1.00
	Part-time	0.74*
	Not in employment	0.98
Attitude to school	Positive	1.00
	Negative	4.23***
Age	11	1.00
	12	1.29
	13	2.18***
	14	3.41***
	15	5.65***
Tenure	Owned	1.00
	Rented	1.72***
High family conflict	No	1.00
	Yes	1.41**
Mother qualifications	Degree	1.00
	A level	1.01
	O level	0.80
	None	1.51*
Poor family communication	No	1.00
	Yes	1.46***
Troubled	No	1.00
	Yes	1.38**
Unhappy	No	1.00
	Yes	1.31*

Statistical significance: *=p<0.05, **=p<0.01, ***=p<0.001.
Constant = 0.027***
% correctly predicted = 86.0%%
Nagelkerke R^2 = 0.259
N=3906
Source: Author's own analysis of BHPS data.

consistent findings. Firstly, paternal unemployment, and for young people in dual parent households, worklessness, had a detrimental effect on the likelihood of having truanted in the last year, and this appeared to operate through a mechanism of economic disadvantage (financial capital), losing significance when housing tenure, as an indicator of longer-term deprivation, was controlled for. Secondly, for those in lone mother families, having ever experienced life in a workless household was associated with higher odds of truanting, and this was not related to economic circumstances. For those in dual parent households, part-time maternal employment appeared to offer young people some protection against truanting (social capital), and again this relationship was not affected by controlling for housing tenure, suggesting that mothers' employment status effects children in ways over and above increasing household economic circumstances (financial capital). Finally, although the relationships between parental employment status and the odds of truanting were significant, having a negative attitude to education and age had a greater impact, with housing tenure, emotional well-being and family relationships also important.

Exclusion from school

This section considers the influences on the likelihood that young people have been excluded from school. Young people in the BHPS survey were asked if they had been expelled or suspended in the last year (as opposed to excluded) and it is important to stress that this question was only asked from Wave Five onwards, and that overall only 5.1 per cent of all youths (241 from a possible 4710) had been excluded in the previous year. Multivariate analysis was therefore restricted, as the numbers involved were too small to split the sample by either family type or gender.

Bivariate analysis Table 5.18 shows the bivariate odds of having been excluded in the previous year by patterns of parental employment, both separately and controlling for housing tenure.

Living with a currently unemployed father doubled the odds of a young person having been excluded in the previous year, in line with previous research evidence discussed above (Daniels et al 2003). However, when housing tenure was controlled for, the impact of paternal unemployment lost statistical significance, which suggests that this relationship operates through the influence on household socio-economic circumstances (financial capital).

Paternal unemployment when the young people were growing up also increased the odds of them being excluded from school in adolescence. As with current unemployment the effect of paternal unemployment when the young person was aged 5–11 lost statistical significance when current housing tenure was controlled for. However, the impact of paternal unemployment at ages 0–1 and 1–5 retained statistical significance when housing tenure was controlled for, suggesting that there is something detrimental about the experience of living with an unemployed father during childhood, over and above the impact on family socio-economic circumstances (financial capital).

The impact of maternal employment is slightly more complex. Maternal employment patterns when the young people were aged 0–1 and 1–5 had no statistically significant association with their later odds of being excluded from school. Young people living with a mother not in employment as opposed to full-time employment, either currently or when they were aged 5–11, had higher odds of having been excluded from school. These associations lost statistical significance when housing tenure was controlled for, suggesting that as with

Table 5.18   Logistic regressions for the odds of having been excluded: Parental employment patterns (controlling for housing tenure)

Variable		N	Bivariate odds	Controlling for tenure
Father current employment	Employed	3243	1.00 (1.0%)	1.00 (2.9%)
	Not in employment	525	1.97***	1.40
Mother current employment	Full-time	1630	1.00 (1.6%)	1.00 (3.6%)
	Part-time	1582	0.61**	0.59**
	Not in employment	1423	1.44*	1.15
Father employment (child 0–1)	Employed	2481	1.00 (1.2%)	1.00 (1.3%)
	Not in employment	208	2.56**	2.41**
Father employment (child 1–5)	Employed	2457	1.00 (1.9%)	1.00 (2.2%)
	Not in employment	228	2.92***	2.46**
Father employment (child 5–11)	Employed	2200	1.00 (0.7%)	1.00 (2.1%)
	Not in employment	265	1.90*	1.31
Mother employment (child 0–1)	Employed full-time	399	1.00 (0.2%)	1.00 (2.4%)
	Employed part-time	406	1.41	1.46
	Not in employment	2798	1.51	1.41
Mother employment (child 1–5)	Employed full-time	582	1.00 (0.2%)	1.00 (2.3%)
	Employed part-time	746	1.06	1.04
	Not in employment	2360	1.37	1.14
Mother employment (child 5–11)	Employed full-time	805	1.00 (1.3%)	1.00 (3.3%)
	Employed part-time	1180	0.91	0.88
	Not in employment	1947	1.73**	1.39

Statistical significance: *=p<0.05, **=p<0.01, ***=p<0.001.
Note: Single observations with substantive significance shown in brackets.
Source: Author's own analysis of BHPS data.

paternal unemployment, these relationships operate through the impact on family socio-economic circumstances (financial capital). However, having a mother currently in part-time as opposed to full-time employment appeared to offer young people some protection against being excluded from school, and this relationship retained significance when housing tenure was controlled for, suggesting that this is related to a nurturing effect (social capital) that a mother may have when she is not employed full-time.

If we take into account paternal and maternal employment patterns together and consider the impact of household worklessness on young people's odds of having been excluded from school, we find a clear pattern (Table 5.19). Experience of life in a workless household at any age was associated with higher odds of having been excluded from school, and these relationships retained significance when housing tenure was controlled for, suggesting that household worklessness has an impact on young people over and above the effects on household income (financial capital). Young people who had ever lived in a workless household were almost

Table 5.19   Logistic regressions for the odds of having been excluded: Parental employment patterns (controlling for housing tenure)

Variable		N	Bivariate odds	Controlling for tenure
Currently workless household	No	3649	1.00 (2.2%)	1.00 (3.8%)
	Yes	561	2.60***	1.84***
Workless household (child 0–1)	No	2386	1.00 (3.5%)	1.00 (3.6%)
	Yes	336	3.45***	3.08***
Workless household (child 1–5)	No	2388	1.00 (4.2%)	1.00 (4.5%)
	Yes	369	3.75***	3.07***
Workless household (child 5–11)	No	2655	1.00 (5.1%)	1.00 (6.0%)
	Yes	566	3.72***	2.78***
Ever workless	No	3474	1.00 (3.6%)	1.00 (4.3%)
	Yes	1058	2.83***	2.20***

Statistical significance: *=p<0.05, **=p<0.01, ***=p<0.001.
Note: Single observations with substantive significance shown in brackets.
Source: Author's own analysis of BHPS data.

three times as likely to have been excluded from school as other young people, and this accounted for 3.6 per cent of the variance in school exclusions.

The impact of other factors on exclusion from school are considered in Table 5.20. Having a negative attitude to education had the most significant association with school exclusion, accounting for around 10 per cent of the variance in exclusion, although this does not suggest causation – are young people who have a negative attitude to education more likely to be excluded, or are young people who have been excluded more likely to have a negative attitude to education? Age and gender were also important predictors of exclusion from school, with boys and older youths more likely to have been excluded. Although household income itself did not have a statistically significant relationship with school exclusion, measures of longer-term deprivation (lower social class, not having at least one car, and living in rented accommodation, compared to owner-occupied) did, with more deprived young people more than twice as likely to have been excluded. Young people living in a lone parent family or stepfamily were more likely to have been excluded than those in intact families (in line with evidence presented above), as were those experiencing high levels of family conflict or low levels of family communication. Having a mother or father with no qualifications, or with poor emotional well-being (high GHQ score) was also associated with being more likely to have been excluded from school in the last year.

Young people's own emotional well-being, in terms of feeling troubled or unhappy, or having low self-esteem or self-efficacy, also had a significant relationship with having been excluded from school (Table 5.21). Again, this does not suggest the direction of this relationship. Young people may not be excluded from school because they have poor emotional well-being, but this may come as a result of having been excluded.

Table 5.20   Logistic regressions for the odds of having been excluded: Other variables

Variable		N	Odds ratios
Equivalent income less than 50% of average after housing costs	No	3800	1.00 (0.1%)
	Yes	900	1.17
Family social class	Man/pro	1343	1.00 (1.5%)
	Non-man	1079	1.25
	Man/unskilled	1579	2.11***
At least one car	Yes	4123	1.00 (1.3%)
	No	587	2.19***
Tenure	Owned	3346	1.00 (2.6%)
	Rented	1353	2.37***
Family type	Intact	3144	1.00 (2.5%)
	Step	995	2.15***
	Lone	601	2.49***
High family conflict	No	3426	1.00 (0.6%)
	Yes	1268	1.55**
Poor family communication	No	3106	1.00 (2.0%)
	Yes	1589	2.11***
Father GHQ+4	No	2861	1.00 (0.6%)
	Yes	669	1.59*
Mother GHQ+4	No	3314	1.00 (0.8%)
	Yes	1227	1.64***
Father qualifications	Degree or higher	439	1.00 (1.1%)
	A level/HND	1052	1.36
	O level/GCSE	1230	1.50
	None	858	2.42**
Mother qualifications	Degree or higher	390	1.00 (1.5%)
	A level/HND	983	0.95
	O level/GCSE	2112	1.19
	None	1101	2.14**
Child gender	Male	2377	1.00 (4.8%)
	Female	2333	0.28***
Child age	11	977	1.00 (4.1%)
	12	993	1.77
	13	952	2.77***
	14	935	4.51***
	15	853	4.84***
Negative school attitude	No	3789	1.00 (10.1%)
	Yes	877	5.82***

Statistical significance: *=p<0.05, **=p<0.01, ***=p<0.001.
Note: Single observations only with substantive significance shown in brackets.
Source: Author's own analysis of BHPS data.

Table 5.21 Logistic regressions for the odds of having been excluded: Emotional well-being variables

Variable		N	Odds ratios
Troubled	No	3063	1.00 (0.2%)
	Yes	1641	1.28
Unhappy	No	3669	1.00 (2.6%)
	Yes	991	2.49***
Low self-efficacy	No	4157	1.00 (1.4%)
	Yes	506	2.31***
Low self-esteem	No	2757	1.00 (0.7%)
	Yes	1922	1.56**

Statistical significance: *=$p<0.05$, **=$p<0.01$, ***=$p<0.001$.
Note: Single observations with substantive significance shown in brackets.
Source: Author's own analysis of BHPS data.

Table 5.22 Logistic regression for having been excluded from school: Model of best fit using mothers' current employment

Variables entered		Odds ratios
Mother current employment	Full-time	1.00
	Part-time	0.80
	Not in employment	1.33
Attitude to school	Positive	1.00
	Negative	3.73***
Gender	Male	1.00
	Female	0.30***
Age	11	1.00
	12	1.49
	13	2.49**
	14	4.39***
	15	4.08***
Tenure	Owned	1.00
	Rented	1.94***
Family type	Intact	1.00
	Step	1.78***
	Lone	1.89***
Low self-efficacy	No	1.00
	Yes	1.90***

Statistical significance: *=$p<0.05$, **=$p<0.01$, ***=$p<0.001$.
Constant = 0.01***
% correctly predicted = 94.4%
Nagelkerke R^2 = 0.214
N=4279
Source: Author's own analysis of BHPS data.

Multivariate analysis With these results in mind, a series of multiple regressions were carried out, firstly using mothers' current employment as the measure of parental employment (Table 5.22).

Table 5.23   Logistic regression for having been excluded from school: Model of best fit using current worklessness

Variables entered		Odds ratios
Current workless household	No	1.00
	Yes	1.73**
Attitude to school	Positive	1.00
	Negative	4.36***
Gender	Male	1.00
	Female	0.26***
Age	11	1.00
	12	1.49
	13	2.68**
	14	4.33***
	15	4.33***
Tenure	Owned	1.00
	Rented	1.90***
Family type	Intact	1.00
	Step	1.89***
	Lone	1.62*
Low self-efficacy	No	1.00
	Yes	1.61*

Statistical significance: *=$p<0.05$, **=$p<0.01$, ***=$p<0.001$.
Constant = 0.01***
% correctly predicted = 94.7%
Nagelkerke R^2 = 0.223
N=4228
Source: Author's own analysis of BHPS data.

A model of best fit was established which accounted for 21.4 per cent of the variance in having been excluded from school, correctly predicting 94.4 per cent of cases. Although mothers' current employment was included in the model of best fit, its relationship with exclusion from school was not statistically significant. The variables which proved important in the bivariate analysis were also included in this multivariate model of best fit. A second regression was thus run using current worklessness as the measure of parental employment (Table 5.23). A model of best fit was established which accounted for 22.3 per cent of the variance in having been excluded from school, correctly predicting 94.7 per cent of cases.

Living in a household where no adult was in employment was associated with a higher likelihood of having been excluded from school. As housing tenure was included in the model, the influence of parental worklessness was not operating solely through the impact on family socio-economic circumstances (financial capital). This provides further evidence that the detrimental effect of living in a currently workless household is not simply due to reduced economic resources, but that there is something else about the experience of worklessness that affects children's behaviour. As was seen in the bivariate analysis, age and gender were important influences, with boys and older youths far more likely to have been excluded from school. As had been seen in previous research (Ashford 1994) young people in lone parent families and stepfamilies were more likely to have been excluded from school than those in intact families. Poor emotional well-being in terms of having low self-efficacy, and having a negative attitude to education were also strongly associated with the likelihood of having been excluded from school in the previous year.

Summary   In summary then, the influence of parental employment patterns on young people's likelihood of having been excluded from school in the last year has been seen to be fairly stable. Living with an unemployed father increased the odds of exclusion from school, as did the experience of paternal unemployment during childhood. In the multivariate analysis, living in a household where no adult was in employment increased the odds that a young person had been excluded from school in the previous year. As this relationship was statistically significant even when housing tenure was controlled for in the model suggests that it is something about the experience of worklessness, over and above the impact on family socio-economic circumstances (financial capital) which influences school exclusion. In the bivariate analysis, having a mother in part-time as opposed to full-time employment appeared to offer young people some protection (social capital) against having been excluded from school. However, this relationship did not achieve statistical significance when other factors were controlled for in the multivariate analysis.

Attitude to education

It has already been seen that having a positive attitude to education is an important influence on young people's fear of being bullied and their likelihood of playing truant or being excluded from school. But do parental employment patterns influence young people's attitudes to education?

Bivariate analysis   Table 5.24 indicates that the picture is complex, illustrating the bivariate odds of having a negative attitude to education for paternal and maternal employment patterns.

It can be seen that living with a currently unemployed father, or having lived with an unemployed father at any stage during childhood had no statistically significant effect on adolescents' attitudes to education. The impact of maternal employment patterns is more complicated. Having a mother currently in part-time as opposed to full-time employment reduced the odds of having a negative attitude to education by around a third, and this relationship retained significance when housing tenure was controlled for. As with the other educational outcomes discussed in this chapter, this suggests that having a mother who is not engaged in

Table 5.24   Logistic regressions for the odds of having a negative attitude to education: Parental employment patterns controlling for housing tenure

Variable		N	Bivariate odds	Controlling for tenure
Father current	Employed	3215	1.00 (0.1%)	1.00 (0.8%)
employment	Not in employment	523	1.22	1.03
Mother current	Full-time	1619	1.00 (1.3%)	1.00 (1.3%)
employment	Part-time	1571	0.62***	0.62***
	Not in employment	1408	1.03	1.03
Father employment	Employed	2463	1.00 (0.2%)	1.00 (0.5%)
(child 0–1)	Not in employment	207	1.41	1.27
Father employment	Employed	2441	1.00 (0.2%)	1.00 (0.6%)
(child 1–5)	Not in employment	225	1.35	1.15
Father employment	Employed	2184	1.00 (0.0%)	1.00 (1.1%)
(child 5–11)	Not in employment	264	1.08	0.83
Mother employment	Employed full-time	395	1.00 (0.4%)	1.00 (1.0%)
(child 0–1)	Employed part-time	404	1.61*	1.63*
	Not in employment	2777	1.57**	1.52*
Mother employment	Employed full-time	577	1.00 (0.3%)	1.00 (0.9%)
(child 1–5)	Employed part-time	743	1.15	1.14
	Not in employment	2340	1.37*	1.27
Mother employment	Employed full-time	801	1.00 (0.6%)	1.00 (1.0%)
(child 5–11)	Employed part-time	1169	1.04	1.03
	Not in employment	1933	1.42**	1.32*

Statistical significance: *=$p<0.05$, **=$p<0.01$, ***=$p<0.001$.
Note: Single observations with substantive significance shown in brackets.
Source: Author's own analysis of BHPS data.

current full-time employment offers young people some protection (social capital) against negative outcomes. However this picture is confused by the fact that living with a mother who was not in the labour market during their childhood was associated with a young person having higher odds of having a negative attitude to education, and that on the whole this retained significance when housing tenure was controlled for. In addition, having a mother who was in part-time as opposed to full-time employment during infancy (aged 0–1) was also associated with higher odds of having a negative attitude to education, and again this retained statistical significance when housing tenure was controlled for.

A series of regressions were then carried out to assess the impact of household worklessness on young people's attitudes to education (Table 5.25).

It can be seen that the experience of household worklessness either currently or at any stage of childhood was associated with higher odds of having a negative attitude to education, and apart from that at ages 1–5 this remained significant

Table 5.25   Logistic regressions for the odds of having a negative attitude to education: Workless households controlling for housing tenure

Variable		N	Bivariate odds	Controlling for tenure
Currently workless household	No	3719	1.00 (0.5%)	1.00 (1.0%)
	Yes	555	1.50***	1.30*
Workless household (child 0–1)	No	2368	1.00 (0.8%)	1.00 (1.1%)
	Yes	335	1.67***	1.45*
Workless household (child 1–5)	No	2372	1.00 (0.5%)	1.00 (0.9%)
	Yes	366	1.51**	1.27
Workless household (child 5–11)	No	2634	1.00 (0.5%)	1.00 (0.6%)
	Yes	562	1.46**	1.34*
Ever workless	No	3447	1.00 (0.4%)	1.00 (0.8%)
	Yes	1048	1.36***	1.19

Statistical significance: *=p<0.05, **=p<0.01, ***=p<0.001.
Note: Single observations with substantive significance shown in brackets.
Source: Author's own analysis of BHPS data.

Table 5.26   Multiple regression for having a negative attitude to education: Workless household variables only

Variables entered		Odds ratios
Currently workless household	No	1.00
	Yes	1.76**
Workless household (child 0–1)	No	1.00
	Yes	1.26
Workless household (child 1–5)	No	1.00
	Yes	0.90
Workless household (child 5–11)	No	1.00
	Yes	1.10

Statistical significance: *=p<0.05, **=p<0.01, ***=p<0.001.
% correctly predicted = 84.4%
Nagelkerke R^2 = 0.011
N = 2449
Source: Author's own analysis of BHPS data.

when housing tenure was controlled for. This suggests that it is not necessarily the economic deprivation (financial capital) that accompanies household worklessness that influences children, but perhaps the lack of a positive working role model (a form of cultural capital) to inspire them to do well at school.

To consider the relative impact of worklessness at the different stages of a child's life, a regression model was run which just contained the 4 workless household variables (Table 5.26). From this it can be seen that when worklessness throughout the young person's life was controlled for, current household worklessness still had a significant detrimental impact on their likelihood of having a negative attitude

Table 5.27   Logistic regressions for the odds of having a negative attitude to education: Other variables

Variable		N	Odds ratios
Equivalent income less than 50% of average after housing costs	No	3769	1.00 (0.0%)
	Yes	893	0.94
Family social class	Man/pro	1334	1.00 (0.1%)
	Non-man	1070	0.97
	Man/unskilled	1567	1.12
At least one car	Yes	4089	1.00 (0.1%)
	No	583	1.19
Tenure	Owned	3324	1.00 (0.7%)
	Rented	1337	1.43***
Family type	Intact	3095	1.00 (0.6%)
	Step	983	1.34**
	Lone	594	1.43**
High family conflict	No	3399	1.00 (3.3%)
	Yes	1257	2.19***
Poor family communication	No	3081	1.00 (4.2%)
	Yes	1576	2.33***
Father GHQ+4	No	2837	1.00 (0.2%)
	Yes	664	1.24*
Mother GHQ+4	No	3285	1.00 (0.4%)
	Yes	1219	1.34***
Father qualifications	Degree or higher	437	1.00 (0.3%)
	A level/HND	1043	1.08
	O level/GCSE	1217	1.07
	None	853	1.38*
Mother qualifications	Degree or higher	387	1.00 (1.1%)
	A level/HND	974	1.24
	O level/GCSE	2093	1.13
	None	1095	1.83***
Child gender	Male	2356	1.00 (0.8%)
	Female	2316	0.70***
Child age	11	969	1.00 (3.1%)
	12	985	1.77***
	13	938	2.51***
	14	933	2.58***
	15	847	2.93***

Statistical significance: *=p<0.05, **=p<0.01, ***=p<0.001.
Note: Single observations only with substantive significance shown in brackets.
Source: Author's own analysis of BHPS data.

to education, whilst that at other stages lost significance. This suggests that it may be the lack of a current employed role model that influences young people, rather their experiences during childhood.

When considering the influence of other factors on the likelihood that young people have a negative attitude to education (Table 5.27) it can be seen that the levels of family conflict and communication had an important influence,

Table 5.28   Logistic regressions for the odds of having a negative attitude to education: Emotional well-being variables

Variable		N	Odds ratios
Troubled	No	3045	1.00 (2.3%)
	Yes	1623	1.87***
Unhappy	No	3656	1.00 (14.9%)
	Yes	978	5.75***
Low self-efficacy	No	4130	1.00 (4.2%)
	Yes	499	3.21***
Low self-esteem	No	2738	1.00 (2.1%)
	Yes	1909	1.79***

Statistical significance: *=p<0.05, **=p<0.01, ***=p<0.001.
Note: Single observations only with substantive significance shown in brackets.
Source: Author's own analysis of BHPS data.

accounting for 3.3 per cent and 4.2 per cent of the variance in having a negative attitude respectively. The only other variables to account for more than 1 per cent of the variance were age and whether the young person's mother had academic qualifications. Of the indicators of socio-economic circumstances, only housing tenure had a statistically significant relationship with young people's attitudes to education, and this only accounted for 0.7 per cent of the variance.

Young people in lone mother families or stepfamilies were more likely to have a negative attitude to education, although again, the relationship was substantively very small, accounting for just 0.6 per cent of the variance. Although a number of other variables have a statistically significant impact on the likelihood that young people have a negative attitude to school, substantively the relationships were very small.

All four indicators of emotional well-being had a significant association with having a negative attitude to school (Table 5.28). Young people who were unhappy were almost 6 times as likely to have a negative attitude to school as other young people, and this accounted for 15 per cent of the variance in having a negative attitude.

Multivariate analysis   With these results in mind multivariate analysis was then conducted. A model of best fit was established (Table 5.29) which accounted for 22.7 per cent of the variance in having a negative attitude to education, correctly predicting 85.1 per cent of cases.

Living in a currently workless household was associated with significantly increased odds of having a negative attitude to education. The other variables to enter the model were those that accounted for most variance individually in the bivariate analyses above: unhappiness and low self-efficacy, poor family communication and high family conflict, the young person's age, and the level of qualifications held by their mother.

Table 5.29 **Logistic regression for having a negative attitude to education: Model of best fit using current worklessness**

Variables entered		Odds ratios
Currently workless household	No	1.00
	Yes	1.57*
Unhappy	No	1.00
	Yes	4.06***
Poor family communication	No	1.00
	Yes	2.15***
Low self-efficacy	No	1.00
	Yes	2.24***
Mother qualifications	Degree	1.00
	A level	1.08
	O level	0.93
	None	1.87*
Age	11	1.00
	12	1.21
	13	1.97**
	14	1.73**
	15	1.81**
High family conflict	No	1.00
	Yes	1.44**

Statistical significance: $*=p<0.05$, $**=p<0.01$, $***=p<0.001$.
Constant $= 0.04***$
% correctly predicted $= 85.1\%$
Nagelkerke $R^2 = 0.227$
N = 2395
Source: Author's own analysis of BHPS data.

Summary   Overall then, living in a currently workless household was associated with young people being more likely to have a negative attitude to education, and this suggests a 'role model' effect of living in a family without a parent in employment. The young person's emotional well-being is also important (although the direction of causality is not determinable), as is the quality of family life, in terms of the level of communication and conflict experienced by young people.

Discussion and conclusions

This chapter has reviewed the existing evidence surrounding bullying, truancy, and school exclusion, reflecting on the scale and nature of these issues, and considering the individual, family, school and societal characteristics which may have an influence. Using data from the youth panel of the BHPS, analysis has been carried out to investigate any associations between parental employment and worrying about being bullied, truancy, school exclusion, and having a negative attitude to education. The impact of other factors has also been considered. Several key points have been observed.

Parental employment, and conversely unemployment, has both positive and negative effects on individual and family levels of economic, social and cultural capital, which is reflected in educational outcomes. It has been suggested that parental employment patterns influence children's educational outcomes in a number of ways: through the impact on household income; through the provision of a role model to children; and through the impact on young people's expectations and aspirations. Differences have been observed regarding the impact of parental employment on the different educational outcomes considered in this chapter.

In terms of worrying about bullying, parental employment patterns were found to have no significant impact. Levels of family conflict and communication were important influences, together with indicators of young people's emotional well-being.

The analysis conducted with regards the impact of parental employment status on young people's likelihood of truanting revealed differences for girls and boys, and for those living in dual parent and lone parent households. Paternal unemployment, and for young people in dual parent households worklessness, had a detrimental effect on the likelihood of having truanted in the last year, and this appears to operate through a mechanism of economic disadvantage (financial capital), losing significance when housing tenure, as an indicator of longer-term deprivation, was controlled for. Having ever experienced life in a workless household was associated with higher odds of truanting for those in lone mother families, and this was not related to economic circumstances. In dual parent households, part-time maternal employment appears to offer young people some protection (social capital) against truanting and again this relationship is not affected by controlling for housing tenure, suggesting that mothers' employment status effects children in ways over and above increasing household economic circumstances. Although the relationships between parental employment status and the odds of truanting were significant, having a negative attitude to education, and age had a greater impact, with housing tenure, emotional well-being and family relationships also important.

Living with an unemployed father increased the odds of exclusion from school, as did the experience of paternal unemployment during childhood. Experience of life in a workless household at any age was associated with higher odds of having been excluded from school, and these relationships retained significance when housing tenure was controlled for, suggesting that it is something about the experience of worklessness, over and above the impact on family socio-economic circumstances (financial capital) which influences school exclusion. In the bivariate analysis, having a mother in part-time as opposed to full-time employment appeared to offer young people some protection (social capital) against having been excluded from school. However, this relationship did not achieve statistical significance when other factors were controlled for in the multivariate analysis.

Similarly, living in a currently workless household, or having experienced household worklessness any stage of childhood was associated with higher odds of having a negative attitude to education. On the whole these relationships remained significant when housing tenure was controlled for, suggesting that it is not the economic deprivation that accompanies household worklessness that influences children, but perhaps the lack of a positive working role model (a form of cultural capital) to inspire children to do well at school. Having a mother currently in part-time as opposed to full-time employment reduced the odds of having a negative attitude to education by around a third, and this relationship retained significance when housing tenure was controlled for. As with the other educational outcomes discussed in this chapter, this suggests that having a mother who is not engaged in current full-time employment offers young people some protection (social capital) against negative outcomes.

Overall then, several conclusions stand out in this chapter. Firstly, it has been observed that young people's fear of bullying shows little or no association with parental employment parental employment patterns. The experience of household worklessness had a detrimental impact upon young people's truanting behaviour, the likelihood that they had been excluded from school in the past year, and on their attitude to education. A residual impact of worklessness during childhood was also observed, particularly for truancy. In general these associations retained statistical significance when housing tenure was controlled for, suggesting that it is something about the experience of worklessness, over and above the impact on family socio-economic circumstances (financial capital) which influences school exclusion. Finally, having a mother engaged in part-time employment (as opposed to full-time) was found to offer young people some protection against truanting, having been excluded from school, and from having a negative attitude to education. Again, these relationships operated independently of family socio-economic circumstances, suggesting that although mothers' employment contributes to the financial capital of a family, mothers employed on a part-time basis also provide increased social capital, or nurturing support to their children, which offers increased protection against negative educational outcomes.

Chapter 6
Educational Well-being:
Attainment and Progression

Introduction

As discussed in the previous chapter, how well children do in school is seen as crucial to their success in later life in terms of both employment opportunities and other factors, such as health and likelihood of criminal activity (Riley and Rustique-Forrester 2002; Department for Work and Pensions 2003). Although young people's attitudes to education and their educational behaviour, in terms of bullying, truancy and exclusion from school (covered in the previous chapter) are important, with the, oft criticised, political emphasis on league tables and educational performance, GCSE attainment levels and staying-on rates are key indicators. There is widespread agreement amongst education policymakers and practitioners that participation in post-16 is desirable for both individuals and society. The attainment of qualifications and skills can enable personal development as well as facilitating access to higher education. It is also important for finding employment in an economy that requires a skilled workforce (Learning and Skills Development Agency 2003). Educational participation and attainment is also fundamental in the transmission of both deprivation and privilege across generations (see for example Goldthorpe 1980; Blanden et al 2003).

There is a vast literature exploring the impact of parental employment patterns on young people's cognitive development and educational attainment (see Haveman and Wolfe 1995 for a review of the evidence, mainly from the US; O'Brien and Jones 1999; Joshi and Verropoulou 2000; Ermisch and Francesconi 2001a). This chapter sets the importance of educational attainment and post-16 participation in context, before considering the individual, parental, family, and other factors which have an influence on these outcomes, using a forms of capital approach to consider the meaning of the empirical evidence. Parental employment and unemployment affect the levels of economic, social and cultural capital available to individuals and within families. Young people's educational outcomes can be influenced by their parents' employment patterns through the impact on household income; through the provision of a role model to children; and through the impact on young people's expectations and aspirations. Data from a special follow-on sample from the British Household Panel Survey (BHPS) (see Chapter 4 for details) are used to consider the impact of parental employment patterns during childhood and adolescence on GCSE attainment, and both the intention and actuality of staying on in full-time education post-16.

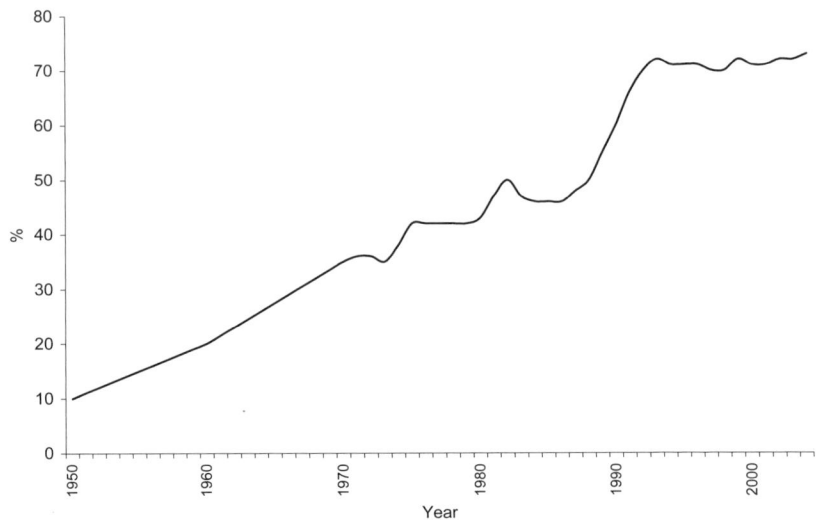

Figure 6.1   Participation of 16-year-olds in full-time education, 1950–2004
Source: Based on DfES figures. 1950–1993 taken from Clark et al (2005); 1994–2004
from DFES (2006).

Historical trends

This section sets the importance of educational attainment and post-16 participation
in context, by firstly considering trends in staying-on rates and attainment of
qualifications at age 16. Figure 6.1 shows that in 1950 around 10 per cent of young
people stayed on at school at age 16, a figure which increased steadily to 35 per
cent in 1970. The 1970s and early 1980s saw a stepped increase in participation,
followed by a much faster rise from 1987 to a peak of around 70 per cent in 1993,
since when staying-on rates have remained fairly constant.

Despite the considerable increase in participation, rates are still low by
international standards (see Figure 6.2, which compares participation rates for
17-year-olds), with the UK just fifth from the bottom of the Organisation for
Economic Co-operation and Development league table in 2002 (OECD 2004),
and according to the recent 14–19 White paper 'that is now the burning problem
facing our education service' (DFES 2005f, 10).

Human capital theory (Becker 1964) would suggest that the decision to stay
on at school at age 16 is made on a cost-benefit basis compared with the available
alternatives, with the other main choice being entry directly into the labour market.
Thus it seems intuitive that some of the trends in staying-on rates will coincide
with trends in unemployment. Between 1979 and 1986, and again between
1989 and 1993, the UK witnessed the sharpest rises in unemployment since the
Second World War (Robinson 1999). Youth unemployment rates, in particular,

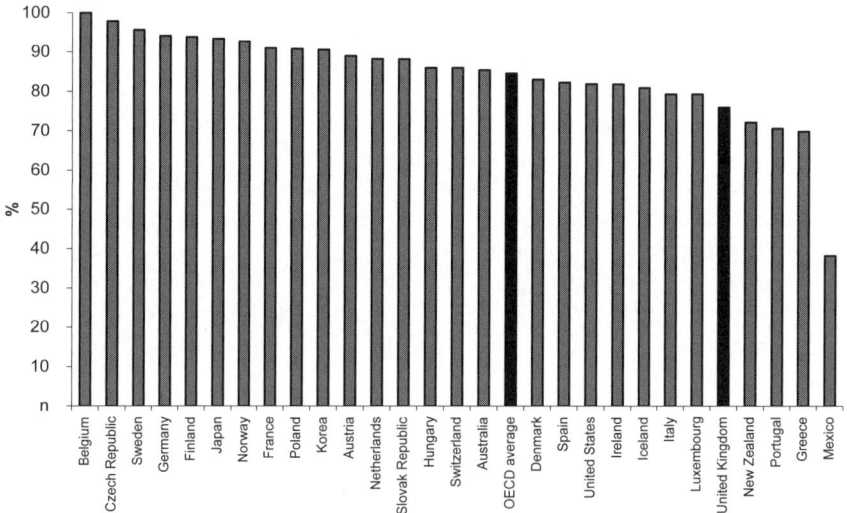

Figure 6.2   International comparison of participation in education and training at age 17, 2002
Source: OECD (2004).

soared to record levels (Hart 1988; White and Smith 1994). The collapse of the manufacturing sector of employment, which began in the mid-1970s, the shift to service occupations, and the growing proportion of part-time work, together with increasing participation by adult women, impacted upon the prospects of school leavers, and radically altered the sorts of jobs available to young people entering the labour market direct from compulsory schooling (Biggart 2002). With a low probability of finding employment in the short-term the costs of remaining in full-time education beyond age 16 are relatively small, and many have argued that the paucity of job opportunities for young people has contributed to the rapid growth in participation in further education over recent years (McVicar and Rice 2001).

The attainment of educational qualifications at age 16 has been found to be a strong predictor of post-16 participation (Pearce and Hillman 1998), and the introduction of GCSEs in 1987/8 has been proposed as the most important explanation for the rise in post-16 participation since this time (Robinson 1999; see also Delorenzi and Robinson 2005). The GCSE 'represented something of a departure from the previous O (Ordinary) level system, in that everyone took the same examination (regardless of ability) and thus (at least in theory) could achieve the top grade' (Clark et al 2005, 72). This seemed to facilitate a sharp increase in both the attainment of students at age 15, and consequently their likelihood of staying on after the compulsory school-leaving age.

Since New Labour came to power in 1997, a number of initiatives have been introduced with the aim of increasing participation in post-compulsory education and reducing the numbers of young people not in education, training or employment (NEET). These have included the Education Maintenance Allowance (EMA), the Connexions Service and Connexions Card, and changes to both academic and vocational education more broadly (DFEE 1999b; DFES 2005f; also see Coles et al 2002 for a discussion). The EMA was piloted and evaluated, before being rolled out nationally in 2004. Evidence from the evaluation (Ashworth et al 2001; Middleton et al 2005) suggests that the introduction of this monetary allowance for young people from low-income families significantly increased participation in post-compulsory education, and had a more moderate impact on attainment. The New Deal for Young People, the new minimum wage for 16- and 17-year-olds, and reforms to the apprenticeship system have also been focussed on reducing youth unemployment.

This section has briefly looked at the background to post-16 participation and the achievement of educational qualifications; the importance of staying on and achieving good qualification will be outlined in the next section.

Importance of staying-on and educational qualifications

Participation levels post-16 are important because of the impact on young people's future life chances, and the costs to individuals, the economy and society of educational failure are high. Young people's achievement and choices at age 16 affect both their own futures and the supply of education and trained labour in the economy. Organisation of Economic Co-operation and Development (OECD) statistics indicate that labour force participation rates rise with educational attainment in most OECD countries, and that better educated populations are a common factor behind economic growth in these countries (OECD 2001).

Educational attainment is strongly related to unemployment and earnings. Teenagers who fail to achieve even basic qualifications are more likely to be unemployed or inactive in later life. When they do get jobs, they tend to be less skilled, less well paid and more insecure (Delorenzi and Robinson 2005). In spring 2005, 88 per cent of working-age people with a degree or equivalent in the United Kingdom were in employment compared with only 48 per cent of those with no qualification. In addition, average gross weekly earnings in the United Kingdom for both men and women with a degree or equivalent were double those of men and women with no qualifications (Office for National Statistics 2006).

The negative impact that lower levels of educational qualifications have on employment and career opportunities in turn affect other outcomes, including happiness and well-being (see, for example, Clark and Oswald 2002a; Layard 2005). Those with lower levels of qualifications were also found to be at greater risk of becoming a teenage or lone parent, suffering mental health problems, and being a smoker (SEU 1999; Hobcraft 2000; SEU 2004), and later mental and physical health problems were also more common amongst those who had significant spells of non-participation between ages 16 and 18 (Stone et al 2000). Educational attainment at age 16 is the most important predictor of future participation in learning and of labour market opportunities. Young people with no formal qualifications were found to be between two and three times more likely to be excluded socially (Riley and Rustique-Forrester 2002), and other research (Bynner and Parsons 1998; Hobcraft 1998; Robinson and Oppenheim 1998) has identified educational attainment to be an effective predictor of social exclusion in adulthood.

As we shall see in the next section, the likelihood of participation in post-compulsory education and high attainment is not equal for all young people. This has important consequences for the perpetuation of social inequalities and intergenerational mobility.

Influences on staying-on and educational qualifications

Introduction

There has been much research conducted on the factors associated with young people's educational attainment and likelihood of staying-on post-16, including the impact of individual, parental and family characteristics, cultural, social, and economic factors. Theoretically, positive educational outcomes are influenced by the different forms of capital – financial, human, cultural and social – available to the young person (Bourdieu 1983; Coleman 1988; Furstenberg and Hughes 1995; Sullivan 2001). To this end, parental employment patterns are important in the extent to which they represent available capital, but other factors including the quality of family relationships, parents own educational qualifications, and young people's own capabilities, attitudes and aspirations are also important.

Parental employment

There is a vast literature exploring the impact of parental employment on children's educational outcomes, together with theoretical explanations of the empirical findings. The development of children's cognitive ability is undoubtedly multi-faceted, potentially affected by parental working patterns in a number of ways. Although considered separately in the next section, increased income derived from employment enables parents to invest more in their children's human capital development, through the purchase of books, personal tuition or private education (Becker 1981; Becker and Tomes 1986).

But parental employment impacts on more than just the financial resources available to the family. Employed parents have less non-work time available to spend interacting with children, reading to them and assisting with homework, which may have negative implications for cognitive development and educational attainment. Parental involvement in children's education, in terms of attending school or class events, or volunteering at the school may be affected by patterns of parental employment, at least in part because parental employment competes for time that could be used participating in school activities. Winquist Nord et al (1997) found that in dual parent families in the US (controlling for other variables including family income, parents' education, child's age, sex and race) mothers who worked more than 35 hours per week were significantly less likely to be involved in their children's schools than mothers who worked part-time, although fathers in these families were more likely to be highly involved. According to Coleman (1988) parents' capacity to forge relationships and networks with other adults in school and in the community is a key element in building social capital, together with the relationships between parents and their children. Consequently, if parental employment reduces the amount of time that parents spend with their children, this would have a detrimental impact on the development of social capital, thereby impairing children's school success. Parental inputs of time, especially from the mother, have been shown to be positively associated with children's educational achievement (Leibowitz 1974), and a recent review of the research (Desforges 2003) concluded that parental involvement, particularly in terms of at-home good parenting has a significant positive effect on children's attainment.

Parental employment patterns also have important implications for the development of educational expectations and aspirations, both amongst parents and children, through the provision of a role model image and cultural expectations. Parents who have acquired high occupational status will be more likely to encourage their children to follow educational routes (Bradley and Nguyen 2003), whilst growing up with an unemployed parent might lower a child's own expectations, by conveying a negative image to children, and not providing them with the incentives to invest in their own education (Ermisch et al 2001). In interviews in both the UK and US, highly educated parents and those from the higher social classes 'confidently assumed things would go well' for their children, whilst those from the lower social classes spoke of how they wanted their children to do well, 'but did not always confidently assume that they would' (Devine 2004, 179–80). This parental confidence, and also 'knowing how the system works' (forms of cultural capital) undoubtedly influence children's aspirations and achievements.

The empirical evidence relating to the effects of early and current parental employment on children's cognitive development and educational attainment is mixed and inconclusive. Indeed, Haveman and Wolfe (1995), in a review of the evidence (mainly from the US) concluded that some studies identify significant adverse effects, whilst others find no significant effect, or even suggest a favourable impact. Research in the US has tended to concentrate solely on the impact of maternal employment on cognitive outcomes for children at different stages of development (Bogenschneider and Steinberg 1994; Muller 1995; Harvey 1999; Smith et al 2000; Han et al 2001; Zick et al 2001).

Turning to UK evidence, Joshi and Verropoulou (2000) studied 1,700 school children whose mothers had been part of the 1958 birth cohort study (National Child Development Study (NCDS)). These children were aged 5–17 at the time of interview in 1991, when they were assessed for reading, maths, and behavioural adjustment, and account was taken of both early and current maternal employment patterns. Fathers' employment was considered in some cases, mainly in relation to whether a child lived in a workless household, but was not studied in it's own right. These analyses suggested that controlling for the economic circumstances of the family, mothers' qualifications and own test scores as a child, maternal employment in the first year of a child's life had a significant negative effect on their later reading ability (at the time of the survey). However, some employment by the mother when the child was aged one to four had a positive significant effect on children's later mathematics scores, but no significant effect on their reading. Having a mother in full-time employment at the time of the survey had a positive effect on a child's maths score, whereas living in a workless household had a negative effect on a child's maths score, but no significant effect on their reading ability. This might tentatively suggest that interaction between mother and child at a very early age, including the introduction of books, may lay the groundwork for a child learning to read later on, although no assessment is made of the actual time a mother spent with her child, or the level of involvement of the father. The development of mathematical ability seems to be more sensitive to the implications of later employment and unemployment. There are some problems with representativeness of the sample of children in the NCDS second generation, as it consisted only of children born to female members of the NCDS by the time they were 28. This excludes older mothers, who are likely to be more highly educated (Dex et al 1996), and this in itself may positively effect children's maths and reading scores.

The second sample used in the Joshi and Verropoulou study (2000) consisted of children who were born in 1970, and tracked into adulthood (The 1970 Birth Cohort Study (BCS)), enabling consideration not only of the effect of maternal employment on children's maths and reading ability at age 10, but also analysis of a series of outcomes in early adulthood. In this instance mothers' employment in their children's pre-school years was not related to either maths or reading scores at age 10. However, a number of other factors, including fathers' social class at birth, either parent leaving school before age 15, and receipt of free school meals did have a significant impact on both maths and reading ability at age 10, suggesting that factors other than maternal employment have a greater impact upon maths and reading ability. Looking at later educational achievement, it is seen that both men and women are slightly less likely to obtain higher levels of qualifications if their mothers had been employed before they were age five. A whole range of other factors need to be taken into account here, such as whether the father, if present, was employed, the number of hours mothers were employed, the job they did and the income they received, information which unfortunately is not available in the BCS70.

One of the problems with both these studies is that there is no information available on the type, quality or quantity of childcare used by families when mothers were employed, which is likely to have contributed to the outcomes observed. In addition it must be noted that the individuals in these studies were pre-schoolers up to 30 years ago, and as Joshi and Verropoulou (2000) recognise, maternal employment then may have been more stressful both for the mother and child, as it was less the norm. The employment patterns of fathers are, on the whole, neglected from these analyses, and thus there is a need for the impact of maternal employment on children to be studied within a whole family context.

Ermisch and Francesconi (2000, 2001a) also considered the effect of parental employment at various stages in a child's life on their later educational attainment, in terms of obtaining A level qualifications or higher. They used various samples of young people drawn from the British Household Panel Survey (BHPS) born between 1970 and 1981, claiming that this data is 'more recent and a better reflection of contemporary family life' than the NCDS and other birth cohort studies (Ermisch and Francesconi 2001a, 10), and has the advantage of providing a partial control for various unmeasured factors by comparing outcomes not just between families but also within families, by comparing outcomes for pairs of siblings. The BHPS also has the advantage of having more detailed information on parents' employment patterns, although no data is available on the type, quality or quantity of childcare used by families. The models used controlled for many child characteristics, including age, gender, and number of siblings, and parental characteristics, including age of father at birth, age of mother at birth, mothers' education, fathers' education, mothers' and fathers' Hope-Goldthorpe measures of occupational prestige, and fathers' working time. Investigations generally found that longer periods of full-time work for mothers of pre-school children tended to reduce the chance of gaining an A level or equivalent, and there was a similar although less pronounced effect of periods of part-time employment. However, longer periods of full-time work when the children were aged 6–10 increased their chance of achieving A level or higher qualifications.

This study also considered the impact of paternal employment, but found no significant associations between fathers' employment and children's outcomes. Missing data on fathers' employment was a real problem, as was the fact that most of the fathers in the samples were employed most of the time, with the lack of variation making it unlikely that any differences in the outcomes for the young adults would be associated with fathers' employment in any significant way (Ermisch and Francesconi 2001a, 33). In a review of US studies, Harvey (1999) similarly concluded that there were few significant effects on children's development that could be attributed to fathers' patterns of employment.

These results suggest that maternal employment when children are very young impacts in different ways to that when children are older. For pre-school children, it could be suggested that the time employed mothers spend away from their children has some negative implications for their cognitive development, both in the short-term (although this evidence is weak), and in terms of later academic achievement. However, when children are older and attending school, maternal employment appears to have positive implications for children's educational achievement, perhaps through the increase in financial resources (economic capital) which maternal employment may bring to a family, and the provision of a role model image to children (cultural capital).

A further study by Kiernan (1996) adds weight to this suggestion. Her analysis of the 1958 National Child Development Study (NCDS) found that having a mother in work when a child was aged 16 was associated with a higher probability of young women gaining qualifications, that this was particularly true in lone parent families, but that there was no similar statistically significant association for young men. This finding refers to a generation of children brought up in an era when employed mothers were less common, divorce was less prevalent and never-married lone parenthood was rare. It is by no means clear that the finding would apply to young people today. But to the extent employed mothers provide a positive role model of self-reliance, then beneficial consequences of having an employed mother might be seen for the current cohort of young people.

Qualitative research suggests that some form of household employment may be important to the acquisition of personal softer skills. Findings suggest that many pupils who grow up in workless households are not exposed to working role models, and as a result fail to learn in the home about the behavioural aspects of work (Kleinman et al 1998).

Examining the relationship between parental employment patterns when children are aged between 13 and 15 and GCSE attainment, O'Brien and Jones (1999) also suggest that maternal employment has positive effects, particularly if the employment is undertaken on a part-time basis. Results showed that children living in dual worker households where the mother was working part-time were 70 per cent less likely to gain low grades (all D-G grades or nil passes at GCSE) than children in households in which the father was the sole earner. They were also 53 per cent less likely to attain low grades than children in dual worker households in which the mother worked on a full-time basis.

There is less evidence regarding the effect of parental employment patterns on young people's staying-on decisions. Leslie and Drinkwater (1999) and Gregg (2000) report a positive effect of parental employment on the staying-on decision. Rice (1999) obtains this result for mothers' employment for boys. Armstrong (1999) reports that young people whose mothers are employed full-time are more likely to stay on but this variable has little effect on other outcomes. More striking is that fathers' employment status has no effect whatsoever on the choice made by students.

In summary, this section has considered some of the evidence relating to the impact of parental employment patterns on young people's educational attainment and on their likelihood of staying on in full-time education post-16. It has been seen that maternal employment, particularly full-time employment, when children are very young may have a detrimental impact upon their later educational achievement, but maternal employment when children are older has a positive effect. These relationships suggest that maternal employment affects children through its impact on household income (financial capital), through the provision of a role model (cultural capital), and nurturing support (social capital), particularly when children are very young.

Socio-economic circumstances

In addition to the impact of parental employment per se, there is much evidence relating to the impact of family social class, income and other socio-economic factors, such as housing tenure, on young people's educational achievement and progression. It is important to stress here that parental employment patterns are strongly correlated with class, income and family socio-economic circumstances.

Family/parental income has long been believed to be an important factor determining educational attainment and achievement, because it is the primary determinant of resources available to finance education, as discussed above. Low income, as indicated by free school meal eligibility, is associated with low levels of educational attainment at all levels. Recent research (West et al 1999) has shown that the proportion of children dependent on income support recipients (at a local authority level) is very strongly related to levels of educational attainment. The strong correlation between low income and GCSE attainment is reiterated in analysis undertaken at school level (Levacic and Hardman 1999). It is possibly the case that those from low income families will be under pressure to be earning rather than studying, although Fletcher and Lockhart (2002) note that it is only for a small minority of learners that financial circumstances influence participation in education. Macdonald and Marsh (2001) offer another explanation for lower rates of participation amongst young people from lower income families, who are found to be disillusioned with the value of education, consider it irrelevant and are sceptical about whether qualifications lead to employment. This again relates to the role model presented to children by their parents, and the expectations that parents have for their children's futures.

Analysis of data from the Youth Cohort Study (YCS) suggested that young people whose parents were in the higher social classes were more likely to both achieve 5 or more GCSE grades at grade A*–C and be in full-time education at age 16 (Cheng 1995; Brooks 1998; Payne 2001). As can be seen in Figure 6.3, the difference is large: in 2004, 85 per cent of the children of parents from higher professional occupations stayed on at school post-16, with 76 per cent of them achieving 5 or more GCSEs at grades A*–C; this compares with 33 per cent of those children of parents from routine occupations staying-on, and 63 per cent achieving at least 5 good GCSEs (DfES 2005d). The relationship between parents' socio-economic status and children's participation in post-compulsory education has also been established using longitudinal data (Rumberger 1983; Micklewright 1989).

The associations between housing tenure, housing conditions and educational attainment and progression are also well established, with individuals living in council housing less likely to attain qualifications and stay on post-16 than those living in other forms of accommodation (Bosworth 1994; Ermisch 2001b; Payne 2001). In the absence of a direct measure of household income, housing tenure was used by O'Brien and Jones (1999) as a proxy of children's material well-being. Children living in owner-occupied accommodation were over three times as likely to achieve good GCSEs than those in rented accommodation.

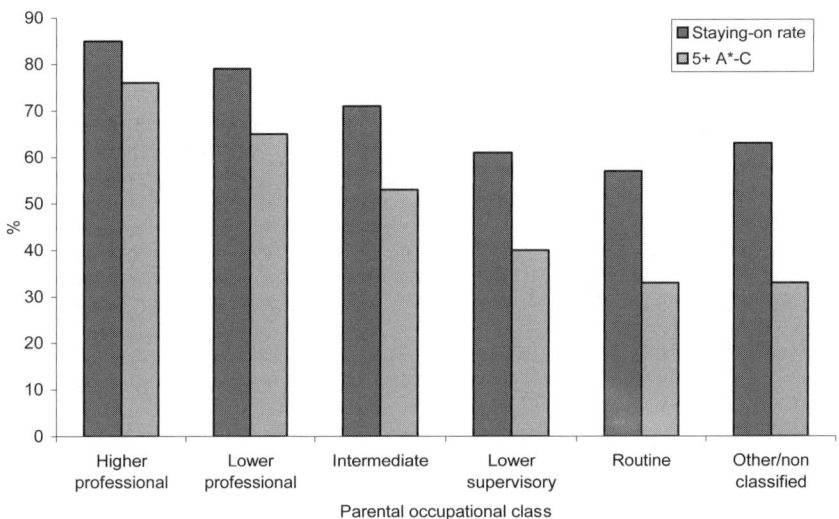

Figure 6.3   GCSE attainment and participation in post-compulsory education at age 16, by parental occupational class, 2004
Source: DFES, 2005d.

Given the strong correlation between parental employment patterns and class, income and family socio-economic circumstances the evidence presented here is not surprising. Young people living in households with lower socio-economic circumstances, whether this be low income, lower social classes, or living in council or poor quality housing, are less likely to achieve good qualifications at age 16 and are less likely to stay on in full-time education post-16.

Parental education

Parental educational attainment has long been recognised as an important predictor of a child's educational attainment and likelihood of staying on in education post-16. Children of parents with higher levels of educational qualifications are more likely to both achieve good GCSE results and stay on in full-time education (Cheng 1995; Ermisch 2001b; Payne 2002). In 2004, 85 per cent of 16-year-olds with at least one parent with a degree were in full-time education, compared to 77 per cent of young people with at least one parent with A levels but not a degree, and 64 per cent of young people with parents who had neither a degree nor A levels (DFES 2005d). The difference in GCSE attainment was even greater.

The means by which better educated parents confer educational advantage to their children remains open to question. Research has highlighted the importance of parents' human, cultural and social capital. Clearly if parents struggle with their own literacy or numeracy, they are less able to assist their child's learning in this respect, and interventions that have increased parents' human capital along side that of the child, such as family literacy projects, have been favourably evaluated (Brooks et al 1998). Whitty et al (1999) suggest that educated parents have higher levels of social capital and that this has a positive impact on their children's attainment. When thinking specifically of the decision to stay on in full-time education at age 16, parents are more likely to encourage their children to stay on despite poor GCSE results if they themselves have had a good education (Payne 2001). In addition, parental education is likely to be an indicator of the amount of intellectual heredity that children receive (Haveman and Wolfe 1995). As Devine 2004, writes well-educated parents 'approached the business of educating their children with more confidence', understanding 'the system', and being able to mobilise their cultural resources to ensure their children's educational and occupational success (180).

Family structure

In the same way that maternal employment reduces the amount of time available to spend with children, thus potentially reducing the development of family social capital, so Coleman (1988) suggested that 'the physical absence of adults may be described as a structural deficiency in family social capital ... [and] ... the most prominent element of structural deficiency in modern families is the single-parent family' (111). The transfer of social capital may be adversely affected, for the contacts and social relations that children receive from absent parents may be reduced. Children raised in lone parent families receive, on average, less parental supervision. To the extent that the absent parent discontinues the investment of human and social capital in their children, the loss of regular contact and support may have a negative effect for children (Amato and Booth 1997). In terms of the impact of life in a stepfamily, whereas parental remarriage often leads to a significant improvement in the financial situation of children, it does not always lead to a significant gain in terms of parental supervision. Although stepparents potentially contribute both in terms of their time and financial resources, some evidence indicates that non-biological parents tend to be less involved with stepchildren as compared with biological parents – and may in some cases disrupt relations with the absent parent (Amato 1998). Indeed, in some situations the concept of stepparent may be too strong, since the adult may be viewed more as the parent's partner rather than a parent (McLanahan 2000). To this end, living in a lone parent or stepfamily can be taken to reduce both parental human capital and family social capital available to children, thus potentially having a detrimental impact on educational attainment and progression.

The evidence however is mixed, suggesting either that lone parenthood is non-significantly or only weakly associated with educational attainment (Gregg and Machin 1997), or that children from couple households are significantly more likely to do well than children from other family types (including lone parent and stepparent families) (Ermisch 2001c; Ermisch et al 2004; Scott 2004).

Ely et al (2000) used data from the BCS70 and a comparable survey conducted in the West of Scotland to consider whether the relationship between family structure and outcomes for children varies between geographical regions. They found that in both studies, the odds of both not achieving any O levels and gaining fewer than 5 O levels were higher for both those in lone parent families and reconstituted families than in intact families. Those in reconstituted families did worse than those in lone parent families, and those who suffered family disruption as a result of separation did worse than those who had a parent die. The apparent disadvantage for those in lone parent families virtually disappears once family income is controlled for. In addition, once elements of family social capital – family time (based on respondents reports of engagement in a range of activities with their families) and relationship with parents (based on respondents' self-reports) – were taken into account, those in lone parent families and those disrupted by the death of a parent were, if anything, more likely to achieve examination success than their counterparts in intact families.

Analysis of the BHPS (Ermisch and Francesconi 2001a) showed that experience of life in a lone mother family at any time during childhood, particularly before the age of 11, was associated with a significantly lower probability of achieving at least one A level or higher. This association becomes weaker when income is controlled for, suggesting that the negative impact of lone parenthood on educational achievement operates partly through lower incomes and wealth (financial capital) in lone parent families.

The circumstances of family disruption are also relevant. The children of widows, for example, seem to experience fewer negative effects than do divorcees. Similarly the addition of a stepparent into a family also appears to have negative effects (Kiernan 1992). In addition, Elliot and Richards (1991), found that children whose parents had divorced were more likely to leave school at the minimum age, less likely at age 23 to have gained a university qualification, and more likely to have no qualifications, compared to those whose parents had remained together. However, there are no significant differences in the chances of getting a university qualification by age 23 between those living with a lone mother or with their mother and a stepfather. The risk of adverse outcomes in terms of educational achievement, for young people in stepfamilies compared with those in lone parent families appears higher for children who were older on entering the stepfamily (Rodgers and Pryor 1998). This is possibly due to the dynamics of relationships with stepparents. Young children in stepfamilies seem to fare better, possibly because it is easier to adapt to a new family structure at an age when they have had a relatively short period of living with either both or just one birth parent.

Family size, birth order, and the sex and ages of other siblings have also been associated with educational attainment. The parental human and social capital available to later-born children and those in larger families is lower, reducing parents' ability to invest in their children's educational attainment. A trade-off exists between quantity and quality of children, since parents' resources and time are limited and must be spread more thinly when they have more children (Becker and Tomes 1976; Becker and Tomes 1979; Hanushek 1992).

Children from larger families were found to do worse in terms of educational attainment (Bosworth 1994), and children lower down the birth order did worse than those higher up the birth order (Iacovou 2001). These findings are consistent with theoretical predictions, but the finding that 'only' children performed worse than those from two-child families, even controlling for a whole range of parental and school characteristics, is not. For the UK, several empirical studies report the negative effect of family size on post-16 participation (Micklewright 1989; Micklewright et al 1990; Armstrong 1999).

Family structure appears to have quite an important influence on children's educational attainment, with those in lone parent or stepfamilies doing less well than those in intact families. The evidence seems to suggest that the negative impact of lone parenthood on educational achievement operates partly through lower income and socio-economic circumstances, but family disruption and instability appear also to play a part.

Other aspects of family

Although family structure has been seen to have an important influence on educational attainment and participation, what those families do, and the strength and quality of the relationships within the family is also vital. What young people think and do by the time they are age 17 is strongly influenced by their family (Durkin 1995), and parental views, attitudes in the family to education, and whether or not there is an expectation that a young person should study (aspects of cultural capital) are strong influences that can sometimes be taken for granted (Payne 2002). Talking within the family about personal matters and parental ambitions for the child's education is an indicator for higher social capital (Coleman 1988), and family relationships also contribute to the social capital available to children in the family, and thus potentially to educational outcomes. Direct parental mentoring such as monitoring homework is associated with favourable educational outcomes, but also associated with such outcomes is more general parent-child communication and parental involvement in wider social networks (Croll 2004).

Indeed, the evidence would suggest that young people who report talking to their parents 'on most days' have greater success at GCSE level than those who 'hardly ever' talk about things that matter, even when socio-economic circumstances are taken into account (Croll 2004; Scott 2004). Quarrelling with parents was found to reduce GCSE success, although the interpretation of this is problematic, as quarrels may have been triggered by problem behaviours or lack of effort at school (Scott 2004).

Aspects of family covered in this section encompass elements of social and cultural capital. Parental attitudes and aspirations, and the quality of family relationships are important influences on children's educational attainment.

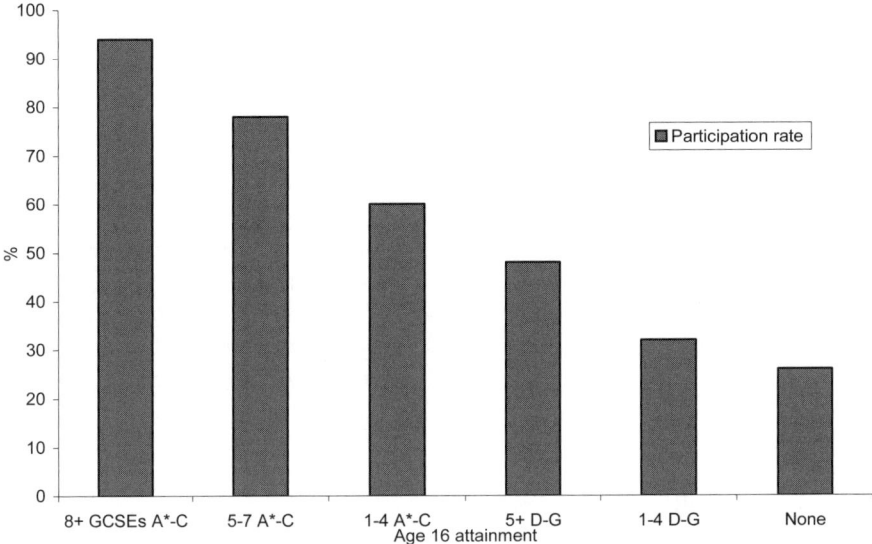

Figure 6.4   Participation in post-compulsory education at age 16 by Year 11 attainment, 2004
Source: DFES, 2005d.

Ability and school behaviour

Human capital theory highlights the importance of an individual's ability in the decision to invest in more education or training (Becker 1993). Young people with higher ability will have a greater demand for more education since they are more able to reap the benefit from investment in post-secondary education. However, testing this theory empirically is not straightforward. There are many relevant dimensions to ability and whatever measure is considered it will reflect both individual inherent attributes and also the outcome of earlier educational experiences. Thus in practice, data availability tends to determine what particular ability measure is used (Machin and Vignoles 2005).

Empirical studies invariably report that ability is a powerful predictor of the decision to stay on (Christensen et al 1975; Micklewright 1989; Averett and Burton 1996; Rice 2000; Payne 2003). Exam achievement is by far the most widely available measure of academic ability. Data from the Youth Cohort Study (Figure 6.4) illustrates that virtually all those who attained 8 or more GCSEs at grades A*–C stayed on post-16, compared with little over a quarter of those who achieved no passes (DfES 2005d).

An alternative is to use data from tests administered to children earlier on in their lives and see how such test scores relate to subsequent achievement or the staying-on decision, and the Birth Cohort Studies (NCDS and BCS) provide such an opportunity. Having a low score in mathematics or reading tests at age 7 was strongly related with being less likely to stay on in post-16 education (Gregg and Machin 1998). Some authors are critical of the use of such scores as indicators of underlying ability, because 'of course by age 7 the social and economic background of a child and indeed their early educational experiences could already be exerting a powerful influence' (Robinson 1999, 159).

In addition to the importance of young people's actual ability in predicting whether they will stay on at school, their perceptions of their ability, and attitudes to education also play a part. The association between negative self-perception, attitudes to school and actual attainment can become self-reinforcing, forming a downward spiral (Payne 2003). As we saw in Chapter 5 truancy and exclusion from school are associated with lower rates of academic achievement and lower staying-on rates.

Emotional well-being

The positive relationship between good emotional well-being, particularly self-esteem, and educational attainment is fairly well established, although the direction of causality is questioned by some (Skaalvik and Hagtvet 1990; Baumeister et al 2003; Flouri 2006; Trautwein et al 2006). Young people with high levels of self-esteem and self-worth are more likely to believe that they will do well and be more motivated, thus achieving better results. On the other hand achieving good results at school can really boost individuals' self-esteem (Ross and Broh 2000). Programmes that teach social and emotional competence have been shown to result in a wide range of educational gains, including improved school attendance, higher motivation, and higher morale (Durlak and Wells 1997; Catalano et al 2002).

Gender

Girls generally outperform boys at GCSE level and are also more likely to enter full-time education at age 16 (DFES 2005d). In 2004, 59 per cent of girls achieved five or more GCSEs at grades A*–C compared with 49 per cent of boys. However, at the lower levels of GCSE attainment, the gender gap is smaller in percentage point terms, with 4 per cent of boys and 3 per cent of girls failing to gain any GCSE qualifications. In terms of staying on in education post-16, the trend is similar, with 67 per cent of boys staying on, compared with 77 per cent of girls.

Summary

This section has reviewed the literature relating to influences on educational attainment and post-16 participation, considering individual, parental, family, and other factors. In many ways educational well-being contributes to young people's quality of life and to their future prospects.

There is a great deal of evidence relating to the impact of parental employment, mainly just maternal employment, on children's educational outcomes. It has been seen that maternal employment, particularly full-time employment, when children are very young may have a detrimental impact upon their later educational achievement, but maternal employment when children are older generally has a positive effect. Paternal employment, where considered, generally had a positive impact on young people's educational outcomes, through improving the family's socio-economic circumstances. These relationships suggest that parental employment affects children through the impact on household income (financial capital), through the provision of a role model (cultural capital), and nurturing support (social capital), particularly when children are very young.

Young people living in households with lower socio-economic circumstances, whether this be low income, lower social class, or living in council or poor quality housing, were less likely to achieve good qualifications at age 16 and were less likely to stay on in full-time education post-16, again suggesting the importance of financial capital for young people's educational outcomes. Children of parents with higher levels of educational qualifications were more likely to both achieve good GCSE results and stay on in full-time education, and parental attitudes and aspirations, and the quality of family relationships were also important influences on children's educational attainment.

Educational attainment and progression in the BHPS

Introduction

So far this chapter has considered the importance of educational attainment and staying on in education post-16. Parental employment patterns have a significant influence on educational attainment and the likelihood of staying on at school post-16 through the impact on household income, through the time that parents have available to spend with their children, through the development of cultural capital, and the presentation of a role model image to children. Other aspects of family life, including the quality of relationships, family structure, parental educational qualifications, and socio-economic circumstances also relate to young people's educational well-being.

The second half of this chapter uses two samples from the BHPS: firstly, a sample of young people aged 11–15 from the youth panel; and secondly, a follow-on sample of young people from the British Household Panel Survey who were interviewed in both the young persons' survey and later in the adult survey (see Chapter 4 for more details). This allows us to examine the effects of parental employment patterns, family life and early adolescent characteristics on later educational attainment and progression into post-compulsory education.

The key questions to be addressed here are: how do parental employment patterns relate to young people's educational outcomes, in terms of the intention and actuality of staying on in full-time education post-16 and the achievement of qualifications at age 16; is there any evidence for mechanisms of financial, social

Table 6.1   Intention to stay on at school post-16, by age

%			Age			Total
	11	**12**	**13**	**14**	**15**	
Stay	66.5	70.1	73.2	74.1	76.2	72.0
Don't know	23.1	19.9	16.6	14.8	10.2	17.0
Leave	10.4	10.0	10.1	11.0	13.6	11.0
N =	1357	1382	1341	1361	1284	6725

Source: Author's own analysis of BHPS data.

and cultural capital; what other factors are important; and are there any differences observed between this sample, and those used in previous research.

Expectation of leaving school at age 16

As we have seen, young people's expectations, together with those of their families and peers have an important influence on attainment and progression. Of the full sample of young people around a tenth (11 per cent) said that they expected to leave school at age 16. Table 6.1 shows that at all ages, a majority of young people knew whether or not they wanted to stay on at school, and not surprisingly, the percentage giving a definite answer increased as they got older. Almost one in four of the young people answered 'don't know' to this question at age 11, whilst by age 15 this figure was one in ten.

The proportion of young people in the sample planning to leave school at age 16 remained fairly constant throughout the first four years of secondary school (ages 11–14), at around 10 per cent, with an increase at age 16 as young people got closer to making the actual decision of whether to leave school or to stay on. In aggregate there was a shift over time from 'don't know' into definite plans to leave or stay, with around three-quarters (77.1 per cent) of the age 11 'don't knows' intending to stay on when interviewed at age 15, and only 11.4 per cent intending to leave. Figure 6.5 shows that girls were consistently more likely to say that they planned to stay on at school than boys.

Influence of parental employment patterns   Here we look at the impact of paternal and maternal employment patterns, considered separately, on the odds that young people expected to leave school at age 16. Table 6.2 shows that having a father out of the labour market, either currently or at any stage during childhood was associated with higher odds of expecting to leave school at age 16. The impact of paternal unemployment when the young people were very young (aged 0–1 or 1–5) had a greater impact on the odds ratios, more than doubling the odds that they expected to leave school at age 16, than that when they were older. These analyses were repeated controlling for current housing tenure, as an indicator of socio-economic circumstances. The negative impact of paternal unemployment

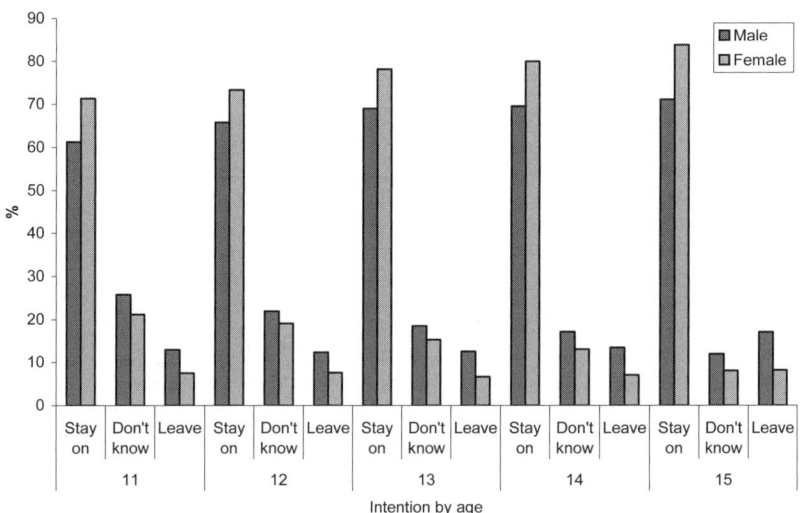

Figure 6.5   Intention to stay on at school post-16, by age and gender
Source: Author's own analysis of BHPS data.

Table 6.2   Logistic regressions for the odds of expecting to leave school at age 16: Parental employment patterns controlling for housing tenure

Variable		N	Odds ratios	Controlling for tenure
Father current employment	Employed	4623	1.00 (1.0%)	1.00 (3.7%)
	Not in employment	826	1.77***	1.22
Mother current employment	Full-time	2361	0.58***	0.74**
	Part-time	2232	0.54***	0.67***
	Not in employment	2132	1.00 (1.5%)	1.00 (4.1%)
Father employment (child 0–1)	Employed	3670	1.00 (1.8%)	1.00 (3.6%)
	Not in employment	298	2.62***	2.03***
Father employment (child 1–5)	Employed	3647	1.00 (1.7%)	1.00 (3.7%)
	Not in employment	329	2.49***	1.88***
Father employment (child 5–11)	Employed	3464	1.00 (0.9%)	1.00 (3.0%)
	Not in employment	413	1.92***	1.27
Mother employment (child 0–1)	Employed full-time	497	0.78	0.79
	Employed part-time	566	0.75	0.84
	Not in employment	4239	1.00 (0.2%)	1.00 (3.4%)
Mother employment (child 1–5)	Employed full-time	759	0.79	0.92
	Employed part-time	1105	0.74*	0.87
	Not in employment	3490	1.00 (0.3%)	1.00 (3.1%)
Mother employment (child 5–11)	Employed full-time	1248	0.60***	0.74*
	Employed part-time	1692	0.58***	0.70**
	Not in employment	2775	1.00 (1.3%)	1.00 (3.7%)

Statistical significance: *=p<0.05, **=p<0.01, ***=p<0.001.
Note: Single observations only with substantive significance shown in brackets.
Source: Author's own analysis of BHPS data.

when the young people were aged 0–1 and 1–5 on the likelihood of expecting to leave school at age 16 remained statistically significant, but the impact of more recent paternal unemployment lost statistical significance. This suggests that the influence of current and recent paternal unemployment on young people's intentions operates through the impact on socio-economic circumstances (financial capital), but that the impact of earlier paternal unemployment appears to operate through some other mechanism.

Looking at the impact of maternal employment patterns on young people's expectations of leaving school at age 16, we find that having a mother in current full-time or part-time employment, as opposed to being out of the labour market, reduced the odds of expecting to leave school by almost half, and that these relationships retained statistical significance when housing tenure was controlled for. The influence of earlier maternal employment patterns is more complex. Whether a young person's mother had been in employment or not when they were very young (0–1) had no statistically significant impact upon their later intention of leaving school at age 16. With non-employment as the base category, part-time maternal employment at age 1–5 reduced the likelihood that a young person expected to leave school at age 16, although this lost statistical significance when housing tenure was controlled for. As with current maternal employment, any maternal employment when young people were aged 5–11 reduced the odds of expecting to leave school at age 16. These results suggest that the presence of an employed maternal role model (a form of cultural capital) is an important influence on young people's expectations of leaving school at age 16.

Combining maternal and paternal employment patterns, we turn to look at the influence of household worklessness on young people's intentions at age 16.

Table 6.3 shows that having lived in a household with no adult in employment at any stage of childhood roughly doubled the odds of expecting to leave school at age 16, as did living in a currently workless household. When a variable encompassing whether young people had ever lived in a workless household was used, again the odds of expecting to leave school at age 16 were roughly doubled. All these associations retained statistical significance, although the odds ratios decreased when housing tenure was controlled for, suggesting that it is something about living in a workless household other than just a reduction in socio-economic circumstances (financial capital) that influences young people's educational expectations.

When the influence of current household worklessness and worklessness at the three stages of childhood were combined into one model (not shown), current worklessness was associated with higher odds of a young person expecting to leave school at age 16, but the influence of worklessness at other ages lost statistical significance. The impact of current parental worklessness retained its significance when housing tenure was controlled for, suggesting that living in a household where no adult is in employment is detrimental to young people's educational expectations, regardless of both their earlier experiences of household worklessness and their current household socio-economic circumstances.

Table 6.3   Logistic regressions for the odds of expecting to leave school at age 16: Workless households

Variable		N	Odds ratios	Controlling for tenure
Currently workless household	No	5664	1.00 (1.7%)	1.00 (3.9%)
	Yes	1060	2.05***	1.42**
Workless household (child 0–1)	No	3526	1.00 (1.8%)	1.00 (3.5%)
	Yes	460	2.29***	1.62**
Workless household (child 1–5)	No	3517	1.00 (1.8%)	1.00 (3.3%)
	Yes	475	2.29***	1.59**
Workless household (child 5–11)	No	3923	1.00 (1.0%)	1.00 (2.3%)
	Yes	697	1.80***	1.30
Ever workless	No	5080	1.00 (1.7%)	1.00 (3.8%)
	Yes	1645	1.91***	1.33**

Statistical significance: *=p<0.05, **=p<0.01, ***=p<0.001.
Note: Single observations only with substantive significance shown in brackets.
Source: Author's own analysis of BHPS data.

Influence of other factors   Table 6.4 provides the odds ratios of expecting to leave school by a variety of other variables relating to the young person, their parents, and family. It can be seen that although most of the variables considered had a statistically significant association with expecting to leave school at age 16, substantively most accounted for very little of the variance.

Reflecting the existing evidence discussed above, parents' levels of academic qualifications had quite a strong association with young people's intentions to leave school at age 16. Young people whose parents had no qualifications were around six times (for fathers) and seven times (for mothers) as likely to expect to leave school at age 16 than those whose parents had degree level qualifications. As discussed above, this suggests that more highly educated parents are more able to mobilise economic, social and cultural capital to improve their children's educational prospects.

Although household income itself only accounted for 0.3 per cent of the variance in expecting to leave school at age 16, housing tenure, a longer-term measure of economic circumstances, accounted for over 3 per cent, with those young people living in rented accommodation more than twice as likely as those in owner-occupied accommodation to expect to leave school at age 16. High levels of family conflict and poor family communication were associated with higher odds of expecting to leave school at age 16, and these factors reflect the importance of social and economic capital.

It is clear from Table 6.5 that indicators of young people's emotional well-being had a fairly small, but statistically significant impact on their likelihood of expecting to leave school at age 16. Having low self-efficacy, which reflects a lack of confidence in one's own capabilities, or being unhappy, roughly doubled the odds of expecting to leave school at age 16, possibly because these young people are less likely to believe that they could do well in post-compulsory education.

Table 6.4   Logistic regressions for the odds of expecting to leave school at age 16: Other variables

Variable		N	Odds ratios
Equivalent income less than 50% of average after housing costs	No	5425	1.00 (0.3%)
	Yes	1373	1.36**
Family social class	Man/pro	1989	1.00 (2.7%)
	Non-man	1466	1.20
	Man/unskilled	2306	2.33***
At least one car	Yes	5915	1.00 (1.4%)
	No	896	2.02***
Tenure	Owned	4921	1.00 (3.2%)
	Rented	1876	2.34***
Family type	Intact	4647	1.00 (0.6%)
	Step	1278	1.43***
	Lone	886	1.48***
High family conflict	No	4852	1.00 (0.4%)
	Yes	1938	1.38***
Poor family communication	No	4497	1.00 (1.1%)
	Yes	2297	1.63***
Father GHQ+4	No	4099	1.00 (0.00%)
	Yes	942	1.12
Mother GHQ+4	No	4806	1.00 (0.2%)
	Yes	1762	1.28**
Father qualifications	Degree or higher	617	1.00 (4.3%)
	A level/HND	1485	2.35**
	O level/GCSE	1678	3.73***
	None	1325	5.99***
Mother qualifications	Degree or higher	526	1.00 (4.0%)
	A level/HND	1360	2.53**
	O level/GCSE	2983	3.43***
	None	1763	6.64***
Child gender	Male	3485	1.00 (2.1%)
	Female	3326	0.51***
Child age	11	1410	1.00 (0.2%)
	12	1419	0.98
	13	1369	0.94
	14	1352	1.02
	15	1261	1.29*
Only child	No	5182	1.00 (0.1%)
	Yes	1629	1.19
Firstborn	No	3705	1.00 (0.4%)
	Yes	2852	0.73***
Number of siblings	0	1629	1.00 (0.2%)
	1	2977	0.78*
	2	1614	0.93
	3+	591	0.94

Statistical significance: *=$p<0.05$, **=$p<0.01$, ***=$p<0.001$.

Note: Single observations only with substantive significance shown in brackets.

Source: Author's own analysis of BHPS data.

Table 6.5   Logistic regressions for the odds of expecting to leave school at 16: Emotional well-being variables

Variable		N	Odds ratios
Troubled	No	4356	1.00 (0.0%)
	Yes	2449	1.02
Unhappy	No	5252	1.00 (1.4%)
	Yes	1498	1.83***
Low self-efficacy	No	5986	1.00 (1.5%)
	Yes	751	2.15***
Low self-esteem	No	3748	1.00 (0.8%)
	Yes	3023	1.49***

Statistical significance: *=p<0.05, **=p<0.01, ***=p<0.001.
Note: Single observations only with substantive significance shown in brackets.
Source: Author's own analysis of BHPS data.

Table 6.6   Logistic regressions for the odds of expecting to leave school at 16: Other education variables

Variable		N	Odds ratios
Negative attitude to education	No	3787	1.00 (8.3%)
	Yes	878	4.27***
Truanted in last year	No	3947	1.00 (5.4%)
	Yes	752	3.43***
Suspended/expelled in last year	No	4462	1.00 (4.6%)
	Yes	238	5.21***
Worried about bullying	No	3888	1.00 (0.1%)
	Yes	2190	0.87

Statistical significance: *=p<0.05, **=p<0.01, ***=p<0.001.
Note: Single observations only with substantive significance shown in brackets.
Source: Author's own analysis of BHPS data.

Not surprisingly, having a negative attitude to education, and having truanted or been excluded from school in the last year have an important influence on whether young people expect to leave school at age 16 (Table 6.6). Those with a negative attitude to education were four and a half times as likely to expect to leave school at age 16 as other young people, and this accounted for 8.3 per cent of the variance in this educational outcome.

Multivariate analysis   With these results in mind, a series of multiple logistic regressions were carried out to establish a model of best fit for expecting to leave school at age 16, using current household worklessness as the measure of parental employment. A model of best fit was obtained which explained 17.0 per cent of the variance in young people expecting to leave school at age 16 (Table 6.7).

Table 6.7   Logistic regression for expecting to leave school at 16: Model of best fit

Variables entered		Odds ratios
Currently workless household	No	1.00
	Yes	1.13
Child gender	Male	1.00
	Female	0.61***
Tenure	Owned	1.00
	Rented	1.62***
Low self-efficacy	No	1.00
	Yes	1.60**
Mother qualifications	Degree or higher	1.00
	A level/HND	2.57**
	O level/GCSE	3.24***
	None	4.03***
Truanted in last year	No	1.00
	Yes	1.95***
Suspended/expelled in last year	No	1.00
	Yes	2.35***
Negative attitude to education	No	1.00
	Yes	2.52***

Statistical significance: *=$p<0.05$, **=$p<0.01$, ***=$p<0.001$.
% correctly predicted = 89.7%
Nagelkerke R^2 = 0.170
N = 4598
Source: Author's own analysis of BHPS data.

Eight variables were included in the model of best fit. Living in a currently workless household had no statistically significant influence on whether young people expected to leave school at age 16 in the final model. If a stepwise regression method was employed (not shown), current worklessness retained a statistically significant influence on young people's expectation of leaving school at age 16 until housing tenure entered the model. Contrary to the bivariate results above, this suggests that the impact of worklessness does operate through a mechanism of financial capital, evident through household socio-economic circumstances.

As was seen in the bivariate analysis, boys were more likely to expect to leave school than girls, as were those young people with low self-efficacy. Unsurprisingly, young people with a negative attitude to education, and those who had been excluded from school or had truanted in the last year, were more likely to expect to leave school at age 16. But perhaps the most significant influence on young people's educational expectations was their mother's level of academic qualifications: those whose mothers had no qualifications were four times as likely as those whose mothers had a degree to expect to leave school at age 16, indicating that parent's human capital is important in determining children's expectations.

Summary In conclusion, the bivariate analysis indicated that early maternal employment, seen as detrimental to young people's educational outcomes in previous research (for example, Joshi and Verropoulou 2000; Ermisch and Francesconi 2001a), had no significant impact upon their expectation of leaving school at age 16. Having lived with an unemployed father during childhood, and having a mother out of the labour market during later childhood and adolescence did however have a small negative effect, suggesting that it is important for young people to have an employed role model during adolescence when they are forming their attitudes and expectations. In turn, living in a household with no adult in employment had a detrimental effect on young people's educational expectations, although when other factors, including socio-economic circumstances were controlled for, this relationship lost statistical significance.

It is clear from the multivariate analysis that factors other than parental employment patterns have an important influence on young people's educational expectations, including mothers' level of academic qualifications, and young people's educational behaviour in the last year (in terms of having been excluded and truanting) and their overall attitude to education. These latter factors do appear to be influenced by parental employment (seen in Chapter 5), so although parental employment, once other factors were controlled for, was found to have no direct association with the expectation of leaving school at age 16, indirectly it might.

Staying on at school

The figures and analysis discussed so far refer of course to young people's statements of intentions rather than to actual behaviour. For those young people who were interviewed in both the young person and the adult survey we know whether or not they stayed at school at age 16, as well as the outcomes of schooling in terms of their performance in GCSE examinations. The following results refer to the 913 young people who were interviewed in the youth study at age 15 and were also interviewed in the main study after they had completed compulsory education. The data come from several waves of the survey, and the 'outcome' variables occurred in the years 1995 to 2001.

Just over 70 percent of the young people stayed in full-time education (Table 6.8). As would be expected, girls were more likely to stay on than boys: 81.1 per cent of girls and 66.7 per cent of boys were still in full-time education towards the end of their first non-compulsory school term. Of the young people who left school, around two-thirds were in employment (lower for girls than boys), a tenth were in training (more girls than boys), with the remaining young people not in education, employment or training (NEET), which includes those who are unemployed, and engaged in family care. These figures are very similar to national statistics (DFEE 2001a) and with those from the Youth Cohort Study (DFEE 2001b).

As the young people in the sample were asked about their intentions with regards to staying in education post-16 it is possible to look at the relationship between intention and the actual outcome. In Table 6.9 comparisons are made

Table 6.8   Staying on in full-time education at age 16

%	Boys	Girls	All
Stayed on	66.7	81.1	73.7
Left	33.3	19.4	26.4
Employment	64.1[a]	52.4[a]	60.0[a]
Training	9.0[a]	16.7[a]	11.7[a]
NEET	26.9[a]	31.0[a]	29.3[a]
N	468	445	913

Note: Proportion of the number leaving school.
Source: Author's own analysis of BHPS data.

Table 6.9   Staying in education and future intentions: Percentage not in full-time education post-16

Intention		Stay on	Don't know	Leave at 16
Age 11	%	19.3	28.2	53.5
	N	192	71	43
Age 12	%	18.1	37.2	56.3
	N	282	94	48
Age 13	%	17.7	38.0	65.5
	N	282	92	55
Age 14	%	18.6	38.9	80.0
	N	539	113	65
Age 15	%	16.1	46.3	73.2
	N	703	95	112

Source: Author's own analysis of BHPS data.

between the answers young people gave to the question about expecting to leave school and their actual decision about staying on or leaving school. Figures are given for intention at age 11, then age 12 and so on until age 15. The sample size increased for the later years as many of the young people who expressed intentions in the earlier years of the young person survey had not reached age 16 and entered the adult survey at the point of this study. The Ns in the table refer to the number of young people who expressed a particular intention (leaving, staying on, don't know) in the young person interview. The percentages are the percentage of each group who did not stay on at school post-16.

It can be seen then that early intentions were a strong predictor of later behaviour with regards to staying in education post-16. Of those who at age 11 said they wanted to leave school at 16, just over half did so, and this increased to three-quarters of those who at age 15 predicted they would leave at age 16. It is not surprising that intentions expressed at age 15, in the last year of compulsory schooling, were accurate predictors of behaviour, or that intentions become better

Table 6.10   Logistic regressions for the odds of leaving school at age 16: Parental employment patterns

Variable		N	Odds ratios
Father current employment	Employed	615	1.00 (3.5%)
	Not in employment	112	2.50***
Mother current employment	Full-time	363	0.67*
	Part-time	306	0.70
	Not in employment	246	1.00 (0.9%)
Father employment (child 0–1)	Employed	536	1.00 (2.3%)
	Not in employment	39	2.86**
Father employment (child 1–5)	Employed	534	1.00 (2.0%)
	Not in employment	44	2.52**
Father employment (child 5–11)	Employed	541	1.00 (2.2%)
	Not in employment	50	2.54**
Mother employment (child 0–1)	Employed full-time	47	1.06
	Employed part-time	74	1.07
	Not in employment	654	1.00 (0.0%)
Mother employment (child 1–5)	Employed full-time	86	1.12
	Employed part-time	169	0.89
	Not in employment	520	1.00 (0.1%)
Mother employment (child 5–11)	Employed full-time	202	0.77
	Employed part-time	360	0.80
	Not in employment	342	1.00 (0.4%)

Statistical significance: *=$p<0.05$, **=$p<0.01$, ***=$p<0.001$.
Note: Single observations only with substantive significance shown in brackets.
Source: Author's own analysis of BHPS data.

predictors closer to the event they are predicting. What is striking, however, is how strong the very early intentions were as predictors of later behaviour.

Influence of parental employment patterns   Earlier we saw that maternal employment had very little association with whether young people expected to leave school at age 16, and that paternal unemployment (both current and during childhood), and similarly household worklessness had a negative influence. Table 6.10 indicates the odds ratios of young people actually leaving school at age 16, and as would be expected to some extent these mirrored the influence of parental employment on young people's intention to leave school.

Of particular note is that maternal employment appeared to have very little influence on young people's leaving school at age 16, with only the relationship for current maternal employment reaching statistical significance, and this only accounting for 0.9 per cent of the variance. Fathers' employment did appear important, accounting for 3.5 per cent of the variance, with young people with a currently unemployed father two and a half times as likely to have left school

Table 6.11   Logistic regressions for the odds of leaving school at age 16: Workless households

Variable		N	Odds ratios
Currently workless household	No	776	1.00 (1.7%)
	Yes	139	1.91**
Workless household (child 0–1)	No	521	1.00 (3.6%)
	Yes	55	3.08***
Workless household (child 1–5)	No	515	1.00 (4.3%)
	Yes	58	3.28***
Workless household (child 5–11)	No	568	1.00 (3.1%)
	Yes	70	2.70***
Ever workless	No	707	1.00 (2.3%)
	Yes	208	1.93***

Statistical significance: *=p<0.05, **=p<0.01, ***=p<0.001.
Note: Single observations only with substantive significance shown in brackets.
Source: Author's own analysis of BHPS data.

at age 16 as those whose fathers were in employment. Paternal unemployment during childhood also had an important influence on young people's behaviour.

When we consider maternal and paternal employment patterns together and look at the impact of household worklessness on whether young people stayed on in full-time education post-16 (Table 6.11), we find that having lived in a workless household at any age was associated with higher odds of leaving school at age 16. Current worklessness accounted for 1.7 per cent of the variance in whether young people had left school, with earlier worklessness accounting for a greater proportion of the variance. This indicates the residual influence of household worklessness on young people's educational outcomes.

Influence of other factors   An earlier section discussed the existing evidence relating to the impact of socio-economic factors, such as family social class, income and housing tenure, on young people's educational achievement and progression. Table 6.12 presents the odds ratios for young people leaving school at age 16 for a variety of factors. Although household income itself did not have a significant association with young people leaving school, in line with previous research, poor socio-economic circumstances (indicated by car ownership and household tenure) did, with housing tenure accounting for 5 per cent of the variance in young people leaving school at age 16.

Other factors are also important. Those in stepfamilies were less likely to stay on post-16 but there was little difference between those in intact and those in lone parent families. The level of parental qualifications accounted for 8.1 per cent of the variance in young people leaving school at age 16, with young people without a parent with any educational qualifications more than 5 times as likely to have left school at age 16 as those with a parent with a degree.

Table 6.12   Logistic regressions for the odds of leaving school at age 16: Other variables

Variable		N	Odds ratios
Equivalent income less than 50% of	No	734	1.00 (0.5%)
average after housing costs	Yes	181	1.36
At least one car	Yes	777	1.00 (1.8%)
	No	138	1.94**
Tenure	Owned	673	1.00 (5.0%)
	Rented	242	2.50***
Family type	Intact	599	1.00 (2.3%)
	Step	128	2.19***
	Lone	188	1.27
High family conflict	No	587	1.00 (0.9%)
	Yes	328	0.69*
Poor family communication	No	587	1.00 (0.4%)
	Yes	328	1.29
Parental qualifications	Degree or higher	143	1.00 (8.1%)
	A level/HND	288	1.57
	O level/GCSE	305	2.65***
	None	174	5.43***
Child gender	Male	470	1.00 (4.1%)
	Female	445	0.46***

Statistical significance: *=$p<0.05$, **=$p<0.01$, ***=$p<0.001$.
Note: Single observations only with substantive significance shown in brackets.
Source: Author's own analysis of BHPS data.

Unsurprisingly, young people with a negative attitude to education were far more likely than other young people to have left school at age 16, as were those who had truanted or been excluded from school in the previous year (Table 6.13). However, having worried about bullying had no statistically significant association with school leaving.

Multivariate analysis   With these results in mind, a series of multiple logistic regressions were carried out to establish a model of best fit for leaving school at age 16, using having ever lived in a workless household as the measure of parental employment. A model of best fit was obtained which explained 20.1 per cent of the variance in young people leaving school at age 16 (Table 6.14).

Young people who had ever lived in a workless household were more likely to have left school at age 16, controlling for a number of other factors. Parental educational qualifications were perhaps the most important influence on whether young people had left school, with those whose parents had no qualifications over six times as likely to have left school at age 16 as those with a parent with a degree. As with young people's expectations of leaving school at age 16, having

Table 6.13   Logistic regression for leaving school at 16: Other education variables

Variable	N	Odds ratios
Negative attitude to education	430	1.00 (8.6%)
	115	3.61***
Truanted in last year	394	1.00 (6.5%)
	153	2.80***
Suspended/expelled in last year	507	1.00 (3.5%)
	41	3.39***
Worried about bullying	574	1.00 (0.2%)
	220	0.85

Statistical significance: *=p<0.05, **=p<0.01, ***=p<0.001.
Note: Single observations only with substantive significance shown in brackets.
Source: Author's own analysis of BHPS data.

Table 6.14   Logistic regression for leaving school at age 16: Model of best fit

Variables entered		Odds ratios
Ever workless household	No	1.00
	Yes	1.55*
Family type	Intact	1.00
	Step	2.26***
	Lone	0.75
Child gender	Male	1.00
	Female	0.41***
Parental qualifications	Degree or higher	1.00
	A level/HND	1.69
	O level/GCSE	2.80***
	None	6.25***
Negative attitude to education	Missing	1.26
	No	1.00
	Yes	3.68***

Statistical significance: *=p<0.05, **=p<0.01, ***=p<0.001.
% correctly predicted = 77.5%
Nagelkerke R^2 = 0.201
N = 910
Source: Author's own analysis of BHPS data.

a negative attitude to education was an important factor in predicting educational progression.

No measures of socio-economic circumstances were included in this model of best fit. However, if housing tenure was entered into the model, the influence of household worklessness on whether young people left school at age 16 lost statistical significance. This suggests that the influence of parental employment patterns, as well as impacting on young people's expectations and aspirations, operates partly through a mechanism of financial capital.

Summary   In the previous section we considered the influences on young people's expectations of leaving school at age 16, as opposed to continuing in full-time education. This section has looked at the results of these expectations, the reality of whether a young person did stay on at school. Early intentions were a strong predictor of later behaviour with regards to staying in education post-16, and even at age 11 young people's intentions were a fairly strong predictor of their later behaviour. This suggests that experiences during childhood may go a long way towards shaping young people's later expectations and behaviours.

In considering the influences on young people's educational decisions at age 16, we found that mothers' employment patterns throughout childhood had no significant association with whether a young person had left school at age 16. However living with an unemployed father, either during childhood or at the time the school-leaving decision was made did appear important. Likewise having lived in a workless household at any age was associated with higher odds of leaving school at age 16. Not only did current household worklessness have a significant association with school-leaving, but the influence of household worklessness during childhood suggests the longer-term impact of this experience on the formation of young people's expectations and behaviours.

As with other educational outcomes, other factors, such as socio-economic circumstances had an important influence on young people's decision whether to leave school at age 16. Earlier educational behaviours, such as truancy and exclusion from school, not surprisingly had a strong association with their later behaviour and decision making. Parental levels of academic qualifications were perhaps the strongest influence on young people staying on in post-16 education, with those with a parent with higher qualifications far more likely to continue their own education.

The multivariate analysis carried out concluded that even controlling for a number of other factors, young people who had ever lived in a workless household were more likely to have left school at age 16. Together with the influence of other factors, such as parental educational qualifications, this suggests the importance of a role model image in young people's decision-making.

Outcomes of education: GCSE results

This section considers the attainment of educational qualifications at age 16 for the sample from the BHPS, looking at the influence of parental employment patterns and other factors. Examination outcomes for the young people in the sample are shown in Table 6.15, for all young people and for girls and boys separately. These have been grouped into those young people who gained five or more GCSE passes at grades A* to C, those who gained at least one pass at grades A* to C, and those

Table 6.15   GCSE attainment in the BHPS, by gender

%	Male	Female	All
5+ grades A* to C	44.9	59.3	51.9
1-4 grades A* to C	21.3	17.8	19.6
No GCSE grades A* to C	33.8	22.9	28.5
N	470	445	915

Source: Author's own analysis of BHPS data.

Table 6.16   Logistic regressions for the odds of achieving 5 good GCSE passes: Parental employment patterns

Variable		N	Odds ratios
Father current employment	Employed	615	1.00 (5.7%)
	Not in employment	112	0.30***
Mother current employment	Full-time	363	1.68**
	Part-time	306	1.91***
	Not in employment	246	1.00 (2.2%)
Father employment (child 0–1)	Employed	536	1.00 (3.8%)
	Not in employment	39	0.24***
Father employment (child 1–5)	Employed	534	1.00 (1.8%)
	Not in employment	44	0.41**
Father employment (child 5–11)	Employed	541	1.00 (3.8%)
	Not in employment	50	0.28***
Mother employment (child 0–1)	Employed full-time	47	0.99
	Employed part-time	74	0.98
	Not in employment	654	1.00 (0.0%)
Mother employment (child 1–5)	Employed full-time	86	1.01
	Employed part-time	169	1.05
	Not in employment	520	1.00 (0.0%)
Mother employment (child 5–11)	Employed full-time	202	1.15
	Employed part-time	260	1.32
	Not in employment	342	1.00 (0.5%)

Statistical significance: *=$p<0.05$, **=$p<0.01$, ***=$p<0.001$.
Note: Single observations only with substantive significance shown in brackets.
Source: Author's own analysis of BHPS data.

who gained no GSCEs at grades A* to C. These figures are very similar to national statistics over the period (DFEE 2001c). Overall just over half of all young people achieved at least five A* to C passes, with a further fifth achieving at least one A* to C grade. Girls outperformed boys quite dramatically in GCSE results: 59 per cent of girls achieved at least five A* to C passes, compared with 45 per cent of boys.

Table 6.17   Logistic regressions for the odds of achieving 5 good GCSE passes: Workless households

Variable		N	Odds ratios
Currently workless household	No	776	1.00 (4.5%)
	Yes	139	0.34***
Workless household (child 0–1)	No	521	1.00 (5.4%)
	Yes	55	0.23***
Workless household (child 1–5)	No	515	1.00 (2.9%)
	Yes	58	0.37**
Workless household (child 5–11)	No	568	1.00 (1.9%)
	Yes	70	0.46**
Ever workless	No	707	1.00 (4.9%)
	Yes	208	0.39***

Statistical significance: *=$p<0.05$, **=$p<0.01$, ***=$p<0.001$.
Note: Single observations only with substantive significance shown in brackets.
Source: Author's own analysis of BHPS data.

The rest of this section considers the influence of parental employment patterns and other factors on whether young people achieved five good GCSE passes (grades A* to C).

Influence of parental employment patterns   There has been much emphasis in previous research (for example, Joshi and Verropoulou 2000; Ermisch and Francesconi 2001a) on the potentially negative impact of early maternal employment on young people's achievement of academic qualifications. Table 6.16 indicates the odds ratios of young people in the follow-on sample achieving at least five good (grades A* to C) GCSE passes, based on their parents' employment status during childhood and adolescence.

Looking first at maternal employment, it can be seen that maternal employment during childhood had no significant association with whether a young person obtained five good GCSEs at age 16. That this is contradictory to previous research indicates the importance of updating information which is based on old data, especially where this has implications for policy. Another important finding is that fathers' employment patterns, often neglected in previous research in this field, do have a significant association with whether young people obtained good educational qualifications. Young people who lived with an unemployed father, or who had experienced paternal unemployment at any stage of their childhood were far less likely to obtain five good GCSE passes than other young people. Current paternal unemployment accounted for 5.7 per cent of the variance in educational achievement at this age.

Combining the influence of parents' employment patterns, Table 6.17 shows the odds ratios of achieving 5 or more good GCSE passes by patterns of household worklessness. Young people living in a currently workless household, or who had

Table 6.18   Logistic regressions for the odds of achieving 5 good GCSE passes: Other variables

Variable		N	Odds ratios
Equivalent income less than 50%	No	734	1.00 (0.7%)
of average after housing costs	Yes	181	0.70*
Family social class	Man/pro	280	1.00 (5.8%)
	Non-man	196	0.75
	Man/unskilled	296	0.38***
At least one car	Yes	777	1.00 (3.5%)
	No	138	0.39***
Tenure	Owned	673	1.00 (5.9%)
	Rented	242	0.37***
Family type	Intact	599	1.00 (2.0%)
	Step	128	0.55**
	Lone	188	0.64**
High family conflict	No	587	1.00 (0.0%)
	Yes	328	0.98
Poor family communication	No	587	1.00 (2.8%)
	Yes	327	0.54***
Father GHQ+4	No	555	1.00 (0.4%)
	Yes	18	0.74
Mother GHQ+4	No	652	1.00 (1.3%)
	Yes	242	0.64**
Parental qualifications	Degree or higher	143	1.00 (12.6%)
	A level/HND	288	0.64*
	O level/GCSE	305	0.31***
	None	174	0.14***
Child gender	Male	470	1.00 (2.8%)
	Female	445	1.79***
Only child	No	571	1.00 (0.1%)
	Yes	344	0.92
Firstborn	No	509	1.00 (1.9%)
	Yes	368	1.62***
Number of siblings	0	344	1.00 (1.4%)
	1	344	1.22
	2	164	1.13
	3+	63	0.52*

Statistical significance: *=p<0.05, **=p<0.01, ***=p<0.001.
Note: Single observations only with substantive significance shown in brackets.
Source: Author's own analysis of BHPS data.

experienced household worklessness at any stage of childhood were far less likely to achieve 5 GCSEs at grade C or above. These results reflect the impact of paternal unemployment, but account for a greater proportion of the variance in educational achievement. Living in a workless household not only affects the financial capital available within the family, but affects the role models (cultural capital) available to young people, influencing their expectations and aspirations.

Influence of other factors Table 6.18 presents the odds ratios of achieving 5 or more GCSEs at grade A*–C for a range of other characteristics. It can be seen that although household income itself had only a small influence on educational achievement, other indicators of socio-economic circumstances were important. Housing tenure accounted for almost 6 per cent of the variance in educational achievement, with those in rented accommodation less likely to achieve 5 good GCSEs than those living in owner-occupied accommodation. Young people whose families did not have access to a car, had a household income less than 50 per cent of the average (after housing costs), or who were in the lower social class were similarly less likely to have achieved 5 good GCSEs than other young people. Family structure was also important, with young people in lone parent families and stepfamilies less likely to get good GCSEs. In keeping with previous results, girls were more likely to have obtained good GCSE results, and firstborn children and those with fewer siblings also had greater success. But as was seen with young people's educational expectations and their decision to stay on in full-time education post-16, the most important influence on educational achievement at age 16, accounting for 13 per cent of the variance, was parental educational qualifications. Young people whose parents had a degree were far more likely than other young people to have gained good GCSE results themselves, again stressing the importance of parental human capital in determining young people's educational success.

Not surprisingly educational behaviour in the last year of compulsory schooling had an important influence on the achievement of GCSE qualifications, shown in Table 6.19. Having a negative attitude to education, having truanted or been expelled were highly related to not achieving 5 good GCSE passes. In addition, young people's intention of leaving school at age 16 was a powerful predictor of their educational achievement. This means that those who expected to leave school at age 16 were also highly likely to leave with low levels of qualifications.

Multivariate analysis With these results in mind, a series of multiple logistic regressions were carried out to establish a model of best fit for attainment of at least 5 GCSEs at grade C or above, using having ever lived in a workless household as the measure of parental employment. A model of best fit was obtained which explained 27.6 per cent of the variance (Table 6.20).

There were 6 variables in the model, including having ever lived in a workless household. Even controlling for a number of other factors, young people who had ever lived in a workless household were around half as likely as other young people to have obtained 5 GCSEs at grade C or above. As was seen in the bivariate analyses truancy and exclusion from school increased the likelihood that young people failed to get good qualifications. The influence of parental educational qualifications was highly significant, again suggesting the importance of both parental human capital, and cultural capital, in the form of a well-educated role model to young people.

No measures of socio-economic circumstances were included in this model of best fit. However, if housing tenure was added to the model, it failed to have any

Table 6.19 Logistic regressions for the odds of achieving 5 good GCSE passes: Other education variables

Variable		N	Odds ratios
Negative attitude to education	No	430	1.00 (4.4%)
	Yes	115	0.40***
Truanted in last year	No	394	1.00 (5.5%)
	Yes	153	0.40***
Suspended/expelled in last year	No	507	1.00 (7.7%)
	Yes	41	0.11***
Worried about bullying	No	574	1.00 (0.0%)
	Yes	220	0.98
Intention at age 16	Stay	703	1.00 (14.9%)
	Don't know	95	0.40***
	Leave	114	0.09***

Statistical significance: *=$p<0.05$, **=$p<0.01$, ***=$p<0.001$.
Note: Single observations only with substantive significance shown in brackets.
Source: Author's own analysis of BHPS data.

Table 6.20 Logistic regression for achieving 5 good GCSE passes: Model of best fit

Variables entered		Odds ratios
Ever workless household	No	1.00
	Yes	0.50**
Parental qualifications	Degree or higher	1.00
	A level/HND	0.74
	O level/GCSE	0.30***
	None	0.17***
Suspended/expelled in last year	No	1.00
	Yes	0.14***
Truanted in last year	No	1.00
	Yes	0.51**
Mother GHQ+4	No	1.00
	Yes	0.57*
Child gender	Male	1.00
	Female	1.65*

Statistical significance: *=$p<0.05$, **=$p<0.01$, ***=$p<0.001$.
Constant = 3.69***
% correctly predicted = 69.9%
Nagelkerke R^2 = 0.276
N = 532
Source: Author's own analysis of BHPS data.

significant influence on whether young people gained good qualifications at age 16. In addition, having ever lived in a workless household retained its negative influence, indicating that this does not operate through the impact on family socio-economic circumstances (financial capital). Overall, the results suggest the role that the experience of household worklessness may play in the formulation of young people's opinions and aspirations.

Summary   This section has considered an attainment-based educational outcome, the achievement of at least 5 GCSEs at grade C or above. Overall around half of all young people, a greater proportion of girls than boys, achieved at least five A* to C passes. In contrast to previous research (Joshi and Verropoulou 2000; Ermisch and Francesconi 2001) maternal employment during childhood was found to have no significant association with whether a young person obtained five good GCSEs at age 16. The experience of paternal unemployment did however have a detrimental impact, with those young people who lived with an unemployed father, or who had experienced paternal unemployment at any stage of their childhood far less likely to obtain five good GCSE passes than other young people. Likewise, the experience of household worklessness had the same negative influence on educational attainment. In the bivariate analysis, other factors, such as socio-economic circumstances, parental levels of educational qualifications and family type were important. Not surprisingly educational behaviour in the last year of compulsory schooling also had an important influence on the achievement of GCSE qualifications, with those who had a negative attitude to education, who had truanted or been expelled far more likely to not have achieved 5 good GCSE passes.

The model of best fit obtained in the multivariate analysis contained 6 variables, including having ever lived in a workless household. Even controlling for a number of other factors, young people who had ever lived in a workless household were around half as likely as other young people to have obtained 5 GCSEs at grade C or above. This appears not to operate through a mechanism of socio-economic circumstances (financial capital), because although no measures of socio-economic circumstances were included in the model, if housing tenure was added having ever lived in a workless household retained its negative influence on whether young people gained good qualifications at age 16. That parental educational qualifications have such a significant influence on whether young people obtain good GCSE results indicates the importance of parental human capital, and indeed the presence of a role model (a form of cultural capital) to children.

Discussion and conclusions

This chapter has reviewed the individual, parental and familial factors which have an influence on young people's educational progression and attainment, adopting a forms of capital approach to understanding these influences. Participation levels post-16 are important because of the impact on young people's future life chances, and the costs to individuals, the economy and society of educational failure are high. Young people's achievement and choices at age 16 affect both their own futures and the supply of education and trained labour in the economy. There are also strong links between educational attainment and progression, and other outcomes including health, employment and earnings, and lone parenthood.

Although there is a vast literature exploring the impact of parental employment on children's educational outcomes, much of this research is based on old data, with the children studied born up to 35 years ago (for example, Joshi and Verroupoulou 2000; Ermisch and Francesconi 2001a). In addition, previous work has tended to neglect the influence of paternal employment, focusing instead on the potentially negative impact of maternal employment, particularly full-time employment when children are very young, on their later educational outcomes. Thus the empirical work carried out in this chapter represented a real opportunity to consider the impact of parental employment patterns on young people's educational outcomes using more up-to-date data.

Of particular note, and in contrast to previous research discussed above, the empirical analysis conducted in this chapter found that maternal employment during early childhood had no statistically significant influence on whether young people expected to leave school at age 16, on whether they did leave school at age 16, or on their attainment of GCSEs at age 16. This is an important finding, as it suggests that whether or not a mother is in employment when her children are young has no impact on their later educational outcomes.

Fathers' employment patterns, often neglected in previous research did have an impact on young people's educational outcomes, with those who lived with an unemployed father or who had experienced paternal unemployment during childhood less likely to both expect to and actually stay on in education post-16, and less likely to obtain 5 or more GCSEs at grade C or above. Similarly the experience of household worklessness, either concurrently or during childhood had a negative impact upon young people's educational outcomes. Even controlling for a number of other factors, including socio-economic circumstances, young people who had ever lived in a workless household were less likely to stay on in education at age 16, and were less likely to obtain 5 or more GCSEs at grade C or above. This suggests that the detrimental effect of household worklessness on young people's educational outcomes operates not through a mechanism of socio-economic circumstances (financial capital) but through the provision of a role model image (a form of cultural capital). That parent's own educational qualifications have such an important influence on young people's educational outcomes also substantiates this.

Chapter 7
Conclusions

Introduction

This study has explored the impact of parental employment and unemployment on outcomes for children and young people. In this final chapter the key findings of the research are discussed. Following a reflection on the limitations of this research, some questions raised by the research, and potential areas for future work are identified.

Over recent decades there have been dramatic changes in the employment patterns of men and women, with particularly significant increases in employment rates among mothers. Government policy has also increasingly given attention to encouraging parents, particularly lone mothers, into work, with a focus on paid work as a defence against poverty. These trends and policy changes affect the everyday lives of both parents and children, and give rise to questions about the potential impact that parental employment patterns have on children and young people.

Using a forms of capital approach, and data from the British Household Panel Survey (BHPS) this research has explored the impact of parental employment and unemployment on the educational and emotional well-being of children and young people.

Key findings

Using the theoretical framework of Bourdieu (1983), parental employment patterns can be understood to impact upon children's outcomes in several ways: through the effect on household income and socio-economic circumstances (economic capital); through the provision of a role model, and cultural norms and expectations (cultural capital); and through family relationships and interaction (social capital). Young people's outcomes were considered in terms of emotional well-being (feeling troubled, being unhappy, having low self-esteem, and having low self-efficacy), and educational well-being (fear of bullying, truanting, exclusion from school, having a negative attitude to education, expectation and actuality of leaving school at age 16, and gaining 5 or more GCSEs at grade C or above).

Economic capital

Parental employment affects household income and socio-economic circumstances, and the amount of economic capital available within families. But for a number of the outcomes considered in this research, the influence of parental employment patterns remained significant even when household socio-economic circumstances were controlled for, suggesting that the economic capital related to employment may be less important for children's outcomes than other factors.

Considered in more detail below, household worklessness was associated with poorer educational outcomes. Young people living in a currently workless household were more likely to have truanted in the past year, and this relationship appeared to operate through a mechanism of economic capital, losing statistical significance when housing tenure (as an indicator of family socio-economic circumstances) was controlled for. A similar effect was seen on young people's expectation and actuality of leaving school at age 16, with those living in a workless household less likely to stay on in full-time education post-16.

Social capital

Supporting the argument of Coleman (1988), that maternal employment weakens family social capital, by reducing women's emotional investment in building relationships with their children, the influence of maternal employment on a number of young people's outcomes, particularly emotional well-being, appeared to operate through a mechanism of nurturing or protection. Young people who had a mother who was not in employment were less likely to feel troubled than those whose mothers were in part-time or full-time employment, and this was also true for feeling unhappy and having low self-esteem, but only for young people in lone mother families. Maternal part-time, as opposed to full-time employment also appeared to offer young people some protection against truancy and having a negative attitude to education. This protective effect of maternal part-time employment is in keeping with the conclusions of O'Brien and Jones (1999). These are important findings, as they suggest that maternal employment during adolescence has an impact on young people's concurrent well-being. Conversely, maternal employment during childhood had very little impact upon the well-being on the young people in our samples, in contrast to some previous research (see below for more details).

Cultural capital

In addition to the impact upon economic and social capital, parental employment patterns have an influence upon the cultural norms and expectations within a family, and upon the role model presented to children by their parents. Particularly important for outcomes which related to attitudes and expectations, the impact of parental employment on some aspects of young people's well-being appeared to operate through a mechanism of cultural capital. Young people who lived in a currently workless household, or who had experienced household worklessness during childhood were more likely to have a negative attitude to education, to expect to leave school at age 16, and to not obtain at least 5 GCSEs at grade C or above, influences which were unaffected by family socio-economic circumstances.

These findings indicate the importance of having an employed role model during adolescence when young people are forming their attitudes and expectations.

Household worklessness

Previous research (such as Joshi and Verroupoulou 2000) tended to consider the impact of maternal employment on children's outcomes in isolation, neglecting to take into account that maternal employment operates within a family employment system. Thus the analysis carried out in this study considered the impact of parental employment patterns both separately, and in terms of the number of earners in a household and whether young people had experienced household worklessness.

The experience of household worklessness, either concurrently or during childhood had a negative impact upon young people's educational outcomes. Even controlling for a number of other factors, including socio-economic circumstances, young people who had ever lived in a workless household were less likely to stay on in education at age 16, and were less likely to obtain 5 or more GCSEs at grade C or above. The experience of household worklessness was also associated with having a negative attitude to education, to exclusion from school, and to being unhappy and having low self-esteem (for those in dual parent families). Housing tenure was controlled for in these analyses, which indicates the influence of parental worklessness was not operating solely through the impact on family socio-economic circumstances (economic capital). This provides further evidence that the detrimental effect of living in a currently workless household is not simply due to reduced economic resources, but that there is something about the experience of worklessness that effects children's behaviour. There was also some evidence that the experience of household worklessness during childhood had a residual negative impact upon their later outcomes. That the experience of worklessness has such a negative impact upon young peoples' outcomes is important, as it relates to the current government's focus on 'work for those who can'. Further research is needed to disentangle the mechanism of impact of household worklessness on outcomes for young people.

Early maternal employment

In the current research, maternal employment when the young people in the samples were children rarely had an impact upon their later well-being. This is in total contrast to previous research, which generally found that maternal employment, particularly full-time employment, when children were very young had a detrimental impact upon their later educational achievement (for example, Ermisch and Francesconi 2000, 2001a; Joshi and Verroupoulou 2000). The empirical analysis conducted in this study found that maternal employment during early childhood had no statistically significant influence on whether young people expected to leave school at age 16, on whether they did leave school at age 16, or on their attainment of GCSEs at age 16. Although a negative finding, in that it has no statistically significant effect, this is critical, as it suggests that whether or not a mother is in employment when her children are young has no impact on their later educational outcomes. Previous research has tended to rely on data from the birth cohort studies, with the children being studied born up to 50 years ago, when maternal employment, lone parenthood and other aspects of family life were very different to modern times. In contrast, the current research used data from the BHPS and its associated youth panel, with the young people in the samples born between 1978 and 1990. Thus the data are a better reflection of contemporary life.

That the findings relating to the impact of early maternal employment on young peoples' outcomes differ from previous research is of vital importance. These findings contribute to the long-standing debate surrounding the impact of parental employment, in reality usually just that of mothers, on children, and highlights the importance of using up-to-date data and research in the formation of policy.

Other factors

Although, as we have seen, parental employment does contribute to young people's well-being, the analysis carried out in this study generally found that other factors matter more. It is also important to note the factors which did not have a statistically significant effect. For young people's emotional well-being outcomes the level of family communication and conflict experienced by individuals appeared to have the most important influence. Indicators of family socio-economic circumstances had a differing influence upon the different indicators of emotional well-being, with income itself having only a very small statistically significant effect on self-esteem, and housing tenure the most substantively significant effects. Young peoples' self-efficacy appeared to be influenced the most by socio-economic circumstances. Gender was important, particularly for feeling troubled and having low self-esteem, and older young people were more likely to be both troubled and unhappy.

For educational behaviours, such as truanting and exclusion from school, the stability of family relationships in terms of the level of communication and conflict were important, as were indicators of family socio-economic circumstances (but not for worrying about bullying) and young people's emotional well-being.

In terms of educational outcomes, the expectation and actuality of leaving school at age 16 and the achievement of good GCSEs, the most important association was with parental levels of qualifications, with those with a parent with a degree far more likely to stay on at school and obtain good qualifications than other young people. This substantiates the above finding that parental role models are a vital motivation in young people's formation of expectations and attitudes, and consequently their later outcomes.

Policy implications

The findings of this research carry important implications for public policy, including employment policies, parental leave policies, and childcare policies. In

Chapter 2 New Labour's anti-poverty strategy with the focus on paid employment as the best route out of poverty was discussed, together with parental leave and childcare policies. The evidence provided by this research tentatively supports the policy of encouraging paid work for all, including mothers, although part-time as opposed to full-time maternal employment might offer young people greater protection against poorer emotional well-being. Parental employment which guards children against the experience of household worklessness would appear to be overwhelmingly positive.

Government policies regarding maternity and paternity leave, and parental leave have improved over recent years, and the findings of this research support these improvements. Maternity leave enables a mother to spend time with her young baby, bringing with it several benefits (discussed in Chapter 2), whilst maintaining a women's connection with the labour market. Entitling parents to more time with their young children can be justified as a potential investment in the labour force of tomorrow.

Childcare policies also have an important part to play in children's well-being, recognised by the government with the introduction of the Sure Start scheme. No information is available on the childcare used by the parents of the young people in this research, and thus more work needs to be done in this area, before the full impact of the current findings for childcare policies can be determined.

Limitations of this study

This research used a quantitative approach to explore the links between parental employment patterns and young people's outcomes. The findings have important implications for public policy and for future research. It is therefore important to acknowledge the limitations of the research.

That the empirical research was based entirely on the secondary analysis of data from the BHPS brings with it certain limitations. Secondary analysis, as discussed in Chapter 3, is restricted by the availability of data, sample sizes, and the questions and response categories included in the original survey. For example, some questions were only asked in some waves of the BHPS, which reduces the available sample size. Although quantitative research enables statistical analysis of how the social world operates, and suited the research questions of this study, there are limitations. The current study does not give an insight into parents' or young people's opinions or attitudes to parental employment patterns, and as discussed below, such research would complement this book.

The research made assumptions about parents' time use, by using the time spent in employment to indicate the amount of time that they otherwise had available to spend with their children. Unfortunately the BHPS does not include information about the type, quantity or quality of childcare used by families where parents were in employment, especially those who were in employment when their children were of pre-school age.

Finally, although the impact of a large number of individual, parental, and family factors were studied in the analysis, these variables are only a few of the many factors that may have a bearing on children's outcomes, many of which may not be measured. The data source used in this research focuses on individual and household level factors, and it is clearly beyond the scope of this study to look at other broader social and structural factors, such as the neighbourhood context and the quality of school that children living in workless households receive compared to children with employed parents. However, these factors may also be important in determining child well-being.

Questions raised and future work

This research concentrated upon outcomes for young people, aged 11–16, for a number of reasons. In previous research, there has been a focus on the outcomes for very young children (for example, Gregg and Washbrook 2003), or the impact of parental employment patterns when children were very young on their later outcomes (for example, Joshi and Verropoulou 2000). Much less attention has been paid to the impact of parental employment patterns on outcomes for adolescents, and this book aimed to address this gap in knowledge. Adolescence is a crucial period in the life course when a young person becomes ready to assume adult responsibility, marking the transition from dependent childhood to independent adulthood (Schoon 2003). Today's adolescents are the parents, teachers, and leaders of the future, and there is clear evidence from life course research that adolescence experiences, and the formation of attitudes and opinions at this stage, have a pronounced influence on adult life. In addition, the opportunities and experiences mark the present quality of young people's lives. However, it would also be interesting and useful to follow the samples of young people used in this research in future years, into young adulthood and beyond. How will parental employment patterns during childhood and adolescence effect individuals' outcomes later in life? The BHPS provides a perfect opportunity to follow these individuals, and consider the future implications of parental employment patterns for these contemporary samples.

As mentioned above, this study used quantitative methods to investigate the relationships between parental employment patterns and outcomes for young people. Further work could be conducted to explore both parents' and young people's opinions and attitudes to parental employment patterns, research which lends itself to the use of qualitative methods.

Options for mothers (and fathers) to spend more time in the self-provision of childcare should be acknowledged and available to all parents. Public policy should not ignore the needs of parents who choose to look after children themselves, to use informal provision or to use a combination of childcare options. Whilst there is a need to ensure that the productivity of all those involved in childrearing is preserved and promoted by encouraging mothers to maintain contact with the labour market after childbirth, the productivity of carers should be recognised and rewarded. The value of direct parental care has been recognised in the progressive extension to maternity leave and pay, paternity leave and pay, and parental leave. In moving away from a climate where any employment of a mother which separated her from a young child was frowned upon, there should not be a swing to a situation where full-time continuous employment is regarded as ideal or compulsory.

Bibliography

6, P. (2002) *The politics of well-being: sense and solidarities: a neo-Durkheimian institutional theory of well-being and its implications for public policy*, paper presented at the Economic and Social Research Council seminar on Wellbeing: social and individual determinants, King's Fund, London.

Adelman, L., Middleton, S. and Ashworth, K. (2003) *Britain's poorest children: severe and persistent poverty and social exclusion*, Save the Children, London.

Ahmed, E. and Braithwaite, E. (2004) 'Bullying and victimization: cause for concern for both families and school', *Social Psychology of Education*, 7, 1, 35–54.

Aldridge, S. (2001) *Social mobility: a discussion paper*, Performance and Innovation Unit, Cabinet Office, London. <www.renewal.net/Documents/RNET/Research/Socialmobilitydiscussion.pdf>

Alexander, L., Currie, C. and Mellor, A. (2004a) *Bullying: health, well-being and risk behaviours*, Briefing Paper 10, Health Behaviour in School-Aged Children, Child and Adolescent Health Research Unit, University of Edinburgh.

Alexander, L., Currie, C. and Mellor, A. (2004b) *Social context of bullying behaviours*, Briefing Paper 9, Health Behaviour in School-Aged Children, Child and Adolescent Health Research Unit, University of Edinburgh.

Alexander, T. (2002) *A bright future for all: promoting mental health in education*, The Mental Health Foundation, London.

Amato, P. (1998) 'More than money? Men's contribution to their children's lives', in A. Booth and A. Crouter (eds) *Men in families: when do they get involved? What difference does it make?* Lawrence Erlbaum, Mahway, NJ.

Amato, P. and Booth, A. (1997) *A generation at risk: growing up in an era of family upheaval*, Harvard University Press, Cambridge, MA.

Andrick, D. and Van Schonbroek, L. (1989) 'The General Health Questionnaire: a psychometric analysis using latent trait theory', *Psychological Medicine*, 19, 2, 469–85.

Arber, S. (2001) 'Secondary analysis of survey data', in N. Gilbert (ed.) *Researching social life*, (second edition), Sage, London.

Arendall, T. (2000) 'Conceiving and investigating motherhood: the decade's scholarship', *Journal of Marriage and the Family*, 62, 4, 1192–207.

Argyle, M. and Crossland, J. (1987) 'Dimensions of positive emotions', *British Journal of Social Psychology*, 26, 2, 127–37.

Armstrong, D. (1999) 'School performance and staying on: a microanalysis for Northern Ireland', *The Manchester School*, 67, 2, 203–30.

Ashford, R. (1994) 'Who is excluded from school? Does family status have an influence?', *Pastoral Care in Education*, 12, 1, 10–11.

Ashworth, K., Hardman, J., Liu, W-C., Maguire, S. and Middleton, S. (2001) *Education Maintenance Allowance: the first year, a quantitative evaluation*, Research Report 257, Department for Education and Employment, London. <www.dfes.gov.uk/research/data/uploadfiles/RR257.pdf>.

Audit Commission (1996) *Misspent youth: young people and crime*, Audit Commission, London.

Audit Commission (1999) *Missing out: LEA management of school attendance and exclusion*, Audit Commission, London.

Averett, S. and Burton, M. (1996) 'College attendance and the college wage premium: differences by gender', *Economics of Education Review*, 15, 1, 37–49.

Balding, J. (1983) 'Developing the Health Related Behaviour Questionnaire', *Education and Health*, 1, 1, 9–13.

Balding, J. (1996) *Bully off*, Schools Health Education Unit, University of Exeter, Exeter.

Balding, J. (2005) *Young people in 2004*, Schools Health Education Unit, University of Exeter, Exeter.

Balding, J., Regis, D. and Wise, A. (1998) *No worries? Young people and mental health*, Schools Health Education Unit, University of Exeter, Exeter.

Baldry, A. (2004) 'The impact of direct and indirect bullying on the mental and physical health of Italian youngsters', *Aggressive Behavior*, 30, 5, 343–55.

Baldry, A. and Farrington, D. (1998) 'Parenting influences on bullying and victimization', *Legal and Criminological Psychology*, 3, 2, 237–54.

Baldry, A. and Farrington, D. (2005) 'Protective factors as moderators of risk factors in adolescence bullying', *Social Psychology of Education*, 8, 3, 263–84.

Banks, M. (1983) 'Validation of the General Health Questionnaire in a young community sample', *Psychological Medicine*, 13, 2, 349–53.

Barlow, A. and Duncan, S. (2000) 'Supporting families? New Labour's communitarianism and the 'rationality mistake': part 1', *Journal of Social Welfare and Family Law*, 22, 1, 23–42.

Barron, R. and Norris, G. (1976) 'Sexual divisions and the dual labour market', in D. Barker and S. Allen (eds) *Dependence and exploitation in work and marriage*, Longman, London.

Baumeister, R., Campbell, J., Krueger, J. and Vohs, K. (2003) 'Does high self-esteem cause better performance, interpersonal success, happiness, or healthier lifestyles?', *Science in the Public Interest*, 4, 1, 1–44.

BBC (1997) 'Missing mum', *Panorama*, BBC1, 3 February 1997.

BBC (2001) 'Phone-in: stay-at-home mums', *Woman's Hour*, Radio 4, 14/11/01. <www.bbc.co.uk/radio4/womanshour/2001_46_wed_01.shtml>

Becker, G. (1964) *Human capital: a theoretical and empirical analysis, with special reference to education*, National Bureau of Economic Research, New York, NY.

Becker, G. (1981) *A treatise on the family*, Harvard University Press, Cambridge, MA.

Becker, G. (1993) *Human capital* (third edition), University of Chicago Press, Chicago, IL.

Becker, G. and Tomes, N. (1976) 'Child endowments and the quantity and quality of children', *Journal of Political Economy*, 84, 4, S143–62.

Becker, G. and Tomes, N. (1979) 'An equilibrium theory of the distribution of income and intergenerational mobility', *Journal of Political Economy*, 87, 6, 1153–89.

Becker, G. and Tomes, N. (1986) 'Human capital and the rise and fall of families', *Journal of Labor Economics*, 4, 3, S1–39.

Becker, S. and Bryman, A. (2004) (eds) *Understanding research methods for social policy*, The Policy Press, Bristol.

Beechey, V. and Perkins, T. (1987) *A matter of hours: women, part-time work and the labour market*, Polity Press, Cambridge.

Belsky, J. (1988) 'Infant day care and socioemotional development in the United States', *Journal of Child Psychology and Psychiatry*, 29, 4, 397–406.

Ben-Zur, H. (2003) 'Happy adolescents: the link between subjective well-being, internal resources, and parental factors', *Journal of Youth and Adolescence*, 32, 2, 67–79.

Beran, T., Hughes, G. and Lupart, J. (Beran) (2005) 'A model of achievement and bullying: analyses of the Canadian National Longitudinal Survey of Children and Youth data', *Manuscript submitted to Educational Research*.

Berdondini, L. and Smith, P. (1996) 'Cohesion and power in the families of children involved in bully-victim problems at school: an Italian replication', *Journal of Family Therapy*, 18, 1, 99–102.

Bergman, M. and Scott, J. (2001) 'Young adolescents' well-being and health-risk behaviours: gender and socio-economic differences', *Journal of Adolescence*, 24, 2, 183–97.

Berridge, D., Brodie, I., Pitts, J., Porteous, D. and Tarling, R. (2001) *The independent effects of permanent exclusion from school on the offending careers of young people*, Occasional Paper 71, Home Office, London. <www.homeoffice.gov.uk/rds/pdfs/occ71-exclusion.pdf>

Besag, V. (1989) *Bullies and victims in schools*, Open University Press, Milton Keynes.

Biggart, A. (2002) 'Attainment, gender and minimum-aged school leavers' early routes in the labour market', *Journal of Education and Work*, 15, 2, 145–62.

Blair, T. (1999) 'Beveridge revisited: the Welfare State for the 21st century', in R. Walker (ed.) *Ending Child Poverty*, The Policy Press, Bristol.

Blanden, J., Goodman, A., Gregg, P. and Machin, S. (2003) 'Changes in intergenerational mobility in Britain', in M. Corak (ed.) *Generational income mobility*, Cambridge University Press, Cambridge.

Blundell, R. (2000) 'Work incentives and in-work benefit reforms: a review', *Oxford Review of Economic Policy*, 16, 1, 27–44.

Blundell, R. (2001) 'Welfare reform for low-income workers', *Oxford Economic Papers*, 53, 2, 189–214.

Bogenschneider, K. and Steinberg, L. (1994) 'Maternal employment and adolescents' academic achievement: a developmental analysis', *Sociology of Education*, 67, 1, 60–77.

Bosworth, D. (1994) 'Truancy and pupil performance', *Education Economics*, 2, 3, 243–65.

Boulton, M. and Underwood, K. (1992) 'Bully/victim problems among middle school children', *British Journal of Educational Psychol*ogy, 62, 1, 73–87.

Bourdieu, P. (1973) 'Cultural reproduction and social reproduction', in R. Brown (ed.) *Knowledge, education and cultural change*, Tavistock, London.

Bourdieu, P. (1983) 'The forms of capital', in J. Richardson (ed.) (1986) *Handbook of theory and research for the sociology of education*, Greenwood Press, New York, NY.

Bourdieu, P. (1984) *Distinction: a social critique of the judgement of taste*, Harvard University Press, Cambridge, MA.

Bourdieu, P. (1987) 'What makes a social class?', *Berkeley Journal of Sociolog*y, 32, 1, 1–17.

Bourdieu, P. (1999) *The weight of the world: social suffering in contemporary society*, Polity Press, Oxford.

Bourdieu, P. (2000) *Masculine domination*, Polity Press, Oxford.

Bourdieu, P. and Coleman, J. (eds) (1991) *Social theory for a changing society*, Westview Press, Boulder, CO.

Bowers, L., Smith, P. and Binney, V. (1992) 'Cohesion and power in the families of children involved in bully/victim problems at school', *Journal of Family Therapy*, 14, 4, 371–87.

Bowers, L., Smith, P. and Binney, V. (1994) 'Perceived family relationships of bullies, victims and bully/victims in middle childhood', *Journal of Social Personal Relationships*, 11, 2, 215–32.

Bowlby, J. (1969) *Attachment and loss: volume 1 – attachment*, Hogarth Press, London.

Bradley, S. and Nguyen, A. (2003) *The school-to-work transition*, Working Paper 44, Lancaster University Management School, Lancaster. <www.lums.lancs.ac.uk/publications/viewpdf/000186/>

Bradshaw, J. (2001) *Poverty: the outcomes for children*, Family Policy Studies Centre/National Children's Bureau, London.

Bradshaw, J. (ed.) (2002a) *The well-being of children in the UK*, Save the Children, London.

Bradshaw, J. (2002b) 'Child poverty and child outcomes', *Children and Society*, 16, 2, 131–40.

Bradshaw, J., Ditch, J., Holmes, H. and Whiteford, P. (1993) *Support for children: a comparison of arrangements in fifteen countries*, Research Report 21, Department of Social Security, London.

Bradshaw, J. and Finch, N. (2002) *A comparison of child benefit packages in 22 countries*, Department for Work and Pensions Research Report 174, Corporate Document Services, Leeds.

Bradshaw, J., Kennedy, S., Kilkey, M., Hutton, S. and Corden, A. (1996) *The employment of lone parents: a comparison of policy in 20 countries*, Family Policy Studies Centre, London.

Bradshaw, J. and Mayhew, E. (eds) (2005) *The well-being of children in the UK* (second edition), Save the Children, London.

Brannen, J., Moss, P., Owen, C. and Wale, C. (1997) *Mothers, fathers and employment: parents and the labour market in Britain 1984–1994*, Research Report 10, Department for Education and Employment, London.

Bridges, L., Margie, N. and Zaff, J. (2001) *Background for community-level work on emotional well-being in adolescence: reviewing the literature on contributing factors*, Child Trends, Washington, DC. <www.childtrends.org/what_works/youth_development/doc/KEmotional.pdf>

Brodie, G. and Berridge, D. (1996) *School exclusions: research themes and issues*, University of Luton Press, Luton.

Brooks, G., Gorman, T., Harman, J., Hutchinson, D. and Wilkin, A. (1998) *Family literacy works*, Basic Skills Agency, London.

Brooks, R. (1998) *Staying or leaving? A literature review of factors affecting the take-up of post-16 options*, National Foundation for Educational Research, Slough.

Bruegel, I. (1979) 'Women as a reserve army of labour: a note on recent British experience', *Feminist Review*, 3, 12–23.

Bruegel, I. (1996) 'Whose myths are they anyway: a comment', *British Journal of Sociology*, 47, 1, 175–7.

Brugha, T., Wing, J., Brewin, C., MacCarthy, B. and Lesage, A. (1993) 'The relationship of social network deficits with deficits in social functioning in long-term psychiatric disorders', *Social Psychiatry and Psychiatric Epidemiology*, 28, 5, 218–24.

Buchanan, A., Flouri, E. and Ten Brinke, J. (2002) 'Emotional and behavioural problems in childhood and distress in adult life: risk and protective factors', *Australian and New Zealand Journal of Psychiatry*, 36, 4, 521–7.

Buchanan, A., Ten Brinke, J. and Flouri, E. (2000) 'Parental background, social disadvantage, public care, and psychological problems in adolescence', *Journal of the American Academy of Child and Adolescent Psychiatry*, 39, 11, 1415–23.

Buchel, F. and Duncan, G. (1998) 'Do parents' social activities promote children's school attainments? Evidence from the German Socio-economic Panel', *Journal of Marriage and the Family*, 60, 1, 95–108.

Buckingham, A. and Saunders, P. (2004) *The survey methods workbook: from design to analysis*, Polity Press, Cambridge.

Burchell, B., Dale, A. and Joshi, H. (1997) 'Part-time work among British women', in H-P. Blossfeld, and C. Hakim (eds) *Between equalisation and marginalisation: women working part-time in Europe and the United States of America*, Oxford University Press, Oxford.

Burt, R. (2000) 'The network structure of social capital', in R. Sutton, and B. Staw (eds) *Research in organizational behaviour*, JAI Press, Greenwich, CT.

Butler, N., Golding, J. and Howlett, B. (1986) *From birth to five: a study of the health and behaviour of Britain's five year olds*, Pergamon Press, Oxford.

Buxton, J. (1998) *Ending the mother war: starting the workplace revolution*, Macmillan, Basingstoke.

Bynner, J. and Parsons, S. (1998) *Influences on adults' basic skills: factors affecting the development of literacy and numeracy from birth to 37*, The Basic Skills Agency, London.

Callender, C., Millward, N., Lissenburgh, S. and Forth, J. (1997) *Maternity rights and benefits in Britain 1996*, Research Report 67, Department of Social Security, London.

Campbell, A., Walker, J. and Farrell, G. (2003) 'Confirmatory factor analysis of the GHQ-12: can I see that again?', *Australian and New Zealand Journal of Psychiatry*, 37, 4, 475–83.

Casey, B. and Smith, D. (1995) *Truancy and youth transitions*, Youth Cohort Study Report 34, Research Strategy Branch, Department for Education and Employment, Sheffield.

Catalano, R., Berglund, L., Ryan, A., Lonczak, H. and Hawkins, J. (2002) 'Positive youth development in the United States: research finding on evaluations of Positive Youth Development programmes', *Prevention and Treatment*, 5, 15.

Chapman, S. and Abbott, W. (1913) 'The tendency of children to enter their father's trades', *Journal of the Royal Statistical Society*, 76, 6, 599–604.

Chapman, S. and Marquis, F. (1912) 'The recruiting of the employing classes from the ranks of the wage earners in the cotton industry', *Journal of the Royal Statistical Society*, 75, 2, 293–306.

Chatterji, P. and Markowitz, S. (2004) *Does the length of maternity leave affect maternal health?*, NBER Working Paper 10206, National Bureau of Economic Research, Cambridge, MA.

Cheng, Y. (1995) *Staying on in full-time education after 16: do schools make a difference?*, Youth Cohort Study Report 37, Research Strategy Branch, Department for Education and Employment, Sheffield.

Childline (2005) *Does back to school mean back to bullying?* Press Release, 31 August 2005, Childline, London. <www.childline.org.uk/doesbacktoschoolmeanbacktobullying.asp>

Children's Society (2002) *Improving behaviour: a report on the consultation with children and young people on their views for improving behaviour in schools*, Children's Society, London.

Christensen, S., Melder, J. and B. Weisbrod (1975) 'Factors affecting college attendance', *Journal of Human Resources*, 10, 2, 174–88.

Clark, A. and Oswald, A. (2002a) 'A simple statistical method for measuring how life events affect happiness', Inter*national Journal of Epidemiology*, 31, 6, 1139–44.

Clark, A. and Oswald, A. (2002b) *Well-being in panels*, Working Paper, Department of Economics, University of Warwick and DELTA, Paris. <www.delta.ens.fr/clark/revClarkOsdec2002.pdf>

Clark, D., Conlon, G. and Galindo-Rueda, F. (2005) 'Post-compulsory education and qualification attainment', in S. Machin and A. Vignoles (eds) *What's the good of education? The economics of education in the United Kingdom*, Princeton University Press, Princeton, NJ.

Clarke, L., Bradshaw, J. and Williams, J. (2000) 'Family diversity and poverty and the mental well-being of young people', in H. Ryan and J. Bull (eds) *Changing family, changing communities: researching health and well-being among children and young people*, Health Development Agency, London.

Coleman, J. (1988) 'Social capital in the creation of human capital', *American Journal of Sociology*, 94, S95–120.

Coles, B., Hutton, S., Bradshaw, J., Craig, G., Godfrey, C. and Johnson, J. (2002) *Literature review of the costs of being not in education, employment or training at age 16–18*, Research Report 347, Department for Education and Skills, London. <www.dfes.gov.uk/research/data/uploadfiles/RR347.pdf>

Collins, D. (1998) *Managing truancy in schools*, Cassell, London.

Collishaw, S., Maughan, B., Goodman, R. and Pickles, A. (2004) 'Time trends in adolescent mental health', *Journal of Child Psychology and Psychiatry*, 45, 8, 1350–62.

Commission for Racial Equality (CRE) (1996) *Exclusion from school: the public cost*, CRE, London.

Corti, L., Foster, J. and Thompson, P. (1995) Archiving qualitative research data, *Social Research Update*, 10, University of Surrey, Guildford. <www.soc.surrey.ac.uk/sru/SRU10.html>

Cowie, H., Boardman, C., Dawking, J. and Jennifer, D. (2004) *Emotional health and well-being: a practical guide for schools*, Paul Chapman Publishing, London.

Craig, W. (1998) 'The relationship among bullying, victimization, depression, anxiety, and aggression in elementary school children', *Personality and Individual Differences*, 24, 1, 123–30.

Croll, P. (2004) 'Families, social capital and educational outcomes', *British Journal of Educational Studies*, 52, 4, 390–416.

Crompton, R. (1980) 'Class mobility in modern Britain', *Sociology*, 14, 1, 117–19.

Crompton, R. (1997) *Women and work in modern Britain*, Oxford University Press, Oxford.

Crompton, R. (1999) *Restructuring gender relations and employment: the decline of the male breadwinner*, Oxford University Press, Oxford.

Crompton, R. (2002) 'Employment, flexible working and the family', *British Journal of Sociology*, 53, 4, 537–58.

Crompton, R. and Harris, F. (1998a) 'A reply to Hakim', *British Journal of Sociology*, 49, 1, 144–9.

Crompton, R. and Harris, F. (1998b) 'Explaining women's employment patterns: 'Orientations to work' revisited', *British Journal of Sociology*, 49, 1, 118–36.

Cummings, E., Davies, P. and Campbell, S. (2000) *Developmental psychopathology and family process: theory, research and clinical implications*, Guildford Press, New York, NY.

Cutright, P. (1995) 'Neighbourhood social structure and the lives of Black and White children', *Sociological Focus*, 27, 3, 243–55.

Dale, A., Arber, S. and Proctor, M. (1988) *Doing secondary analysis*, Unwin Hyman, London.

Dalziel, D. and Henthorne, K. (2005) *Parents'/carers' attitudes towards school attendance*, Research Report 618, Department for Education and Skills, London. <www.dfes.gov.uk/research/data/uploadfiles/RR618.pdf>

Daniels, H., Cole, T., Sellman, E., Sutton, J. and Visser, J. with Bedward, J. (2003) *Study of young people permanently excluded from school*, Research Report 405, Department for Education and Skills, London. <www.dfes.gov.uk/research/data/uploadfiles/RR405.pdf>

Davies, J. (ed.) (1993) *The family: is it just another lifestyle choice?*, Institute of Economic Affairs, London.

Daycare Trust (2004) *A new era for universal childcare?*, Leading the Vision Policy Papers 1, Daycare Trust, London.

Dearden, L., Ferrier, J. and Meghir, C. (2000) *The effects of school quality on educational attainment and wages*, Working Paper 00/22, Institute of Fiscal Studies, London. <www.ifs.org.uk/wps/wp0022.pdf>

Delorenzi, S. and Robinson, P. (2005) *Choosing to learn: improving participation after compulsory education*, Institute for Public Policy Research, London.

Department of Education and Science (1989) *Discipline in schools (Report of the committee of enquiry chaired by Lord Elton)*, HMSO, London.

Department for Education (1994) *Bullying – don't suffer in silence: an anti-bullying pack for schools*, HMSO, London.

Department for Education and Employment (1997) *Excellence in schools*, Cm 3681, HMSO, London.

Department for Education and Employment (1998a) *Meeting the childcare challenge*, Cm 3959, HMSO, London.

Department for Education and Employment (1998b) *Pupil absence and truancy from schools in England 1993/94–1997/98*, Statistical Bulletin 14, DFEE, London.

Department for Education and Employment (1999a) *The National Healthy Schools Standard*, HMSO, London. <www.wiredforhealth.gov.uk/PDF/Brochurenew.pdf>

Department for Education and Employment (1999b) *Learning To Succeed: a new framework for post-16 learning*, Cm 4392, HMSO, London.

Department for Education and Employment (2000a) *Work life balance: changing patterns in a changing world*, HMSO, London.

Department for Education and Employment (2000b) *Youth cohort study: education, training and employment of 16–18 year olds in England and the factors associated with non-participation*, Statistical Bulletin 2, DFEE, London.

Department for Education and Skills (2001a) *Participation in education, training and employment by 16–18 year olds in England: 1999 and 2000*, Statistical First Release 30, DFES, London.

Department for Education and Skills (2001b) *Youth cohort study: the activities and experiences of 16 year olds: England and Wales, 2000*, Statistical First Release 2, DFES, London.

Department for Education and Skills (2001c) *Statistics of education: public examinations GCSE/GNVQ and GCE/AGNVQ in England 2000*, Statistical Volume, HMSO, London.

Department for Education and Skills (2002a) *Bullying – don't suffer in silence: an anti-bullying pack for schools (revised version)*, HMSO, London.

Department for Education and Skills (2002b) *14–19: extending opportunities, raising standards*, Cm 5342, HMSO, London.

Department for Education and Skills (2003) *Guidance on exclusion from schools and pupil referral units*, Circular 87/03, DFES, London.

Department for Education and Skills (2004a) *Improving behaviour and attendance: guidance on exclusion from school and pupil referral units*, HMSO, London.

Department for Education and Skills (2004b) *Permanent and fixed period exclusions from schools and exclusion appeals in England, 2002/03*, Statistical First Release 42, DFES, London.

Department for Education and Skills (2005a) *Managing behaviour and attendance: handling signs of disaffection*, DFES, London.

Department for Education and Skills (2005b) *Pupil absence in schools in England 2004/05 (revised)*, Statistical First Release 56, DFES, London.

Department for Education and Skills (2005c) *Trends in education and skills online*, HMSO, London. <www.dfes.gov.uk/trends/>

Department for Education and Skills (2005d) *Youth cohort study: the activities and experiences of 16 year olds: England and Wales, 2004*, Statistical First Release 4, DFES, London

Department for Education and Skills (2005e) *Permanent and fixed period exclusions from schools and exclusion appeals in England, 2003/04*, Statistical First Release 23, DFES, London.

Department for Education and Skills (2005f) *14–19 education and skills, White Paper*, Cm6476, HMSO, London.

Department for Education and Skills (2006) *Participation in education and training by 16 and 17 year olds in each local area in England: 2003 and 2004*, Statistical First Release 13, DFES, London

Department for Education and Skills/Home Office (2002) *Tackling it together: truancy and crime*, HMSO, London. <www.dfes.gov.uk/schoolattendance/uploads/TacklingitTogether.pdf>

Department of Health/Department for Education and Skills (2004) *National service framework for children, young people and maternity services*, HMSO, London.

Department of Social Security (1998a) *New ambitions for our country: a new contract for welfare*, Cm 3805, HMSO, London.

Department of Social Security (1998b) *A new contract for welfare: the gateway to work*, Cm 4102, HMSO, London.

Department of Social Security (1999) *Opportunity for all: tackling poverty and social exclusion*, Cm 4445, HMSO, London.

Department of Social Security (2000a) *Households below average income: a statistical analysis 1994/5 – 1998/9*, Corporate Document Services, Leeds.

Department of Social Security (2000b) *Opportunity for all – one year on: making a difference*, Cm 3865, HMSO, London.

Department of Trade and Industry (2000) *Work and parents – competitiveness and choice: a Green Paper*, Cm 5005, HMSO, London.

Department for Work and Pensions (2001) *Opportunity for all: making progress*, Cm 5260, HMSO, London.

Department for Work and Pensions (2002) *Opportunity for all: fourth annual report 2002*, Cm 5598, HMSO, London.

Department for Work and Pensions (2003) *Opportunity for all: fifth annual report 2003*, Cm 5956, HMSO, London.

Department for Work and Pensions (2004) *Opportunity for all: sixth annual report 2004*, Cm 6329, HMSO, London.

Department for Work and Pensions (2005) *Opportunity for all: seventh annual report 2005*, Cm 6673, HMSO, London.

Department for Work and Pensions (2006a) *Opportunity for all: eighth annual report*, Cm 6915, HMSO, London.

Department for Work and Pensions (2006b) *Households below average income: a statistical analysis 1994/5 – 1998/9*, Corporate Document Services, Leeds.

Desforges, C. (2003) *The impact of parental involvement, parental support and family education on pupil achievement and adjustment: a review of the literature*, Research Report 433, Department for Education and Skills, London. <www.dfes.gov.uk/research/data/uploadfiles/RR433.pdf>

De Vaus, D. (1996) *Surveys in social research* (third edition), UCL Press, London.

Devine, F. (2004) *Class practices: how parents help their children get good jobs*, Cambridge University Press, Cambridge.

Dex, S. (1995) 'The reliability of recall data: a literature review', *Bulletin de Methodologie Sociologique*, 49, 58–80.

Dex, S. (ed.) (1999) *Families and the labour market*, Family Policy Studies Centre/Joseph Rowntree Foundation, London.

Dex, S. and Joshi, H. (2005) *Children of the 21st century: from birth to nine months*, The Policy Press, Bristol.

Dex, S., Joshi, H. and Macran, S. (1996) 'A widening gulf among Britain's mothers', *Oxford Review of Economic Policy*, 12, 1, 65–75.

Dex, S., Joshi, H., Macran, S. and McCullogh, A. (1998) 'Women's employment transitions around childbearing', *Oxford Bulletin of Economics and Statistics*, 60, 1, 79–98.

Dickens, R., Gregg, P. and Wadsworth, J. (eds) (2003) *The labour market under New Labour*, Palgrave Macmillan, Basingstoke.

Diener, E. (2000) 'Subjective well-being: the science of happiness, and a proposal for a national index', *American Psycho*logist, 55, 1, 34–43.

Diener, E., Suh, E., Lucas, R., and Smith, H. (1999) 'Subjective well-being: three decades of progress', *Psychological Bulletin*, 125, 2, 276–302.

Donnelley, M. (1999) 'Factors associated with depressed mood among adolescents in Northern Ireland', *Journal of Community and Allied Social Psychology*, 9, 1, 47–59.

Dunn, J., Deater-Deckard, K., Pickering, K., O'Connor, T., Golding, J. and the ALSPAC Study Team (1998) 'Children's adjustment and prosocial behaviour in step-, single, and non-stepfamily settings: findings from a community study', *Journal of Child Psychology and Psychiatry*, 39, 8, 1083–95.

Durkin, K. (1995) *Developmental social psychology: from infancy to old age*, Blackwell, Oxford.

Durlak, J. and Wells, A. (1997) 'Primary prevention mental health programs for children and adolescents: a meta-analytic review', *American Journal of Community Psychology*, 25, 2,115–52.

Dustmann, C., Rajah, N. and Smith, S. (1997) 'Teenage truancy, part-time working and wages', *Journal of Population Economics*, 10, 4, 425–42.

Edwards, L. (2003) *Promoting young people's well-being: a review of research on emotional health*, Research Report 15, Scottish Council for Research in Education, University of Glasgow, Glasgow. <www.scre.ac.uk/resreport/pdf/115.pdf>

Elander, J. and Rutter, M. (1996) 'Use and development of the Rutter parents' and teachers' scales', *International Journal of Methods in Psychiatric Research*, 6, 2, 63–78.

Elias, P. (1991) 'Methodological, statistical and practical issues arising from the collection and analysis of work history information by survey techniques', *Bulletin de Methodologie Sociologique*, 31, 3–31.

Elliot, J. and Richards, M. (1991) 'Children and divorce: educational performance and behaviour before and after parental separation', *International Journal of Law and the Family*, 5, 3, 258–76.

Elliott, M. (2002) *Bullying pays! A survey of young offenders*, Kidscape, London.

Elliott, M. and Kilpatrick, J. (1994) *How to stop bullying: a Kidscape guide to training*, Kidscape, London.

Ely, M., West, P., Sweeting, H. and Richards M. (2000) 'Teenage family life, lifechances, lifestyles and health: a comparison of two contemporary cohorts', *International Journal of Law, Policy and the Family*, 14, 1, 1–30.

Ermisch, J. and Francesconi, M. (2000) *The effect of parent's employment on children's educational attainment*, Working Paper 31, Institute for Social and Economic Research, University of Essex, Colchester. <www.iser.essex.ac.uk/pubs/workpaps/pdf/2000-31.pdf>

Ermisch, J. and Francesconi, M. (2001a) *The effects of parents' employment on children's lives*, Family Policy Studies Centre/Joseph Rowntree Foundation, London.

Ermisch, J. and Francesconi, M. (2001b) 'Family matters: impacts of family background on educational attainment', *Economica*, 68, 270, 137–56.

Ermisch, J. and Francesconi, M. (2001c) 'Family structure and children's achievements', *Journal of Population Economics*, 14, 2, 249–70.

Ermisch, J., Francesconi, M. and Pevalin, D. (2001) *Outcomes for children of poverty*, Department for Work and Pensions Research Report 158, Corporate Document Services, Leeds. <www.dwp.gov.uk/asd/asd5/rrep158.asp>

Ermisch, J., Francesconi, M. and Pevalin, D. (2004) 'Parental partnership and joblessness in childhood and their influence on young people's outcomes', *Journal of the Royal Statistical Society A*, 167, 1, 69–101.

Esping-Anderson, G. (1990) *The three worlds of welfare capitalism*, Polity Press, Cambridge.

European Economic Community (EEC) (1992) *Pregnant workers directive, 92/85/EEC*, EEC, Luxembourg.

Fagan, C. and O'Reilly, J. (eds) (1998) *Part-time prospects: international comparison of part-time work in Europe, North America and the Pacific Rim*, Routledge, London.

Farrington, D. (1993) 'Understanding and preventing bullying', *Crime and Justice*, 17, 381–458.

Farrington, D. (1998) 'Predictors, causes and correlates of male youth violence', *Crime and Justice*, 24, 421–76.

Felce, D. and Perry, J. (1995) 'Quality of life: its definition and measurement', *Research in Developmental Disabilities*, 16, 1, 51–74.

Ferero, R., McLellan, L., Rissel, C. and Bauman, A. (1999) 'Bullying behaviour and psychosocial health among school children in New South Wales, Australia: cross-sectional study', *British Medical Journal*, 319, 344–8.

Ferri, E. and Smith, K. (1996) *Parenting in the 1990s*, Family Policy Studies Centre/Joseph Rowntree Foundation, London.

Fletcher, M. and Lockhart, I. (2002) *The impact of financial circumstances on engagement with post-16 learning: a systematic map of research*, Learning and Skills Research Centre, London.

Flood-Page, C., Campbell, S., Harrington, V. and Miller, J. (2000) *Youth crime: findings from the 1998/99 Youth Lifestyles Survey*, Research Study 209, Home Office, London

Flouri, E. (2006) 'Parental interest in children's education, children's self-esteem and locus of control, and later education attainment: twenty-six year follow-up of the 1970 British Birth Cohort', *British Journal of Educational Psychology*, 76, 1, 41–55.

Flouri, E. and Buchanan, A. (2002) 'What predicts good relationships with parents in adolescence and partners in adult life: findings from the 1958 British birth cohort', *Journal of Family Psychology*, 16, 2, 186–98.

Fogelman, K. (1983) *Growing up in Great Britain: collected papers from the National Child Development Study*, Macmillan, London.

Fraser, N. (1997) *Justice interruptus: critical reflections on the postsocialist condition*, Routledge, London.

Furstenberg, F. and Hughes, M. (1995) 'Social capital and successful development among at-risk youth', *Journal of Marriage and the Family*, 57, 3, 580–92.

Gilbert, N. (ed.) (2001) *Researching social life* (second edition), Sage, London.

Gillborn, D. and Gipps, C. (1996) *Recent research on the achievement of ethnic minority pupils*, Reviews of Research by The Office for Standards in Education, HMSO, London.

Gilmartin, B. (1987) 'Peer group antecedents of severe love-shyness in males', *Journal of Personality*, 55, 3, 467–89.

Ginn, J., Arber, S., Brannen, J., Dale, A., Dex, S., Elias, P., Moss, P., Pahl, J., Roberts, C. and Rubery, J. (1996) 'Feminist fallacies: a reply to Hakim on women's employment', *British Journal of Sociology*, 47, 1, 167–74.

Ginsberg, H. (1929) 'Interchange between social classes', *Economic Journal*, 39, 156, 554–65.

Gittins, D. (1998) *The child in question*, Macmillan Press, Basingstoke.

Glass, D. (ed.) (1954) *Social mobility in Britain*, Routledge and Kegan Paul, London.

Glass, N. (1999) 'Sure Start: the development of an early intervention programme for young people in the United Kingdom', *Children and Society*, 13, 4, 257–64.

Glendinning, A., Kloep, M. and Hendry, L. (2000) 'Parenting practices and well-being in youth: family life in rural Scotland and Sweden', in H. Ryan and J. Bull (eds) *Changing families, changing communities: researching health and well-being among children and young people*, Health Development Agency, London.

Glew, G., Fan, M., Katon, W., Rivara, F. and Kernic, M. (2005) 'Bullying, psychosocial adjustment and academic performance in elementary school', *Archives of Paediatrics and Adolescent Medicine*, 159, 11, 1026–31.

Glover, D., Cartwright, N. and Gleeson, D. (1998) *Towards bully-free schools: interventions in action*, Open University Press, Milton Keynes.

Goldberg, D. (1972) *The detection of minor psychiatric illness by questionnaire*, Oxford University Press, Oxford.

Goldberg, D., Oldehinkel, T. and Ormel, J. (1998) 'Why GHQ threshold varies from one place to another', *Psychological Medicine*, 28, 4, 915–21.

Goldberg, D. and Williams, P. (1988) *A user's guide to the General Health Questionnaire*, NFER-Nelson, Windsor.

Golding, J., Pembrey, M., Jones, R. and the ALSPAC Study Team (2001) 'ALSPAC – The Avon Longitudinal Study of Parents and Children: Study methodology', *Paediatric and Perinatal Epidemiology*, 15, 1, 74–87.

Goldthorpe, J. (1980) *Social mobility and class structure in modern Britain*, Clarendon Press, Oxford.

Goldthorpe, J. and Payne, C. (1986) 'Trends in intergenerational class mobility in England and Wales, 1972–1983', *Sociology*, 20, 1, 1–24.

Goodman, R. (1997) 'The Strengths and Difficulties Questionnaire: a research note', *Journal of Child Psychology and Psychiatry*, 38, 5, 581–6.

Goodman, R. (1999) 'The extended version of the Strengths and Difficulties Questionnaire as a guide to child psychiatric caseness and consequent burden', *Journal of Child Psychology and Psychiatry*, 40, 5, 791–9.

Goodman, R., Ford, T., Richards, H., Gatward, R. and Meltzer, H. (2000a) 'The development and well-being assessment: description and initial validation of an integrated assessment of child and adolescent psychopathology', *Journal of Child Psychology and Psychiatry*, 41, 5, 645–55.

Goodman, R., Ford, T., Simmons, H., Gatward, R. and Meltzer, H. (2000b) 'Using the Strengths and Difficulties Questionnaire (SDQ) to screen for child psychiatric disorders in a community sample', *British Journal of Psychiatry*, 177, 6, 534–9.

Graetz, B. (1991) 'Multidimensional properties of the General Health Questionnaire', *Social Psychiatry and Psychiatric Epidemiology*, 26, 3, 132–8.

Graham, J. and Bowling, B. (1995) *Young people and crime*, Home Office Research Report 145, HMSO, London.

Granovetter, M. (1973) 'The strength of weak ties', *American Journal of Sociology*, 78, 6, 1360–80.

Granovetter, M. (1974) *Getting a job: a study of contacts and careers*, Harvard University Press, Cambridge, MA.

Gray, G., Smith, A. and Rutter, M. (1980) 'School attendance and the first year of employment', in L. Hersov, and I. Berg (eds) *Out of school*, John Wiley, Chichester.

Green, H., McGinnity, A., Meltzer, H., Ford, T. and Goodman, R. (2005) *Mental health of children and young people in Great Britain 2004*, Palgrave MacMillan, London.

Gregg, P. (2000) *The impact of youth unemployment on adult unemployment in the NCDS*, Working paper 00/495, Economics Department, Bristol University, Bristol.

Gregg, P. and Machin, S. (1997) *Blighted lives*, Centre Piece, Centre for Economic Performance, London School of Economics, London.

Gregg, P. and Machin, S. (1998) *Child development and success or failure in the youth labour market*, Discussion Paper 397, Centre for Economic Performance, London School of Economics, London. <http://cep.lse.ac.uk/pubs/download/dp0397.pdf>

Gregg, P. and Wadsworth, J. (eds) (1999) *The state of working Britain*, Manchester University Press, Manchester.

Gregg, P. and Wadsworth, J. (2004) *Two sides to every story: measuring the polarisation of work*, Discussion Paper 632, Centre for Economic Performance, London School of Economics, London. <http://cep.lse.ac.uk/pubs/download/dp0632.pdf>

Gregg, P., Hansen, K. and Wadsworth, J. (1999) 'The rise of the workless household', in P. Gregg and J. Wadsworth (eds) *The state of working Britain*, Manchester University Press, Manchester.

Gregg, P., Waldfogel, J. and Washbrook, E. (2005) *Family expenditures post-welfare reform in the UK: are low-income families starting to catch up?*, Working Paper 119, Centre for Market and Public Performance, University of Bristol. <www.bris.ac.uk/Depts/CMPO/workingpapers/wp119.pdf>

Gregg, P., Washbrook, E. and the ALSPAC Study Team (2003) *The effects of early maternal employment on child development in the UK*, Working Paper 70, Centre for Market and Public Performance, University of Bristol. <www.bris.ac.uk/cmpo/workingpapers/wp70.pdf>

The Guardian (2003) 'Working mothers "bad for children"', November 14. <www.guardian.co.uk/uk_news/story/0,3604,1084834,00.html>

Gureje, O. (1991) 'Reliability and the factor structure of the Yoruba version of the 12-item General Health Questionnaire', *Acta Psychiatrica Scandinavica*, 84, 2, 125–9.

Hakim, C. (1982) *Secondary analysis in social research*, Allen and Unwin, London.

Hakim, C. (1991) 'Grateful slaves and self-made women: fact and fantasy in women's work orientation', *European Sociological Review* 7, 2, 101–21.

Hakim, C. (1995) 'Five feminist myths about women's employment', *British Journal of Sociology*, 46, 3, 429–55.

Hakim, C. (1996a) *Key issues in women's work: female heterogeneity and the polarisation of women's employment*, Athlone Press, London.

Hakim, C. (1996b) 'The sexual division of labour and women's heterogeneity', *British Journal of Sociology*, 47, 1, 178–88.

Hakim, C. (1998) 'Developing a sociology for the twenty-first century: preference theory', *British Journal of Sociology*, 49, 1, 137–43.

Hakim, C. (2000) *Work-lifestyle choices in the 21st century: preference theory*, Oxford University Press, Oxford.

Hakim, C. (2002) 'Lifestyle preferences as determinants of women's differential labour market careers', *Work and Occupations*, 29, 4, 428–59.

Hakim, C. (2003) *Models of the family in modern societies: ideals and realities*, Ashgate, Aldershot.

Halpin, B. (1997) *Unified BHPS work-life histories: combining multiple sources into a user-friendly format*, Technical Paper 13, ESRC Research Centre on Micro-Social Change, University of Essex, Colchester.

Halpin, B. (2000) *BHPS work-life history files*, Version 2, Institute for Social and Economic Research, University of Essex, Colchester.

Halsey, A. (ed.) (1988) *British social trends since 1900: a guide to the changing social structure of Britain* (second edition), Macmillan, Basingstoke.

Halsey, A. (1993) 'Changes in the family', *Children and Society*, 7, 2, 125–36.

Han, W.-J., Waldfogel, J. and Brooks-Gunn, J. (2001) 'The effect of early maternal employment on later cognitive and behavioural outcomes', *Journal of Marriage and Family*, 63, 2, 336–54.

Hanushek, E. (1992) 'The trade-off between child quantity and quality', *Journal of Political Economy*, 100, 1, 84–117.

Harkness, S. (1996) 'The gender earnings gap: evidence from the UK', *Fiscal Studies*, 17, 2, 1–36.

Harrop, A. and Moss, P. (1995) 'Trends in parental employment', *Work, Employment and Society*, 9, 3, 421–44.

Hart, P. (1988) *Youth unemployment in Great Britain*, Cambridge University Press, Cambridge.

Hartmann, H. (1976) 'Capitalism, patriarchy, and job segregation by sex', *Signs*, 1, 3, 137–69.

Harvey, E. (1999) 'Short-term and long-term effects of early parental employment on children of the National Longitudinal Survey of Youth', *Developmental Psychology*, 35, 2, 445–59.

Haveman, R. and Wolfe, B. (1995) 'The determinants of children's attainments: a review of methods and findings', *Journal of Economic Literature*, 33, 4, 1829–78.

Hawker, D. and Boulton, M. (2000) 'Twenty years' research on peer victimization and psychosocial maladjustment: a meta-analytic review of cross-sectional studies', *Journal of Child Psychology and Psychiatry*, 41, 4, 4411–55.

Hawton, K., Rodham, K., Evans, E. and Weatherall, R. (2002) 'Deliberate self - harm in adolescents: self-report survey in schools in England', *British Medical Journal*, 325, 1207–11.

Hayden, C. and Dunne, S. (2001) *Outside, looking in: children's and families' experiences of exclusion from school*, The Children's Society, London.

Heath, A. (1981) *Social mobility*, Fontana, Glasgow.

Hewitt, P. (1993) *About time: the revolution in work and family life*, Rivers Oram Press, London.

Hibbert, A. and Fogelman, K. (1990) 'Future lives of truants: family formation and health-related behaviour', *British Journal of Educational Psychology*, 60, 2, 171–9.

Hibbert, A., Fogelman, K. and Maoner, O. (1990) 'Occupational outcomes of truancy', *British Journal of Educational Psychology*, 60, 1, 23–36.

Hird, S. (2003) *What is well-being? A brief review of current literature and concepts*, Public Health Institute of Scotland and Scottish Executive. <www.phis.org.uk/doc.pl?file=pdf/What%20is%20wellbeing%202.doc>

HM Treasury (1998) *Working Families Tax Credits and work incentives*, The Modernisation of Britain's Tax and Benefit System No 3, HM Treasury, London. <www.hm-treasury.gov.uk/media/65B/66/wftc.pdf>

HM Treasury (2000) *Tackling poverty and making work pay – tax credits for the 21st century*, The Modernisation of Britain's Tax and Benefit System No 6, HM Treasury, London. <www.hm-treasury.gov.uk/media/CDE/54/432.pdf>

HM Treasury (2002) *The Child and Work Tax Credits*, The Modernisation of Britain's Tax and Benefit System No 10, HM Treasury, London. <www.hm-treasury.gov.uk/media/8D5/BD/new_tax_credits.pdf>

HM Treasury (2004a) *Choice for parents, the best start for children: a ten-year strategy for children*, HMSO, London. <www.hmtreasury.gov.uk/media/426/F1/pbr04childcare_480upd050105.pdf>

HM Treasury (2004b) *Child poverty review*, HMSO, London. <www.hmtreasury.gov.uk/media/985/CC/childpoverty_complete_290704.pdf>

Hobcraft, J. (1998) *Intergenerational and life-course transmission of social exclusion: influences and childhood poverty, family disruption and contact with the police*, CASE Paper 15, Centre for the Analysis of Social Exclusion, London School of Economics, London.

Hobcraft, J. (2000) *The roles of schooling and educational qualifications in the emergence of adult social exclusion*, CASE Paper 43, Centre for Analysis of Social Exclusion, London School of Economics, London.

Hobcraft, J. and Sigle-Rushton, W. (2005) *An exploration of childhood antecedents of female adult malaise in two British birth cohorts: combining bayesian model averaging and recursive partitioning*, CASE Paper 95, Centre for the Analysis of Social Exclusion, London School of Economics, London.

Holliday, J. (2002) *Bullying*, Policy, Research and Influencing Unit, Barnardos, London. <www.barnardos.org.uk/bullying.pdf>

House of Commons Treasury Committee (2006) *The administration of tax credits*, Sixth Report of Session 2005–06, HC 811, HMSO, London.

Hudson, M., Lissenburgh, S. and Sahin-Dikmen, M. (2004) *Maternity and paternity rights in Britain 2002: survey of parents*, In-house research report 131, Department for Work and Pensions, London.

Iacovou, M. (2001) *Family composition and children's educational outcomes*, Working Paper 2001-12, Institute for Social and Economic Research, University of Essex, Colchester. <www.iser.essex.ac.uk/pubs/workpaps/pdf/2001-12.pdf>

Johnson, P. and Reed, H. (1996) 'Intergenerational mobility among the rich and poor: results from the National Child Development Survey', *Oxford Review of Economic Policy*, 12, 1, 127–42.

Joshi, H. and Verropoulou, G. (2000) *Maternal employment and child outcomes*, Smith Institute, London.

Kasparova, D., Marsh, A., Vegeris, S. and Perry, J. (2003) *Families and children 2001: work and childcare*, Department for Work and Pensions Research

Report 191, Corporate Document Services, Leeds. <www.dwp.gov.uk/asd/asd5/rrep191.asp>

Katz, A., Buchanan, A. and Bream, V. (2001) *Bullying in Britain: testimonies from teenagers*, Young Voice, London.

Kerr, D., Beaujot, R. and Fernando, R. (2001) *Family relations, low income and child outcomes: a comparison of Canadian children in intact, step and lone parent families*, Paper presented at the 2001 International Union for the Scientific Study of Population, Brazil.

Kidd, M. and Shannon, M. (2001) 'Convergence in the gender wage gap in Australia over the 1980s: identifying the role of counteracting forces via the Juhn, Murphy and Pierce decomposition', *Allied Economics*, 33, 7, 929–36.

Kidscape (1999) *Kidscape Survey: long-term effects of bullying*. <www.kidscape.org.uk/assets/downloads/kslongtermeffects.pdf>

Kiernan, K. (1992) 'The impact of family disruption in childhood on transitions made in young adult life', *Population Studies*, 46, 2, 213–34.

Kiernan, K. (1996) 'Lone motherhood, employment and outcomes for children', *International Journal of Law, Policy and the Family*, 10, 3, 233–49.

Kinder, K., Harland, J., Wilkin, A. and Wakefield, A. (1995) *Three to remember: strategies for disaffected pupils*, National Foundation for Educational Research, Slough.

Kinder, K., Wakefield, A. and Wilkin, A. (1996) *Talking back: pupils' views on disaffection*, National Foundation for Educational Research, Slough.

Kleinman, M., West, A. and Sparkes, J. (1998) *Investing in employability: the role of business and government in the transition to work*, London School of Economics and Political Science, London.

Kuh, D., Power, C., Blane, D. and Bartley, M. (1997) 'Social pathways between childhood and adult health', in D. Kuh, and B. Shlomo (eds) *A life course approach to chronic disease epidemiology*, Oxford University Press, Oxford.

Lamb, M. (ed.) (1986) *The fathers' role: applied perspectives*, Wiley, New York, NY.

Lawrence, D. (1981) 'Development of a self esteem questionnaire', *British Journal of Educational Psychology*, 51, 245–51.

Layard, R. (2005) *Happiness: lessons from a new science*, Allen Lane, London.

Learning and Skills Development Agency (2004) *Participation by 17 year olds: a systematic review of the factors that influence participation in the second year of post-compulsory education or training*, Learning and Skills Development Agency, London. <www.lsda.org.uk/files/pdf/4176_sysrev.pdf>

Leibowitz, A. (1974) 'Home investment in children', *Journal of Political Economy*, 82, 2, S111–131.

Leslie, D. and Drinkwater, S. (1999) 'Staying on in full-time education: reasons for higher participation rates among ethnic minority males and females', *Economica*, 66, 261, 63–77.

Levacic, R. and Hardman, J. (1999) 'The performance of grant maintained schools in England: an experiment in autonomy', *Journal of Education Policy*, 14, 2, 185–210.

Lewis, S. and Lewis, J. (1996) *The work-family challenge: rethinking employment*, Sage, London.

Ma, X., Stewin, L. and Mah, D. (2001) 'Bullying in school: nature, effects, and remedies', *Research Papers in Education*, 16, 3, 247–70.

Macdonald, R. and Marsh, J. (2001) *Youth, the underclass and social exclusion: end of award report*, Economic and Social Research Council, Swindon.

Machin, S. (1998) 'Childhood disadvantage and intergenerational transmission of economic status', in A. Atkinson, and J. Hills (eds) *Exclusion, employment and opportunity*, CASE Paper 4, London, Centre for the Analysis of Social Exclusion, London School of Economics, London. <http://sticerd.lse.ac.uk/dps/case/cp/Paper4.PDF>

Machin, S. and Vignoles, A. (eds) (2005) *What's the good of education? The economics of education in the United Kingdom*, Princeton University Press, Princeton, NJ.

Magadi, M. and Middleton, S. (2005) *Britain's poorest children revisited: evidence from the BHPS (1994–2002)*, CRSP Research Report 3, Centre for Research in Social Policy, Loughborough University, Loughborough. <www.savethechildren.org.uk/scuk_cache/scuk/cache/cmsattach/3796_BPC2_Research_Report.pdf>

Malcolm, H., Wilson, V., Davidson, J. and Kirk, S. (2003) *Absence from school: a study of its causes and effects in seven LEAs*, Research Report 424, Department for Education and Skills, London. <www.dfes.gov.uk/schoolattendance/uploads/Absence%20from%20school.doc>

Marks, G. and Houston, D. (2002) 'Attitudes towards work and motherhood held by working and non-working mothers', *Work, Employment and Society*, 16, 3, 523–36.

Marshall, G., Newby, H., Rose, D. and Vogler, C. (1988) *Social class in modern Britain*, Hutchinson, London.

Martin, A. (1999) 'Assessing the multidimensionality of the 12-item general health questionnaire', *Psychological Reports*, 84, 3, 927–35.

Martin, J. and Roberts, C. (1984) *Women and employment: a lifetime perspective*, Department of Employment/OPCS, London.

Mathai, J., Anderson, P. and Bourne, A. (2004) 'Comparing psychiatric diagnoses generated by the Strengths and Difficulties Questionnaire with diagnoses made by clinicians', *Australian and New Zealand Journal of Psychiatry*, 38, 8, 639–43.

Mayer, S. (1997) *What money can't buy: family income and children's life chances*, Harvard University Press, Cambridge, MA.

Mayer, S. (2002) *The influence of parental income on children's outcomes*, Ministry of Social Development, Wellington, New Zealand. <www.msd.govt.nz/documents/publications/csre/influence-of-parental-income.pdf>

McAra, L. (2004) *Truancy, school exclusion and substance misuse*, Report 4, The Edinburgh Study of Youth Transitions and Crime, Centre for Law and Society, The University of Edinburgh, Edinburgh. <www.law.ed.ac.uk/cls/esytc/findings/digest4.pdf>

McCulloch, A. and Joshi, H. (2000) *Child development and family resources: an exploration of evidence from the second generation of the 1958 British Birth Cohort*, Working Papers 2000-24, Institute for Social and Economic Research, University of Essex, Colchester. <www.iser.essex.ac.uk/pubs/workpaps/pdf/1999-15.pdf>

McLanahan, S. (2000) *The future of the family: fragile families in the 21st century*, Paper presented at the 2000 Population Association of America Meetings, Los Angeles.

McMunn, A., Nazroo, J., Marmot, M., Boreham, R. and Goodman, R. (2001) 'Children's emotional and behavioural well-being and the family environment: findings from the Health Survey for England', *Social Science and Medicine*, 53, 4, 423–40.

McNamee, S. and Miller, R. (2004) *The meritocracy myth*, Rowman and Littlefield Publishers, Lanham, MD.

McRae, S. (1991a) 'Occupational change over childbirth: evidence from a national survey', *Sociology*, 25, 4, 589–605.

McRae, S. (1991b) *Maternity rights in Britain*, Policy Studies Institute, London.

McRae, S. (2003) 'Constraints and choices in mothers' employment careers: a consideration of Hakim's Preference Theory', *British Journal of Sociology*, 54, 3, 317–38.

McVicar, D. and Rice, P. (2001) 'Participation in further education in England and Wales: an analysis of post-war trends', *Oxford Economic Pa*pers, 53, 1, 47–66.

Meltzer, H., Gatward, R. with Goodman, R. and Ford, T. (2000) *The mental health of children and adolescents in Great Britain*, HMSO, London. <www.statistics.gov.uk/downloads/theme_health/ChildAdol_Mental_Health_v1.pdf>

Meltzer H., Gatward, R., Corbin, T., Goodman, R. and Ford, T. (2003) *Persistence, onset, risk factors and outcomes of childhood mental disorders*, HMSO, London. <www.statistics.gov.uk/downloads/theme_health/PMAchildPersist.pdf>

Meltzer, H., Gill, B., Petticrew, M. and Hinds, K. (1995) *The prevalence of psychiatric morbidity among adults living in private households*, HMSO, London.

Micklewright, J. (1989) 'Choice at sixteen', *Economica*, 56, 1, 25–39.

Micklewright, J., Pearson, M. and Smith, S. (1990) 'Unemployment and early school leaving', *Economic Journal*, 100, 400, 163–9.

Middleton, S. (2002) 'Child poverty in lone parent families: progress or procrastination?' in Gingerbread, *A quality life for lone parents and their children*, Report of Gingerbread annual conference, 17 April 2002 Gingerbread, London. <www.gingerbread.org.u/information-and-advice/documents/qualrep.pdf>

Middleton, S., Perren, K., Maguire, S., Rennison, J., Battistin, E., Emmerson, C. and Fitzsimons, E. (2005) *Evaluation of Education Maintenance Allowance pilots: young people aged 16 to 19 years: final report of the quantitative evaluation,*

Research Report 678, Department for Education and Skills, London. <www. dfes.gov.uk/research/data/uploadfiles/RR678.pdf>

Millar, J. (2000) *Keeping track of welfare reform*, York Publishing Services/Joseph Rowntree Foundation, York. <www.jrf.org.uk/bookshop/eBooks/1859353436. pdf>

Millar, J. and Ridge, T. (2001) *Families, poverty, work and care*, Department for Work and Pensions Research Report 153, Corporate Document Services, Leeds. <www.dwp.gov.uk/asd/asd5/rrep153.asp>

Miller, P. (1987) 'The wage effect of the occupational segregation of women in Britain', *The Economic Journal*, 97, 388, 885–96.

Morgan, A., Malam, S., Muir, J. and Barker, R. (2006) *Health and social inequalities in English adolescents: exploring the importance of school, family and neighbourhood*, Findings from the WHO Health Behaviour in School-aged Children study, National Institute for Health and Clinical Excellence, London. <www.hbsc.org/countries/downloads_countries/England/ NationalReport2006.pdf>

Morley, D. and Wilson, P. (2001) *Child and adolescent mental health: its importance and how to commission a comprehensive service: guidance for primary care trusts*, Young Minds, London. <www.youngminds.org.uk/pctguidance/YM_ PCT_Guidelines.pdf>

Moseki, M. (2004) *The nature of truancy and the life world of truants in secondary schools*, MA dissertation, University of South Africa, Pretoria, South Africa. <http://etd.unisa.ac.za/ETD-db/theses/available/etd-05252005-132718/ unrestricted/01dissertation.pdf>

Moss, P. (1996) 'Parental employment in the European Union, 1985–1993', *Labour Market Trends*, 104, 12, 517–22.

Muller, C. (1995) 'Maternal employment, parental involvement, and mathematics achievement among adolescents', *Journal of Marriage and the Family*, 57, 1, 85–100.

Murray, C. (1994) *The underclass: the crisis deepens*, Institute of Economic Affairs, London.

Nathan, G. (1999) A review of sample attrition and representativeness in three longitudinal surveys, Office for National Statistics, London.

National Audit Office (2005) *Improving school attendance in England*, HC 212 Session 2004-2005, HMSO, London. <www.nao.org.uk/publications/nao_ reports/04-05/0405212.pdf>

Neiderhiser, J. and Reiss, D. (2002) *Understanding the influence of family processes on family adjustment: the role of genetic research*, Paper to the Joint Centre for Poverty Research Conference, Chicago, IL, 19–20 September. <www.jcpr. org/conferences/SRI_2002/neiderhiser_reiss.pdf>

Newman, S., Bland, R. and Orn, H. (1988) 'A comparison of methods of scoring the General Health Questionnaire', *Comprehensive Psychiatry*, 29, 4, 402–8.

National Society of Prevention of Cruelty to Children (NSPCC) (2004) *Someone to turn to? Who can children and young people trust when they are worried and need to talk?*, NSPCC, London. <www.nspcc.org.uk/Inform/Publications/ Downloads/STTT_pdf_gf25336.pdf>

O'Brien, M. and Jones, D. (1999) 'Children, parental employment and education attainment: an English case study', *Cambridge Journal of Economics*, 23, 5, 599–621.

O'Brien, M., Singleton, N., Sparks, J., Meltzer, H. and Brugha, T. (2002) *Adults with a psychotic disorder living in private households 2000*, HMSO, London. <www.statistics.gov.uk/downloads/theme_health/PMA_Psycho_v2.pdf>

Oakley, A. (1974) *Housewife*, Penguin Books, London.

The Observer (2005) 'Official: babies do best with mother', October 2. <http:// observer.guardian.co.uk/uk_news/story/0,6903,1583072,00.html>

Office for National Statistics (2001a) *Social trends 31*, HMSO, London.

Office for National Statistics (2001b) *Social focus on men*, HMSO, London.

Office for National Statistics (2002) *Social trends 32*, HMSO, London.

Office for National Statistics (2005a) *Focus on families*, HMSO, London.

Office for National Statistics (2005b) *Families and work: An analysis of the employment patterns of families and parents with dependent children*, Labour Market Trends July, HMSO, London.

Office for National Statistics (2005c) *Census 2001 quality report for England and Wales*, HMSO, London.

Office for National Statistics (2006a) *Social trends 36*, HMSO, London.

Office for National Statistics (2006b) *Work and worklessness amongst households*, First Release, July, ONS, London.

Office for Standards in Education (OFSTED) (1995) *Pupil referral units – the first twelve inspections*, HMSO, London.

Office for Standards in Education (OFSTED) (1996) *Exclusion from secondary schools 1995/6*, HMSO, London.

Office for Standards in Education (OFSTED) (2001) *Improving attendance and behaviour in secondary schools: strategies to promote educational inclusion*, Office for Standards in Education, London. <www.ofsted.gov.uk/assets/1021. pdf>

Oliver, C. and Candappa, M. (2003) *Tackling bullying: listening to the views of children and young people*, Research Report 400, Department for Education and Skills, London. <www.dfes.gov.uk/research/data/uploadfiles/RR400.pdf>

Olweus, D. (1993) *Bullying at school: what we know and what we can do*, Blackwell, Oxford.

Olweus, D. (1994) 'Bullying at school: basic facts and effects of a school based intervention programme', *Journal of Child Psychology and Psychiatry*, 35, 7, 1171–90.

Organisation for Economic Co-operation and Development (OECD) (2001) *Education at a glance: OECD indicators 2001*, OECD, Paris.

Organisation for Economic Co-operation and Development (OECD) (2004) *Education at a glance: OECD Indicators 2004*, OECD, Paris.

Oskrochi, G. and Crochley, R. (2000) *Using SPSS and Gauss to unify the BHPS work history data*, Working Paper 2000/03, Centre for Applied Statistics, University of Lancaster, Lancaster. <www.cas.lancs.ac.uk/papers/unifbhps5.pdf>

Osler, A., Street, C., Lall, M. and Vincent, K. (2001) *Not a problem? Girls and school exclusion*, National Children's Bureau, London. <www.npi.org.uk/reports/schools%20exclusions%20girls.pdf>

Parcel, T. and Menaghan G. (1994) 'Early parental work, family social capital and early childhood outcomes', *American Journal of Sociology*, 99, 4, 972–1109.

Park, A., Phillips, M. and Johnson, M. (2004) *Young people in Britain: the attitudes and experiences of 12 to 19 year olds*, Research Report 564, Department for Education and Skills, London. <www.dfes.gov.uk/research/data/uploadfiles/RR564.pdf>

Parliamentary and Health Service Ombudsman (2005) *Tax credits: putting things right*, Third Report of Session 2005-06, HC 124, HMSO, London. <www.publications.parliament.uk/pa/cm200506/cmselect/cmpubadm/577/577.pdf>

Parsons, C. (1996) *Exclusions from school: the public cost*, Routledge, London.

Parsons, C. (1999) *Education, exclusions and citizenship*, Routledge, London.

Pascall, G. (1997) 'Women and the family in the British Welfare State: the Thatcher/Major legacy', *Social Policy and Administration*, 31, 3, 290–305.

Payne, J. (2001) *Patterns of participation in full-time education after 16: an analysis of the England and Wales Youth Cohort Studies*, Research Report 307, Department for Education and Skills, London. <www.dfes.gov.uk/research/data/uploadfiles/RR307.pdf>

Payne, J. (2002) *Attitudes to education and choices at age 16: a brief research review*, Department for Education and Skills, London. <www.dfes.gov.uk/research/data/uploadfiles/Attitudes%20to%20Education,%20and%20Choices%20at%20Age%2016.doc>

Payne, J. (2003) *Vocational pathways at age 16–19: an analysis of the England and Wales Youth Cohort Study*, Research Report 501, Department for Education and Skills, London. <www.dfes.gov.uk/research/data/uploadfiles/RR501.pdf>

Payne, S. (1999) *Poverty, social exclusion and mental health: findings from the 1999 PSE survey*, Working Paper 15, Townsend Centre for International Poverty Research, University of Bristol, Bristol.

Pearce, N. and Hillman, J. (1998) *Wasted youth: raising achievement and tackling social exclusion*, Institute for Public Policy Research, London.

Perfect, D. and Hurrell, K. (2003) *Pay and income*, Women and Men in Britain series, Equal Opportunities Commission, Manchester.

Pfau-Effinger, B. (1999) 'The modernisation of family and motherhood in Western Europe', in R. Crompton (ed.) *Restructuring gender relations and employment: the decline of the male breadwinner*, Oxford University Press, Oxford.

Phillips, M. (1999) *The sex change society: feminised Britain and neutered male*, The Social Market Foundation, London.

Phoenix, A., Woollett, A. and Lloyd, E. (1991) *Motherhood: meanings, practices and ideologies*, Sage Publications, London.

Polachek, S. (1981) 'Occupational self-selection: a human capital approach to sex differences in occupational structure', *Review of Economics and Statistics*, 63, 1, 60–69.

Politi, P., Piccinelli, M. and Wilkinson, G. (1994) 'Reliability and validity and factor structure of the 12-item General Health Questionnaire among young males in Italy', *Acta Psychiatrica Scandinavia*, 90, 432–7.

Powis, B., Griffiths, P., Gossop, M., Lloyd, C. and Strang, J. (1998) 'Drug use and offending among young people excluded from school', *Drugs: Education, Prevention and Policy*, 5,3, 245–56.

Prescott-Clarke, P. and Primatesta, P. (eds) (1998) *Health survey for England 1997: the health of young people 95–97*, HMSO, London. <www.archive. official-documents.co.uk/document/doh/survey97/hse95.htm>

Prince, P. and Prince, C. (2001) 'Subjective quality of life in the evaluation of programs for people with serious and persistent mental illness', *Clinical Psychology Review*, 21, 7, 1005–36.

Procter, I. and Padfield, M. (1999) 'Work orientations and women's work: a critique of Hakim's theory of the heterogeneity of women', *Gender, Work and Organization*, 6, 3, 152–62.

Putnam, R. (2000) *Bowling alone: the collapse and revival of American community*, Simon and Shuster, New York, NY.

Radavanovic, Z. and Eric, L. (1983) 'Validity of the General Health Questionnaire in a Yugoslav student population', *Psychological Medicine*, 13, 205–7.

Randall, G. and Brown, S. (1999) *Prevention is better than cure*, Crisis, London. <www.crisis.org.uk/downloads.php/272/PreventionIsBetterThanCure.pdf>

Ravens-Sieberer, U., Kokonyei, G. and Thomas, C. (2004) 'School and health', in C. Currie, C. Roberts, A. Morgan, R. Smith, W. Settertobulte, O. Samdal, and V. Barnekow-Rasmussen (eds) *Young people's health in context: Health Behaviour in School-aged Children (HBSC) study: international report from the 2001/2002 survey*, Health Policy for Children and Adolescents, No 4, World Health Organisation, Copenhagen. <www.euro.who.int/Document/ e82923.pdf>

Ray, S. and McLoyd, V. (1986) 'Fathers in hard times: the impact of unemployment and poverty of paternal and marital relations', in M. Lamb (ed.) *The father's role: applied perspectives*, Wiley, New York, NY.

Reid, K. (1999) *Truancy and schools*, Routledge, London.

Rennison, J., Maguire, S., Middleton, S. and Ashworth, K. (2005) *Young people not in education, employment or training: evidence from the Education Maintenance Allowance pilots database*, Research Report 628, Department for Education and Skills, London. <www.dfes.gov.uk/research/data/uploadfiles/ RR628.pdf>

Rice, P. (1999) 'The impact of local labour markets on investment in further education: evidence from the England and Wales Youth Cohort Studies', *Journal of Population Economics*, 12, 2, 287–312.

Rice, P. (2000) *Participation in further education and training: how much do gender and race matter?*, Department of Economics, University of Southampton, Southampton.

Rigby, K. (1994) 'Psychosocial functioning in families of Australian adolescent schoolchildren involved in bully/victim problems', *Journal of Family Therapy*, 16, 21, 173–87.

Rigby, K. (1996) *Bullying in schools – and what to do about it*, ACER Melbourne, Australia.

Rigby, K. (2003a) 'Consequences of bullying in schools', *Canadian Journal of Psychiatry*, 48, 9, 583–90.

Rigby, K. (2003b) *Addressing bullying in schools: theory and practice*, Trends and Issues in Crime and Criminal Justice 259, Australian Institute of Criminology, Canberra, Australia.

Riley, K. and Rustique-Forrester, E. (2002) *Working with disaffected students*, Paul Chapman Publishing, London.

Roberts, R., Atkinson, C. and Rosenblatt, A. (1998) 'Prevalence of psychopathology among children and adolescents', *American Journal of Psychiatry*, 155, 6, 715–25.

Robinson, P. (1999) 'Education, training and the youth labour market', in P. Gregg and J. Wadsworth (eds) *The state of working Britain*, Manchester University Press, Manchester.

Robinson, P. and Oppenheim, C. (1998) *Social exclusion indicators*, Institute of Public Policy Research, London.

Robson, C. (2002) *Real world research* (second edition), Blackwell, Oxford.

Robson, K. (2003) *Teenage time use as investment in cultural capital*, Working Paper 2003-12, Institute for Social and Economic Research, University of Essex, Colchester. <www.iser.essex.ac.uk/pubs/workpaps/pdf/2003-12.pdf>

Rodgers, B., Pickles, A., Power, C., Collishaw, S. and Maughan, B. (1999) 'Validity of the Malaise Inventory in general population samples', *Social Psychiatry and Psychiatric Epidemiology*, 34, 6, 333–41.

Rodgers, B. and Pryor, J. (1998) *Divorce and separation: the outcomes for children*, Joseph Rowntree Foundation, York.

Rojas, M. (2004) *The complexity of well-being: a life satisfaction conception and a domains-of-life approach*, Paper for the International Workshop on Researching Well-being in Developing Countries, Hanse Institute for Advanced Study, Delmenhorst, Germany. <www.flacso.or.cr/fileadmin/documentos/FLACSO/Dialogos_Bienestar/Luis_Mariano4.pdf>

Rose, D. (ed.) (2000) *Researching social and economic change: the uses of household panel studies*, Routledge, London.

Rosenberg, M. (1965) *Society and the adolescent self-image*, Princeton University Press, Princeton, NJ.

Ross, C. and Broh, B. (2000) 'The roles of self-esteem and the sense of personal control in the academic achievement process', *Sociology of Education*, 73, 4, 270–84.

Ross, D. and Roberts, P. (1999) *Income and child well-being: a new perspective on the poverty debate*, Canadian Council on Social Development, Ottawa, Canada. <www.ccsd.ca/pubs/inckids/es.htm>

Rowlingson, K. (2004) 'Secondary analysis', in S. Becker, and A. Bryman (eds) *Understanding research methods for social policy*, The Policy Press, Bristol.

Rubery, J., Horrell, S. and Burchell, B. (1994) 'Part-time work and gender inequality in the labour market', in A. Scott (ed.) *Gender segregation and social change*, Oxford University Press, Oxford.

Rumberger, R. (1983) 'Dropping out of high school: the influence of race, sex and family background', *American Educational Research Journal*, 20, 2, 199–220.

Rutter, M. (1995) *Psychosocial disorders in young people: time trends and their causes*, Wiley, Chichester.

Rutter, M., Tizard, J. and Whitmore, K. (1970) *Education, health and behaviour*, Longman, London.

Ryan, H. and Bull, J. (eds) (2000) *Changing families, changing communities: researching health and well-being among children and young people*, Health Development Agency, London.

Ryff, C. (1989) 'Happiness is everything or is it? Explorations on the meaning of psychological well-being', *Journal of Personal Social Psychology*, 57, 6, 1057–81.

Sacker, A., Schoon, I. and Bartley, M. (1999) 'Childhood influences on socio-economic inequalities in adult mental health: path analysis as an aid to understanding', *Health Variations*, The Official Newsletter of the Economic and Social Research Council (ESRC) Health Variations Programme, 4, 8–10.

Salmon, G., James, A. and Smith, D. (1998) 'Bullying in schools: self-reported anxiety, depression, and self-esteem in secondary school children', *British Medical Journal*, 317, 924–5.

Schools Health Education Unit (2004) *Trends: young people and emotional health and well-being 1983–2003*, Schools Health Education Unit, University of Exeter, Exeter.

Schoon, I. (2003) *Teenage aspirations for education and work and long-term outcomes: evidence from two British Cohort Stud*ies, paper presented to the Economic and Social Research Council (ESRC) seminar on How to motivate (demotivated) 14–16 year old learners, 16 May 2003 at the Centre for Economic Performance, London <http://cep.lse.ac.uk/events/seminars/motivation/schoon.pdf>

Scott, J. (2000) 'Children as respondents: the challenge for quantitative methods', in P. Christensen and A. James (eds) *Research with children: perspectives and practices*, Falmer Press, London.

Scott, J. (2004) 'Family, gender, and educational attainment in Britain: a longitudinal study', *Journal of Comparative Family Studies*, 35, 4, 655–89.

Scott, J., with Brynin, M. and Smith, R. (1995) 'Interviewing children in the British Household Panel Survey', in J. Hox and B. van der Meulen (eds) *Advances in family research*, Thesis Publishers, Amsterdam.

Sharp, S. (1995) 'How much does bullying hurt? The effects of bullying on the personal well-being and educational progress of secondary aged students', *Educational Child Psychology*, 12, 2, 81–8.

Shelter (2004) *Toying with their future: the hidden cost of the housing crisis, Shelter*, London. <www.shelter.org.uk/files/docs/4489/Toyingfuture.pdf>

Sigle-Rushton, W. (2004) *Intergenerational and life-course transmission of social exclusion in the 1970 British Cohort Study*, CASE Paper 78, Centre for Analysis of Social Exclusion, London School of Economics, London. <http://sticerd.lse.ac.uk/dps/case/cp/CASEpaper78.pdf>

Skaalvik, E. and Hagtvet, K. (1990) 'Academic achievement and self-concept: an analysis of causal predominance in a developmental perspective', *Journal of Personality and Social Psychology*, 58, 2, 292–307.

Smeaton, D. (2006) 'Work return rates after childbirth in the UK – trends, determinants and implications: a comparison of cohorts born in 1958 and 1970', *Work, Employment and Society*, 20, 1, 5–25.

Smith, J., Brooks-Gunn, J., Klebanov, P. and Lee, K. (2000) 'Welfare and work: complementary strategies for low-income women?', *Journal of Marriage and the Family*, 62, 3, 808–21.

Smith, R. (1998) *No lessons learnt: a survey of school exclusions*, The Children's Society, London.

Smith, P. (ed.) (1999) *The nature of school bullying: a cross-national perspective*, Routledge, London.

Smith, P., Cowie, H. and Blades, M. (1998) *Understanding children's development* (third edition), Blackwell, Oxford.

Smith, P. and Madsen, K. (1997) *A follow-up survey of the DFE anti-bullying pack for schools: its use, and the development of anti-bullying work in schools*, Research Brief 3, Department for Education and Employment, London. <www.dfes.gov.uk/research/data/uploadfiles/RB3.doc>

Smith, P. and Samara, M. (2003) *Evaluation of the DfES anti-bullying pack*, Research Brief 6, Department for Education and Skills, London. <www.dfes.gov.uk/research/data/uploadfiles/RBX06-03.pdf>

Smith, P. and Sharp, S. (eds) (1994) *School bullying: insights and perspectives*, Routledge, London.

Smith, P., and Shu, S. (2000) 'What good schools can do about bullying: findings from a survey in English schools after a decade of research and action', *Childhood*, 7, 2, 193–212.

Smith, P., Talamelli, L., Cowie, H., Naylor, P. and Chauhan, P. (2004) 'Profiles of non-victims, escaped victims, continuing victims and new victims of school bullying', *British Journal of Educational Psychology*, 74, 4, 565–81.

Social Exclusion Unit (1998) *Truancy and school exclusion*, HMSO, London. <www.socialexclusionunit.gov.uk/downloaddoc.asp?id=239>

Social Exclusion Unit (1999) *Bridging the gap: new opportunities for 16–18 year olds*, Cm4405, HMSO, London. <www.socialexclusionunit.gov.uk/downloaddoc.asp?id=31>

Social Exclusion Unit (2004) *Breaking the cycle: taking stock of progress and priorities for the future*, Office of the Deputy Prime Minister, London. <www.socialexclusionunit.gov.uk/downloaddoc.asp?id=262>

Sparkes, J. (1999) *Schools, education and social exclusion*, CASE Paper 29, Centre for Analysis of Social Exclusion, London School of Economics, London. <http://sticerd.lse.ac.uk/dps/case/cp/CASEpaper29.pdf>

Sproston, K. and Primatesta, P. (eds) (2003) *Health Survey for England 2002: volume 1: the health of children and young people*, London: HMSO. <www.archive2.officialdocuments.co.uk/document/deps/doh/survey02/hse02.htm>

Stephenson, P. and Smith, D. (1989) 'Bullying in the junior school', in D. Tattum and D. Lane (eds) *Bullying in schools*, Trentham Books, Stoke-on-Trent.

Stirling, M. (1992a) 'How many pupils are being excluded?', *British Journal of Special Education*, 19, 4, 128–30.

Stirling, M. (1992b) 'Absent with leave', *Special Children*, 52.

Stone, V., Cotton, D. and Thomas, A. (2000) *Mapping troubled lives: young people not in education, employment or training*, Research Brief 181, Department for Education and Skills, London. <www.dfes.gov.uk/research/data/uploadfiles/ACF3192.doc>

Sullivan, A. (2001) 'Cultural capital and educational attainment', *Sociology*, 35, 4, 893–912.

Swadi, H. (1989) 'Adolescent substance use and truancy: exploring the link', *European Journal of Psychiatry*, 3, 2, 108–15.

Sweeting, H. and West, P. (1995) 'Family life and health in adolescence: a role for culture in the health inequalities debate?', *Social Science and Medicine*, 40, 2, 163–75.

Sweeting, H., West, P. and Richards, M. (1998) 'Teenage family life, lifestyles and life chances: associations with family structure, conflict with parents and joint family activity', *International Journal of Law, Policy and the Family*, 12, 1, 15–46.

Tabachnick, B. and Fidell, L. (1996) *Using multivariate statistics* (third edition), Harper Collins, New York, NY.

Taylor, M. with Brice, J., Buck, N. and Prentice-Lane, E. (2001) *British Household Panel Survey user manual volume A: introduction, technical report and appendices*, University of Essex, Colchester. <www.iser.essex.ac.uk/bhps/doc>

The Telegraph (2005) 'What if mums don't actually want to go out to work?', June 16. <www.telegraph.co.uk/opinion/main.jhtml?xml=/opinion/2005/06/16/do1601.xml>

Todd, J. and Currie, C., with Mellor, A., Johnstone, M. and Cowie, M. (2004) *Bullying and fighting among schoolchildren in Scotland: age and gender patterns, trends, and cross-national comparisons*, Briefing Paper 8, Health Behaviour in School-Aged Children, Child and Adolescent Health Research Unit, University of Edinburgh, Edinburgh. <www.education.ed.ac.uk/cahru/publications/BriefingPaper8.pdf>

Trautwein, U., Ludtke, O., Koller, O. and Baumert, J. (2006) 'Self-esteem, academic self-concept, and achievement: how the learning environment moderates the dynamics of self-concept', *Journal of Personality and Social Psychology*, 90, 2, 334–49.

Trivellato, U. (1999) 'Issues in the design and analysis of panel studies: a cursory review', *Quality and Quantity*, 33, 3, 339–52.

Utting, W. (1997) *People like us: the report of the review of safeguards for children living away from home*, HMSO, London.

Varhama, L. and Björkqvist, K. (2005) 'Relation between school bullying during adolescence and subsequent long-term unemployment in adulthood in a Finnish sample', *Psychological Reports*, 96, 2, 269–72.

Waddell, G. (2006) 'Labor-market consequences of poor attitude and low self-esteem in youth', *Economic Inquiry*, 44, 1, 69–97.

Walby, S. (1986) *Patriarchy at work*, Polity Press, Cambridge.

Walby, S. (ed.) (1988) *Gender segregation at work*, Open University Press, Buckingham.

Walby, S. (1990) *Theorising patriarchy*, Blackwell, Oxford.

Walby, S. (1997) *Gender transformations*, Routledge, London.

Walby, S. and Olsen, W. (2002) *The impact of women's position in the labour market on pay and implications for UK productivity*, Report to Women and Equality Unit, Department of Trade and Industry, London. <www.womenandequalityunit.gov.uk/publications/weu_pay_and_productivity.pdf>

Waldfogel, J. (1998) 'The family gap for young women in the United States and Britain: can maternity leave make a difference?', *Journal of Labor Economics*, 16, 3, 505–45.

Walker, R. (1999) *Ending child poverty*, The Policy Press, Bristol.

Warren, T. (2000) 'Women in low status part-time jobs: a class and gender analysis', *Sociological Research Online*, 4, 4. <www.socresonline.org.uk/4/4/warren.html>

Warren, T. and Walters, P. (1998) 'Appraising a dichotomy: a review of the use of 'part-time/full-time' in the study of women's employment in Britain', *Gender, Work and Organisation*, 5, 2, 102–18.

Weare, K. and Gray, G. (2003) *What works in developing children's emotional and social competence and well-being?*, Research Report 456, Department for Education and Skills, London. <www.dfes.gov.uk/research/data/uploadfiles/RR456.pdf>

Weinburg, B. (2001) 'An incentive model of the effect of parental income on children', *Journal of Political Economy*, 109, 2, 266–80.

West, A., Pennell, H., West, R. and Travers, T. (1999) *The financing of school based education: end of Award Report*, Economic and Social Research Council, Swindon. <www.esrc.ac.uk>

West, P. and Sweeting, H. (2003) 'Fifteen, female and stressed: changing patterns of psychological distress over time', *Journal of Child Psychology and Psychiatry*, 44, 3, 399–411.

White, M. and Kaufman, G. (1997) 'Language usage, social capital, and school completion among immigrants and native-born ethnic groups', *Social Science Quarterly*, 78, 2, 385–98.

White, M. and Smith, D. (1994) 'The causes of persistently high unemployment', in A. Peterson, and J. Mortimer (eds) *Youth unemployment and society*, Cambridge University Press, Cambridge.

Whiteford, P., Mendelson, M. and Millar, J. (2003) *Timing it right? Tax credits and how to respond to income changes*, Joseph Rowntree Foundation, York.

Whitney, I. and Smith, P. (1993) 'A survey of the nature and extent of bullying in junior/middle and secondary schools', *Educational Research*, 35, 1, 3–25.

Whitty, G., Power, S., Gamarnikow, E., Aggleton, P., Tyrer, P. and Youdell, D. (1999) 'Health, housing and education', in A. Hayton (ed.) *Tackling disaffection and social exclusion*, Kogan Page, London.

Wilson, W. (1987) *The truly disadvantaged: the inner city, the underclass, and public policy*, University of Chicago Press, Chicago, IL.

Winquist-Nord, C., Brimhall, D. and West, J. (1997) *Fathers' involvement in their children's schools*, Statistical Analysis Report 98-091, National Center for Educational Statistics, Washington, DC. <http://nces.ed.gov/pubs98/98091.pdf>

Wolke, D., Woods, S., Bloomfield, L. and Karstadt, L. (2001) 'Bullying involvement in primary school and common health problems', *Archives of Disease in Childhood*, 85, 3, 197–201.

Woodland, S., Miller, M. and Tipping, S. (2002) *Repeat study of parents' demand for childcare*, Research Report 348, Department for Education and Skills, London. <www.dfes.gov.uk/research/data/uploadfiles/RR348.pdf>

Woods, S. and Wolke, D. (2004) 'Direct and relational bullying among primary school children and academic achievement', *Journal of School Psychology*, 42, 135–55.

World Health Organisation (WHO) (1994) *The ICD-10 classification of mental and behavioural disorders: diagnostic criteria for research*, WHO, Geneva, Switzerland.

Worsely, A. and Gribbin, C. (1977) 'A factor analytic study of the 12-item General Health Questionnaire', *Australia and New Zealand Journal of Psychiatry*, 11, 4, 260–72.

Wright, C., Weekes, D. and McGlaughlin, A. (2000) *'Race', class and gender in exclusion from school*, Falmer, London.

Young, J. (1999) *The exclusive society*, Sage, London.

Youth Justice Board (2004) *MORI Youth Survey 2004*, Youth Justice Board, London.

Zick, C., Bryant, W. and Osterbacka, E. (2001) 'Mothers' employment, parental involvement, and the implications for intermediate child outcomes', *Social Science Research*, 30,1, 25–49.

Statutes

Education (No 2) Act 1986
Education Act 2002
School Standards and Framework Act 1998
Work and Families Bill, 2005

Appendix A
Constructing the Samples

The data analysed for this research came from the British Household Panel Survey (BHPS), an annual household panel survey which began in Autumn 1991 with a representative sample of 5,500 households, containing around 10,000 people. The same individuals are re-interviewed each year, and if an individual leaves their original household to form a new household, all members of that household are also then interviewed. Since 1994 (Wave Four) young people (aged 11–15) in the households are also interviewed, and it is these young people which form the sample used in this research.

The purpose of this study was to assess any impact of parents' employment patterns on outcomes for their children. It was thus necessary to match young people to their parents, and then determine the patterns of family structure and parental employment that applied both when children were growing up, and currently (ie when the interview was conducted).

The first stage of the matching process was to isolate the youths at each wave, a straightforward procedure as all members of a household who were aged 11 to 15 at the time of interview were asked a different set of questions to the adults, and their responses are therefore to be found in a separate data file (wYOUTH, where w corresponds to the wave letter (wave 1=A, wave 2=B, etc)). The youth survey began in 1994, there were eight years of youth data available for analysis up to 2003. To boost the sample size respondents from each wave were pooled to give an overall sample of 7347 person-wave observations, with each of the 2770 individuals included between one and five times.

The next stage was to link youths to their parents in the main survey of the BHPS. It was necessary to distinguish between biological parents, stepparents, adoptive parents, and cases where a parent was known to be absent. The second Wave (1992) of the BHPS gathered retrospective information of complete fertility, marital and cohabitation histories for all the adult panel members interviewed that year. In subsequent waves information was collected from individuals about births, marriage, divorce and cohabitation in that year. This information was used to establish the type of family youths had lived in during each year since their birth. For the purpose of this research, the different family types identified were; intact family (living with both biological parents); lone-parent family (living with a biological parent who is neither cohabiting or married); and stepfamily (living with a biological parent who is cohabiting or married to, a person other than the child's (other) biological parent). As their numbers were very small, those youths living with two adoptive parents (N=66) were excluded from the research, but youths living with one biological parent and one adoptive parent were included, and treated as stepfamilies. Lone father families (N=172), and those living in other family types (N=109) were also excluded as their numbers were small.

Once family details had been established for each year of youths' lives, including parental identification numbers, the third stage of sample construction was to match in the parents' employment details in each year. The BHPS collects extensive labour market history information, both during the panel period and retrospectively, from first leaving full-time education. In Wave Two (1992) a complete employment status history was collected, recording non-employed states in detail, and in Wave Three (1993) a complete job history was collected, with detailed information on every job held. At each wave, information is recorded on labour market status both at the time of interview and for the period beginning on 1 September a year (or more) prior to the interview. Thus the information exists to construct a complete employment/labour market history status for nearly every individual (except those who entered the BHPS after Wave Three) in the survey, from the time they left full-time education to the latest wave of the panel. However, this information is by necessity collected at different times, in somewhat different ways, and recorded in different locations. The Work-Life History Project, based at the ESRC Research Centre on Micro-Social Change (see Halpin, 1997, 2000) undertook the necessary work required to reconcile this data into a form more convenient for analysis, depositing the resulting data files with the Data Archive (SN3954). These files have been updated several times, as new waves of information have become available. Some of the problems associated with creating work-life histories, including measurement or coding error, and recall error are discussed in Halpin (1997), and elsewhere (see Elias, 1991; Dex, 1995; Oskrochi and Crouchley, 2000). Specifically, measurement or coding error relates to the incorrect coding of a spell of economic activity, and is a serious problem with occupational data, when coders may code a particular job description differently at different times. This can lead to the same period of time being coded in more than one way, resulting in problems when reconciling work-life history information. Halpin (1997) acknowledges this problem, and maintains that whilst it presents difficulties in adjudicating a single 'best' form of the data, the multiple overlapping in the work-life data available in the BHPS is a very important resource for analysing the nature, extent and effect of measurement error. Recall error represents a different problem (see Dex, 1995), and comes as a result of the failure of the human memory to remember all events with equal consistency. In general, the more time that has passed since an event, the less accurately we remember it, but the type of event also effects recall reliability. For example, short episodes are more easily forgotten, as perhaps are less pleasant events, such as unemployment. Certain transitions (such as starting a job) may be better remembered than others (such as moving from one non-employed state to another, for example, from family care to unemployment). One positive feature of the retrospective employment history collected from individuals at Wave Two of the BHPS is that other retrospective information, such as marriages and fertility history was collected at the same time, and this may have aided respondents' recollection of their employment history.

Once parental employment details had been established for each year of the young people's lives, several measures of parental employment were constructed. These were determined for each of three developmental stages in the young people's lives: birth to first birthday; first birthday to fifth birthday; fifth birthday to eleventh birthday. Other details about the young people's parents, (such as level of qualifications, age) and families (such as region of residence, number of children in the household) were also matched to each young person in the sample.

To construct the follow-on sample, data from interviews with fifteen-year-olds in the BYP (from all waves) were matched with data from the first wave of the BHPS after the young people had completed compulsory education (the first BHPS interview for most young people, but the second for those with September to November births). Each individual is included just once, with a total sample size of 915.

Appendix B

Parental Employment in the BHPS

This section examines parental employment patterns in the entire BHPS, comparing these with figures from other datasets, in order to validate the employment histories for parents of the young people in our sample, which are discussed in the next section.

Figure B.1 indicates the economic activity rates for all fathers in the BHPS over the period 1991–2001. It can be seen that the rates for fathers have altered little over time with the majority of fathers each year being in employment. The proportion of fathers not in employment stands at around a fifth each year.

For mothers, three categories of economic activity, employed full-time, employed part-time and not in employment were established for each available wave of BHPS data. Figure B.2 shows the economic activity rates for all lone mothers and coupled mothers in the BHPS over the period 1990–2001. Overall, the proportion of mothers in full-time employment has increased during the period, albeit slowly, balanced by a slight fall in the proportion of mothers not

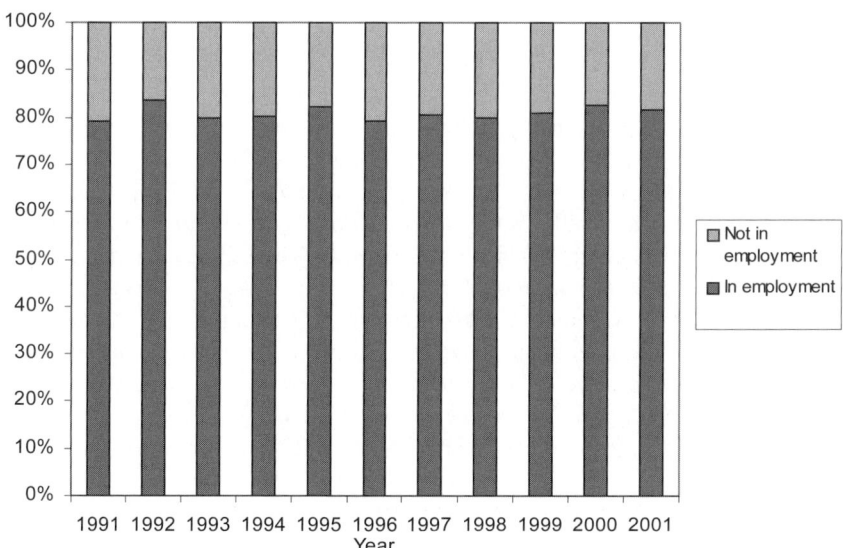

Figure B.1   Fathers' economic activity in the BHPS, 1991–2001
Source: Author's own analysis of BHPS data.

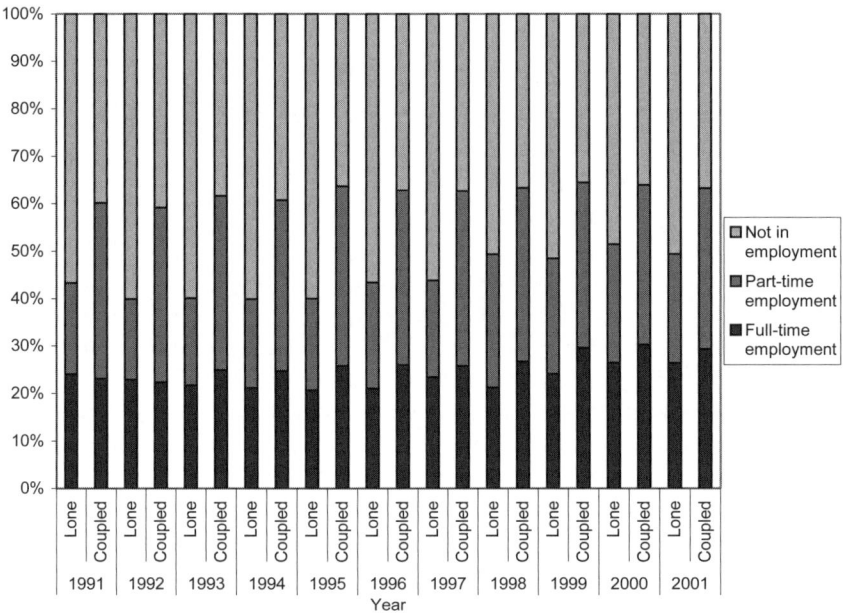

Figure B.2   Mothers' economic activity in the BHPS, lone and coupled mothers, 1991–2001

Source: Author's own analysis of BHPS data.

in employment. For lone mothers the proportion not in employment has fallen, whilst the proportions employed both full-time and part-time have increased. For coupled mothers the proportion employed full-time has increased, balanced by a fall in the proportion of mothers not in employment.

Figures for parents' current economic activity from the BHPS were then compared with data available from other data sources, the Labour Force Survey (LFS) and the Families and Children Study (FACS). The LFS is a quarterly sample survey of around 60,000 households covering a wide range of demographic and employment related information. Classifications of economic activity are based on respondents' self-assessment, and thus full-time employed and part-time employment are not based on a uniform assessment of the actual number of hours worked. The FACS is a refreshed panel survey, which began in 1999 (as the Survey of Low-Income Families), and at the third wave in 2001 was representative of all families with children (see Kasparova et al 2003). Respondents were asked what they were currently doing where 'working 16 hours and under' and 'working over 16 hours' were 2 of the categories. If employed, they were later asked how many hours they worked (0–15, 16–23, 24–29, 30 or more). 30 hours has been used as the line dividing full-time and part-time employment. For the BHPS figures responses to the questions relating to current economic activity, and the derived

Table B.1   Economic activity rates, BHPS and LFS, 1991

Economic activity %	All	Women aged 16–59				No dependent children	Men aged 16–64
		With youngest dependent child					
		Under 5	5–10	11–15	16–18		
LFS							
Full-time employed	38.3	14.2	21.1	31.0	37.5	49.3	75.5
Part-time employed	27.5	29.1	45.2	42.2	37.7	21.1	4.0
Not in employment	34.2	56.7	33.7	26.8	24.8	29.6	20.5
BHPS							
Full-time employed	40.3	14.7	24.5	32.0	38.9	52.3	71.1
Part-time employed	23.5	24.5	41.2	41.4	16.7	17.0	3.5
Not in employment	36.1	60.8	34.3	26.7	44.4	30.6	25.3

Source: Labour Force Survey, ONS, 2002; Author's own analysis of BHPS data.

Table B.2   Economic activity rates, lone and coupled mothers, LFS, FACS and BHPS, 2001

Economic activity %	Women aged 16–59					
	Lone mothers			Coupled mothers		
	LFS	FACS	BHPS	LFS	FACS	BHPS
Full-time employment	22.1	22.8	28.5	27.6	30.4	29.1
Part-time employment	27.2	26.7	18.9	42.9	40.9	39.9
Not in employment	50.7	50.2	52.7	29.1	28.9	31.0

Source: Labour Force Survey – ONS, 2002; Author's own analysis of BHPS data.

variable for full-time/part-time employment (which is calculated on a 30-hours basis for those both in employment and self-employed) were used.

Table B.1 indicates the economic activity rates for men and women by the presence and age of youngest child, for the LFS and BHPS in 1991, the first year of the BHPS. It can be seen that the figures compare fairly accurately, with a few exceptions. Slightly higher, but not statistically significantly different, proportions of part-time employment are seen in the LFS figures than in the BHPS figures, which may be accounted for by the difference in the measurement of these categories, based on 30 hours for the BHPS but self-report for the LFS. The mismatch of figures for women with a youngest dependent child aged 16–18 may be accounted for by the small number of women in this category in the BHPS figures.

In Chapter 2, differences in the employment rates of lone and coupled mothers were discussed, and Table B.2 provides a comparison of figures for the BHPS with the LFS and FACS.

The full-time employment rates are slightly higher for lone mothers in the BHPS compared with the other sources, although again this could be due to differences in definition. Overall the figures compare well, and offer support for the reliable use of data from the BHPS in this thesis.

Index